TALES OF WITCHCRAFT

TALES OF
WITCH-
CRAFT

Edited by Richard Dalby

CASTLE BOOKS

Typeset by DP Photosetting, Aylesbury, Bucks, England
Printed in the United States of America

ISBN: 0-7858-0137-5

CONTENTS

FOREWORD

Belief in witches and magicians dates back to prehistoric times among primitive tribes in all corners of the world. When nothing was known about the transmission of diseases, or about science and natural phenomena, sorcerers and witch-doctors were accepted as manipulators of health and life, respected and feared at the same time, and credited with supernatural powers by their fellow tribesmen.

As 'civilization' increased and Christianity became more firmly rooted, persecutions of 'witches' (usually innocent and reclusive women) grew enormously in the 16th and 17th centuries, and stories about them inevitably passed widely into folklore and literature.

Tales of witchcraft have always been a staple of both adult and children's literature, from the Bible and Shakespeare, through 'Hansel and Gretel', 'The Tinder Box', 'Snow White' and countless other fairy tales, to a vast range of modern classics including L. Frank Baum's *The Wizard of Oz*, Roald Dahl's *The Witches*, and John Updike's *The Witches of Eastwick*.

For the present anthology, I have selected some of the best stories to be found in witchcraft literature, ranging from early classics by Nathaniel Hawthorne and Saki to the modern masters, Robert Bloch and Stephen King. There are also several less familiar pieces, including two new stories by Ron Weighell and Jessica Amanda Salmonson, and a rare tale by M.R. James, 'The Fenstanton Witch', recently discovered by Rosemary Pardoe.

R.D.

THE PEACE OF
MOWSLE BARTON

Saki

'Saki' (Hector Hugh Munro, 1870–1916) ranks
as one of the most skilful, humorous and cynical
masters of the short story, with a special talent
for weaving the comic with the supernatural.
This tale is taken from *The Chronicles of Clovis*
(1911).

Crefton Lockyer sat at his ease, an ease alike of body and soul, in the little patch of ground, half-orchard and half-garden, that abutted on the farmyard at Mowsle Barton. After the stress and noise of long years of city life, the repose and peace of the hill-begirt homestead struck on his senses with an almost dramatic intensity. Time and space seemed to lose their meaning and their abruptness; the minutes slid away into hours, and the meadows and fallows sloped away into middle distance, softly and imperceptibly. Wild weeds of the hedgerow straggled into the flower-garden, and wallflowers and garden bushes made counter-raids into farmyard and lane. Sleepy-looking hens and solemn preoccupied ducks were equally at home in yard, orchard, or roadway; nothing seemed to belong definitely to anywhere; even the gates were not necessarily to be found on their hinges. And over the whole scene brooded the sense of a peace that had almost a quality of magic in it. In the afternoon you felt that it had always been afternoon, and must always remain afternoon; in the twilight you knew that it could never have been anything else but twilight. Crefton Lockyer sat at his ease in the rustic seat beneath an old medlar tree, and decided that here was the life-anchorage that his mind had so fondly pictured and that latterly his tired and jarred senses had so often pined for. He would make a permanent lodging-place among these simple friendly people, gradually increasing the modest comforts with which he would like to surround himself, but falling in as much as possible with their manner of living.

As he slowly matured this resolution in his mind an elderly woman came hobbling with uncertain gait through the orchard. He recognized her as a member of the farm household, the mother or possibly the mother-in-law of Mrs Spurfield, his present landlady, and hastily formulated some pleasant remark to make to her. She forestalled him.

'There's a bit of writing chalked up on the door over yonder. What is it?'

She spoke in a dull impersonal manner, as though the question had been on her lips for years and had best be got rid of. Her eyes, however, looked impatiently over Crefton's head at the door of a small barn which formed the outpost of a straggling line of farm buildings.

'Martha Pillamon is an old witch,' was the announcement that met Crefton's inquiring scrutiny, and he hesitated a moment before giving the statement wider publicity. For all he knew to the contrary, it might be Martha herself to whom he was speaking. It was possible that Mrs Spurfield's maiden name had been Pillamon. And the gaunt, withered old dame at his side might certainly fulfil local conditions as to the outward aspect of a witch.

'It's something about someone called Martha Pillamon,' he explained cautiously.

'What does it say?'

'It's very disrespectful,' said Crefton; 'it says she's a witch. Such things ought not to be written up.'

'It's true, every word of it,' said his listener with considerable satisfaction, adding as a special descriptive note of her own, 'the old toad.'

And as she hobbled away through the farmyard she shrilled out in her cracked voice, 'Martha Pillamon is an old witch!'

'Did you hear what she said?' mumbled a weak, angry voice somewhere behind Crefton's shoulder. Turning hastily, he beheld another old crone, thin and yellow and wrinkled, and evidently in a high state of displeasure. Obviously this was Martha Pillamon in person. The orchard seemed to be a favourite promenade for the aged women of the neighbourhood.

''Tis lies, 'tis sinful lies,' the weak voice went on. ''Tis Betsy Croot is the old witch. She an' her daughter, the dirty rat. I'll put a spell on 'em, the old nuisances.'

As she limped slowly away her eye caught the chalk inscription on the barn door.

'What's written up there?' she demanded, wheeling round on Crefton.

'Vote for Soarker,' he responded, with the craven boldness of the practised peacemaker.

The old woman grunted, and her mutterings and her faded red shawl lost themselves gradually among the tree trunks. Crefton rose presently and made his way towards the farmhouse. Somehow a good deal of the peace seemed to have slipped out of the atmosphere.

The cheery bustle of tea-time in the old farm kitchen, which Crefton had found so agreeable on previous afternoons, seemed to have soured today into a certain uneasy melancholy. There was a dull, dragging silence around the board, and the tea itself, when Crefton came to taste it, was a flat, lukewarm concoction that would have driven the spirit of revelry out of a carnival.

'It's no use complaining of the tea,' said Mrs Spurfield hastily, as her guest stared with an air of polite inquiry at his cup. 'The kettle won't boil, that's the truth of it.'

Crefton turned to the hearth, where an unusually fierce fire was banked up under a big black kettle, which sent a thin wreath of steam from its spout, but seemed otherwise to ignore the action of the roaring blaze beneath it.

'It's been there more than an hour, an' boil it won't,' said Mrs Spurfield, adding, by way of complete explanation, 'we're bewitched.'

'It's Martha Pillamon as has done it,' chimed in the old mother; 'I'll be even with the old toad. I'll put a spell on her.'

'It must boil in time,' protested Crefton, ignoring the suggestions of foul influences. 'Perhaps the coal is damp.'

'It won't boil in time for supper, nor for breakfast tomorrow morning, not if you was to keep the fire a-going all night for it,' said Mrs Spurfield. And it didn't. The household subsisted on fried and baked dishes, and a neighbour obligingly brewed tea and sent it across in a moderately warm condition.

'I suppose you'll be leaving us, now that things has turned up uncomfortable,' Mrs Spurfield observed at breakfast; 'there are folks as deserts one as soon as trouble comes.'

Crefton hurriedly disclaimed any immediate change of plans; he observed, however, to himself that the earlier heartiness of manner had in a large measure deserted the household. Suspicious looks, sulky silences, or sharp speeches had become the order of the day. As for the old mother, she sat about the kitchen or the garden all day, murmuring threats and spells against Martha Pillamon. There was something alike terrifying and piteous in the spectacle of these frail old morsels of humanity consecrating their last flickering energies to the task of making each other wretched. Hatred seemed to be the one faculty which had survived in undiminished vigour and intensity where all else was dropping into ordered and symmetrical decay. And the uncanny part of it was that some horrid unwholesome power seemed to be distilled from their spite and their cursings. No amount of sceptical explanation could remove the undoubted fact that neither kettle nor saucepan would come to boiling-point over the hottest fire. Crefton clung as long as possible to the theory of some defect in the coals, but the wood fire gave the same result, and when a small spirit lamp kettle, which he ordered out by carrier, showed the same obstinate refusal to allow its contents to boil he felt that he had come suddenly into contact with some unguessed-at and very evil aspect of hidden forces. Miles away, down through an opening in the hills, he could catch glimpses of a road where motor-cars sometimes passed, and yet here, so little removed from the arteries of the latest civilization, was a bat-haunted old homestead, where something unmistakably like witchcraft seemed to hold a very practical sway.

Passing out through the farm garden on his way to the lanes beyond, where he hoped to recapture the comfortable sense of peacefulness that was so lacking around house and hearth – especially hearth – Crefton came across the old mother, sitting mumbling to herself in the seat beneath the medlar tree. 'Let un sink as swims, let un sink as swims,' she was repeating over and over again, as a child repeats a half-learned lesson. And now and then she would break off into a shrill laugh, with a note of malice in it that was not pleasant to hear. Crefton was glad when he found himself out of earshot, in the quiet and seclusion of the deep overgrown lanes that seemed to lead away to nowhere; one, narrower and deeper than the rest, attracted his footsteps, and he was almost annoyed when he found that it really did act as a miniature roadway to a human dwelling. A forlorn-looking cottage with a scrap of ill-tended cabbage garden and a few aged apple trees stood at an angle where a swift-flowing stream widened out for a space into a decent-sized pond before hurrying away again through the willows that had checked its course. Crefton leaned against a tree trunk and looked across the swirling eddies of the pond at the humble little homestead opposite him; the only sign of life came from a small procession of dingy-looking ducks that marched in single file down to the water's edge. There is always something rather taking in the way a duck changes itself in an instant from a slow, clumsy waddler of the earth to a graceful, buoyant swimmer of the waters, and Crefton waited with a certain arrested attention to watch the leader of the file launch itself on to the surface of the pond. He was aware at the same time of a curious warning instinct that something strange and unpleasant was about to happen. The duck flung itself confidently forward into the water, and rolled immediately under the surface. Its head appeared for a moment and went under again, leaving a train of bubbles in its wake, while wings and legs churned the water in a helpless swirl of flapping and kicking. The bird was obviously drowning. Crefton thought at first that it had caught itself in some weeds, or was being attacked from below by a pike or water-rat. But no blood floated to the surface, and the wildly bobbing body made the circuit of the pond current without hindrance from any entanglement. A second duck had by this time launched itself into the pond, and a second struggling body rolled and twisted under the surface. There was something peculiarly piteous in the sight of the gasping beaks that showed now and again above the water, as though in terrified protest at this treachery of a trusted and familiar element. Crefton gazed with something like horror as a third duck poised itself on the bank and splashed in, to share the fate of the other two. He felt almost relieved when the remainder of the flock, taking tardy alarm from the commotion of the slowly drowning bodies, drew themselves up with tense outstretched necks, and sidled away from the scene of danger, quacking a deep note of disquietude as they went. At the same moment Crefton became aware that he was not the only human witness of the scene; a bent and withered old woman, whom he recognized at once as Martha Pillamon, of sinister reputation, had limped down the cottage path to the water's edge, and was gazing fixedly at the gruesome whirligig of dying birds that went in horrible procession round the pool. Presently her voice rang out in a shrill note of quavering rage:

''Tis Betsy Croot adone it, the old rat. I'll put a spell on her, see if I don't.'

Crefton slipped quietly away, uncertain whether or no the old woman had noticed his presence. Even before she had proclaimed the guiltiness of Betsy Croot, the latter's muttered incantation 'Let un sink as swims' had flashed uncomfortably across his mind. But it was the final threat of a retaliatory spell which crowded his mind with misgiving to the

[5]

exclusion of all other thoughts or fancies. His reasoning powers could no longer afford to dismiss these old wives' threats as empty bickerings. The household at Mowsle Barton lay under the displeasure of a vindictive old woman who seemed able to materialize her personal spites in a very practical fashion, and there was no saying what form her revenge for three drowned ducks might not take. As a member of the household Crefton might find himself involved in some general and highly disagreeable visitation of Martha Pillamon's wrath. Of course he knew that he was giving way to absurd fancies, but the behaviour of the spirit-lamp kettle and the subsequent scene at the pond had considerably unnerved him. And the vagueness of his alarm added to its terrors; when once you have taken the Impossible into your calculations its possibilities become practically limitless.

Crefton rose at his usual early hour the next morning, after one of the least restful nights he had spent at the farm. His sharpened senses quickly detected that subtle atmosphere of things-being-not-altogether well that hangs over a stricken household. The cows had been milked, but they stood huddled about in the yard, waiting impatiently to be driven out afield, and the poultry kept up an importunate querulous reminder of deferred feeding-time; the yard pump, which usually made discordant music at frequent intervals during the early morning, was today ominously silent. In the house itself there was a coming and going of scuttering footsteps, a rushing and dying away of hurried voices, and long, uneasy stillnesses. Crefton finished his dressing and made his way to the head of a narrow staircase. He could hear a dull, complaining voice, a voice in which an awed hush had crept, and recognized the speaker as Mrs Spurfield.

'He'll go away, for sure,' the voice was saying; 'there are those as runs away from one as soon as real misfortune shows itself.'

Crefton felt that he probably was one of 'those', and that there were moments when it was advisable to be true to type.

He crept back to his room, collected and packed his few belongings, placed the money due for his lodging on a table, and made his way out by a back door into the yard. A mob of poultry surged expectantly towards him; shaking off their interested attentions he hurried along under cover of cow-stall, piggery, and hayricks till he reached the lane at the back of the farm. A few minutes' walk, which only the burden of his portmanteaux restrained from developing into an undisguised run, brought him to a main road, where the early carrier soon overtook him and sped him onward to the neighbouring town. At a bend of the road he caught a last glimpse of the farm; the old gabled roofs and thatched barns, the straggling orchard, and the medlar tree, with its wooden seat, stood out with an almost spectral clearness in the early morning light, and over it all brooded that air of magic possession which Crefton had once mistaken for peace.

The bustle and roar of Paddington Station smote on his ears with a welcome protective greeting.

'Very bad for our nerves, all this rush and hurry,' said a fellow-traveller; 'give me the peace and quiet of the country.'

Crefton mentally surrendered his share of the desired commodity. A crowded, brilliantly over-lighted music-hall, where an exuberant rendering of '1812' was being given by a strenuous orchestra, came nearest to his ideal of a nerve sedative.

THE
FENSTANTON
WITCH

M. R. James

Montague Rhodes James (1862–1936) was this
country's most influential and widely reprinted
writer of ghost stories. In his essay 'Stories I
have Tried to Write', James described some of
his shorter tales 'which got as far as the stage of
being written down', but were never enlarged or
published. Among these was 'the story of two
students of King's College, Cambridge, in the
sixteenth century (who were, in fact, expelled
thence for magical practices), and their
nocturnal expedition to a witch at Fenstanton', a
small village near the Huntingdon road.
This story lay neglected and unpublished until
the recent sterling efforts of Rosemary Pardoe
who discovered the original manuscript at
King's College, and printed it in her journal
Ghosts & Scholars 12 (1990). It now appears here
in book form for the first time.

Nicholas Hardman and Stephen Ashe were two Fellows of King's
College in Cambridge; they had come like all their contempor-
aries from the sister college at Eton where they had spent their
lives from about the age of six to that of sixteen, and at the time we
encounter them they were both men of about thirty years old. Hardman
was the son of a Lincolnshire parson, living at Thorganby-on-the-
Wolds, while Ashe's father was a yeoman-farmer of Ospringe in Kent.

Hardman was black, dour and saturnine with a rasping voice and a strong Lincolnshire accent which I will not reproduce here. Ashe had the sturdy and somewhat slow intelligence of his Kentish ancestors: 'a good friend and a bad enemy' represents the opinion which the men of his year held of him. Both were in priests' orders, and each, we might suppose, looked forward in the fullness of time to occupying college livings, marrying and bringing up a son or two; one most likely to reproduce his father's career, another perhaps to go on the land and become a reputable farmer in a small way.

I say we might suppose their aspirations to have been of this nature, for such was the programme of a majority of Fellows of colleges at that time. But there is an entry in the book called Harwood's *Alumini* which shows that they entertained ideas of a very different sort, and it has occurred to me that it may be worthwhile to tell the story of what they adventured and what came of it.

I have alluded more than once to 'their times' but I have not yet told you when they lived. Queen Anne was on the throne of England, Scotland, Ireland and France, and Dr James Roderick was Provost of the College, having been elected by the Fellows in preference to Sir Isaac Newton, whom the Prince of Orange, King William the Third of Blessed Memory, would have intruded into that position. The Fellows of King's had indicated their right and so the Lower Master of Eton occupied the Lodge, while Sir Isaac lived over Trinity Great Gate with his dog Diamond. The University was a happy, sleepy place in those days, one is apt to think; but after all, what with the Church in danger and the excitement of depriving Dr Richard Bentley, then Master of Trinity, of his degrees, there was probably no lack of sport to be had within the precincts. Certainly just outside them there was more than there is now. Snipe were shot on Parker's Piece and the dreary expanse of undrained fen was the haunt of many a strange fowl. Of other inhabitants of the above I may one day find an occasion to tell.

But it is time to leave such generalities. The two sheep to whom we must return – and I am afraid they were black ones – were very close friends; but few men in the University, or indeed in King's College itself, could boast of more than a speaking acquaintance with either. They occupied one room in the Old Schools of King's, north of the Chapel, which room was always locked when they were out. These were not days when Fellows, nor still less Scholars, were in the habit of dropping into each other's abodes to partake of casual hospitality in the way of tobacco or whiskey and water. The common life, such as it was, was confined to Chapel, Hall and the Fellows' Parlour.

All that was known of Hardman and Ashe's way of employing their leisure was that they went for long walks together and smoked apparently very bad tobacco when they came back.

It was a fine afternoon in October when the events began, or to speak more truly, came to a head, which seemed to show what manner of men were Nicholas Hardman and Stephen Ashe. Chapel service, we may be sure, was at three o'clock, and both our friends were there, staring at each other from opposite stalls. The reedy and pedalless organ helped the rather infirm and jaded choir through a new verse anthem by Dr Blow during which the snoring of Provost Roderick was undoubtedly heard. At near four o'clock Dr Tudway, the organist, played out the scant congregation with a march of his own composition. The choirmen hurried off to go through a similar performance at Trinity. The boys rushed off to whatever haunts in the town they had emerged from. The Provost strolled to his Lodge, which was then at the east end of the Chapel, and the Fellows and Scholars made their way across the strip of ground on the north side, holding on their caps – for a strong west wind was blowing the yellow leaves about – and so into the Old Court and to dine in Hall. A coarse meal, I expect it was, and a silent one. The Vice-Provost and three or four Seniors occupied one table on the dais, the Masters of Arts – among whom were Hardman and Ashe – filled a second along with the Fellow Commoners, and the Bachelors and Undergraduate Fellows and Scholars, two more. There may have been about fifty people in the room. Not much passed at dinner, which lasted about forty minutes; but afterwards the Fellows returned to the parlour and the Scholars to their rooms. With these last we are not concerned, but we may as well follow the Seniors. They are sitting at a large table, clothless, with some decanters of wine (I don't know whether port or claret: much depends upon the date of Lord Methuen's treaty with Portugal), and something like a conversation has broken out.

'Where did ye ride today, Mr Bates?' said Mr Glynne.

'Only as far as Fenstanton.'

'Fenstanton. Ah, isn't that where the witch was ducked last week? Lord Blandford was riding by at the time' (this was the Duke of Marlborough's son and heir who was then a Fellow Commoner but died shortly afterwards), 'and his Lordship made some hot-headed show at rescuing the old creature. Has there been any stir made? Dodgson of Magdalene has the living, but I doubt, if he hath not acted, no one will.

'Tis a lost place, Fenstanton, for all it be on the Huntingdon road.' Mr Glynne, it should be noted, had rather a knack for monopolizing conversation.

'Well, to tell the truth,' said Bates, 'I had not heard of the matter, but the bell was tolling for the burying as I rode through, and I happened to meet Dodgson coming from his beer and pipe as I passed by the churchyard. He did let fall something which could fit with what you say. Pray, Glynne, did you hear of the name Galpin or Gibson; some word with a 'G' in it?'

'Gibson? Mother Gibson! That was the name for a guinea! So that ducking had finished the poor creature,' said the good-natured Glynne. 'These fen people are little but hate. I know the coroner should have sat, and there should have been a dozen strung up at the Assizes, and in any but Dodgson's parish there would have been. But Lord! the man thinks of nothing but his tithes and his beer.'

'Matthews had the parsonage before Dodgson,' said Bates, 'and in his time there were four attempts at ducking that old woman. Not a boy nor man in the parish, he told me, but was ready to swear she had signed herself away. But Matthews threatened to call in the sheriff, and he would have done it, and so they kept mum in his time.'

'For all that,' said Glynne, 'I remember his saying in this parlour that when he looked at her he was half in a mind to believe the tale. He painted her once, and it is true that she might have sat for a portrait of the evening as far as her eyes were concerned. They were as red as blood and the pupils like a goat's'; with which Mr Glynne was silent and shuddered slightly.

'Did they bury her in the churchyard, Bates?' said Dr Morell, the Vice-Provost.

'Yes, Mr Vice-Provost. I noticed a grave dug on the north side, which I take it was for her.'

'All this talk about burying witches puts me in mind of William of Malmesbury's tale that Dr Gates printed not so long back.' This was from a new contributor to the conversation; Mr Newborough, afterwards Headmaster of Eton, who was more bookish and learned than many of his peers. 'Do you know it, Mr Glynne? You should look at Malmesbury,' and he proceeded to tell the story which William had put under the name of the 'Old Woman of Berkeley'. After that came a short discussion of the Witch of Endor, then the conversation drifted to Dr Hodges' book on the Versions of the Bible, then by a not uncommon fate to Dr Bentley's last enormities and thence back to the old question of college livings and probable vacancies.

In the midst of this, Hardman and Ashe made their bow to the Vice-President and went out. They had neither of them made any remark since dinner but Dr Morell, an observant man, noticed that they had taken a very considerable interest in the early part of the conversation.

When the door closed behind them, Mr Glynne said, 'I pity their wives if ever they marry and their parishes if ever they take one.'

'Still,' said Newborough, 'they are quiet enough.'

'I don't know about that, Newborough,' said Morell. 'The man that has chambers under theirs doesn't always sleep well. What can keep the two men treading about the whole night, as I am told they do, and what have they on their mind that makes them sigh and moan like sick owls, as Burton says? You know everyone in college, Glynne; tell me, pray, were you ever in Hardman and Ashe's chambers?'

'Not I,' said Glynne. 'I knocked on their door one day, I recollect, last year. Such a clatter as they made before they opened it, I know I never heard, but all I can tell of the matter is that Hardman was as pale as death when he opened to me, and that the place smelled as sweet as a bonfire of old rags and bones. Hardman made swift to ask my business, and then shut the door in my face!'

'Well,' said Mr Vice-Provost, 'he might have spared himself the question, Glynne, for I never knew you to have any business in this life yet. Never matter! 'Tis time to turn unto the coffee house, gentlemen. I have told Dr Gates that we should be there before eight o'clock, and the clocks are giving the quarter now.'

The company adjourned therefore to a coffee house on the Market Place, and smoked clay pipes till ten with Dr Roger Gates and some other gentlemen from Trinity, Queens' and Bene't Colleges.

The curfew bell was ringing and it was a fine night when Hardman and Ashe, each with a packet and a stick, emerged from the gates of King's College and told the porter – a fiddling old ruffian as were most college servants of that day – that they were not likely to return that night. Neither said any more until they were clear of the town and on the Huntingdon road. Then Nicholas Hardman said, 'If all goes as it should tonight, Ashe, we shall know a matter well worth knowing.'

'Yes, Nick, and there will be a matter worth knowing in one of these bundles,' said Ashe. 'I dare swear though that there will be some disappointment. Newborough's tale of the old witch set me a-thinking. Have you got the book upon you, Nick?'

'Book, what book? Dr Gates' of Malmesbury, I suppose? A fat folio of some weight. Is it likely?'

'No, no! Not Malmesbury. *Our* book, *the* book, I mean.'

'Call me a fool if you like, Stephen, but don't ask me such a question. Have I a tooth outside my head? That is as likely as it would be for me to leave the book in my chambers. Buy why, pray, does that ass Newborough's old story set you thinking?'

'Why, only that if the same gentry that came for their friend in that story were thinking of waiting upon *our* friend at Fenstanton tonight, it is like we may see trouble.'

Hardman gave a snort. 'And if they did, do you think a circle is broken so easily? Have I nothing here that can avail to make them give back? Still, you are right in a way, Stephen, as you have been before. If we are later in the field than they, there may be trouble, even danger. If we get the three locks of hair and the winding-sheet, we are masters of the elementals. The others want the soul.'

It was a thought that seemed to give them pause for a moment, and they were silent. So the clouds flew across the moon, and the wind blew over the bare fields, and the bells of Cambridge came more faintly to the ear, as they walked quietly on towards the sleeping village of Fenstanton.

Those who remember the road between Cambridge and Fenstanton will bear me out when I say that it is eleven miles long, and presents few features of interest. There is an occasional wayside inn, a few farms a little off the road, and on a clear day we may see the lantern and western tower of Ely Cathedral, and a good many church towers. The church nearest to the road is that of Lolworth, on the left hand, some five or six miles out. There was something doing at Lolworth when Hardman and Ashe passed it. The bell was going, and the windows lighted. Nocturnal funerals were not uncommon in Queen Anne's time, so it did not surprise the onlookers when they saw two lines of torches working their way slowly through the trees near the church, and when they saw a figure in white flit out of the south porch to meet the cortege, they knew that it must be the parson. Yet a few moments more and the procession was in the church. Then Hardman and Ashe walked on again, for they had paused a moment.

The turning out of the main road towards Lolworth church lay some little distance ahead, and down the lane was coming a group of figures at a great pace. They reached the road and turned down it towards the travellers, who were a little daunted thereby, because they did not wish to be recognized as Cambridge parsons at that hour of the night. There appeared to be seven people clustering round one in the middle, and their action and gait were like those of watchmen who had taken a prisoner. The party came on, and it seemed as if this conjecture might fit the situation, for the person in the midst was plainly reluctant, and as plainly was being hurried on by the rest. Hardman and Ashe drew toward the hedge to let the men pass, and their eyes were riveted upon the face of the captured man. It was not lightly to be forgotten, for it is not often that one beholds the face of a man who has lost all hope, and yet has room in his brain for an unspeakable fear. This is the sight which the two ill-starred priests were now looking at, and they saw moreover that in spite of his fear and desperation, the captive could look nowhere save straight in front of him, for anything seemed tolerable rather than to see the faces of the seven who were about him. When they pictured the scene themselves thereafter, they realized that his was the only face of which they had caught sight at all; nay, it even seemed to them that there was no other face for their eyes to catch.

The group passed quite silently and for many moments the two men were stayed breathless to within an ace of sudden flight or swooning. They knew that they had seen that which no mourner at the funeral had seen, and it was in their mind that it is not always well for those whose eyes are opened. It may happen to some to see the mountain full of issues and vaults of fire, but to others are also shown very different sights. Yet the natures of both were so obstinate and dogged that neither would broach to the other the thought of returning, and giving up the dismal project they had in their mind. They soon sighted Fenstanton spire, and half a mile further they left the road and made their way over the fields to the side where the churchyard was accessible out of sight of the street. It was not a difficult wall to climb, yet they were unnerved and took several minutes to get over it. Then they proceeded to go through the sinister rites and ceremonies which were to safeguard them against those powers with which they supposed themselves to be leagued, for they are treacherous allies, as those tell who claim to know the heart of the matter. In the shadow of the dark church, on the north side, not more than ten yards from the only new-made grave on that side of the building, the men picked out a space where the grass was shortest and there they drew two large circles, one within the other. In the space between the circles they marked out with some pains the symbols of the planets and a few Hebrew letters which were meant to indicate the names of angels and of the great Power, whose aid by one of the strange incantations of magic they promised themselves they would gain for the work they were at. When their defence was completed they stopped, and Ashe looked at his timepiece. The time was something short of a quarter to twelve, so they had but a brief wait until the middle of the night was reached.

And now, we might ask what was it that these two educated clergymen proposed to themselves? And how came it that they were on an enterprise which is associated not always kindly with the darkest medievalism and the most decadent civilization?

You will have guessed that they were earnest and credulous students of magic. How came such men to Cambridge in the reign of Queen Anne? I can only answer that in that day there were many such men in Germany, and the instinct which prompts men to seek intercourse with the unseen peoples of the air is one that may come to any civilization and in any century. Many believe the intercourse has been sometimes gained, but that is little to the point.

That which Hardman and Ashe were determined upon was the obtaining of an ingredient for future spells. This would, they hoped, enable them to command the forces of nature to a degree which they believed many to have obtained before them. They meant on this night, and they were confident of accomplishing it, to go through certain forms of words which would have the power to make the corpse of the old woman buried that day rise out of the grave and come to them. Hard as it is to think of, they intended to get from her the portion of graveclothes and the locks of hair of which Hardman spoke when they were on the road. Then the body would return to the earth as it was, and the soil be replaced over it. They were to go back to their college the next day, and in seven days' time, few would be so rich and powerful as Nicholas Hardman and Stephen Ashe.

It was with a strange kind of exaltation that, as midnight came near, Hardman drew from his bosom a paper book, about a hundred years old, ill-written and full of diagrams like those which had just been drawn upon the ground, and within whose compass both of them were standing. He began to read, or intone, a Latin form of conjuration, a sinister kind of church service in which the most sacred of names were freely employed. To this Ashe made the set appropriate refrains. The night had been disturbed throughout and windy, but no rain had fallen and thin cloud kept covering the moon, which was by this time low and near the horizon. The wind rattled in the louvres of the tower, and every now and then swung the tongue of a bell so that it sounded in a dim and far off fashion. Nicholas Hardman read on, faster and louder, and Ashe responded at short intervals. They had now entered upon the 91st Psalm:

[15]

'*Qui Habitat*' ('Whoso dwelleth'), and they were just promising themselves deliverance from the terror that walks in darkness when a blacker cloud than usual left the moon's face and Stephen Ashe fell like an ox at the feet of Hardman. For it seemed that it had been determined that these fools should be answered according to their folly.

I have said that the miserable and unfortunate old woman whom the fen-men had killed was buried a bare ten yards away from the two conjurors. This was the point to which their spells were directed. Looking over at the grave, Hardman beheld crouched there a shape which there was small likelihood of his ever forgetting. It was the figure, one might say at first sight, of an enormous bat, with folded wings and a head approaching the human form. In a short moment, Hardman caught sight of the folds of wrinkled skin or hide that hung down from the cheeks, of the wide ears which shone transparent in the moonlight, and of the two lines of flickering fire which marked the almost closed eyes. And further, as he declared afterwards, he saw the earth heap upon which this being was crouched stir and wave beneath it. Nor was he allowed to remain a spectator, for this terrible apparition rose to its full height and for a minute seemed to look about for a victim whom it knew to be near. Hardman, almost at the pitch of despair, trusted only in his charmed circle, but the creature on a sudden turned full in his direction and stepped straight towards him, plucking for but an instant at the angelic names and planetary symbols. In another moment its palms were raised before his face and he knew no more.

It was Ashe who helped him back to Cambridge in the morning of the next day, and it was Ashe too who, though himself a stricken man, sheltered and ministered to him in the parsonage of Willoughton for the twenty years that he survived. But Hardman never saw light again.

The College never learned the rights of the matter. Two days after the catastrophe, Mr Glynne asked Mr Morell, the Vice-Provost, 'What did you do at the Fellows' meeting this morning, Mr Vice?'

'Sealed the presentation to Weedon Lois, and received a declaration.'

'A Royal declaration or what?'

'No, Glynne, Mr Provost will tell you what it may be, if you ask him.'

So off goes Mr Glynne to the Lodge. But Provost Roderick is pale, which is not natural to him, and not smoking, which is decidedly unnatural, and disturbed and uncommunicative. Mr Glynne can only learn that it is a matter which the Seniors have decided to keep private. During the next week, a wagonload of items from one set of chambers in King's College is wheeled off in the direction of Barton and does not

[16]

come back; and most of the Seniors are very regular in their attendance in the Chapel for some months.

I cannot help concluding the events I have set down with that entry in the *Alumni* book, which states that two gentlemen, being Fellows of the College, were permitted to register a solemn abjuration of all unlawful acts in the practice of which they had grievously transgressed. It was agreed that the Provost and Seniors should exercise their utmost discretion to the end that this matter be kept strictly private to the Seniority.

UNBURIED BANE

N. Dennett

N. Dennett's story originally appeared in the
anthology *Horrors*, published in 1933.

It all began (said Frances Windthrop) when I was led by my husband excitedly over three and a half miles of wet moor to inspect the old farm he had recently discovered. It was not only the fact that it was incredibly lonely, was at least two hundred years old, and probably possessed, as he explained with enthusiasm, Lord knew what queer history, but it was – though dilapidated to a degree – occupied by an old scrag of a woman whom he declared gave him the shivers.

Beyond demurring mildly that neither could possibly interest me to the extent it did himself, I consented to tramp along to see the farmhouse and its grim-sounding occupant. I had discovered long ago, in the early days of my marriage, that it was not everything to be the wife of a popular playwright; one, moreover, who specialized in those of a sensational character, and was, consequently, ever on the look-out for likely material.

I realized that for some months now his pen had been idle; that, possibly through overwork or lack of change, no themes had come to his harassed brain except those which had been used countless times before. Here in the old farm he had found the necessary impetus: he declared the very look of the place inspired him; that, if he could only obtain admission, he was sure he would find his plot already made within its four walls. Further, so better to soak in its atmosphere, he suggested that we occupied the place ourselves until such time as the play was written, providing, of course, the old woman now living there was agreeable. There was a village of a sort three and a half miles away, and probably she would be only too glad to move there, he said; unless, as an alternative, she agreed to stay and 'do' for us while letting us have a room or two for a consideration.

I was against it from the first; but seeing him so eager and hopeful, and dreading a continuance of his moody irritability, the restless pacing and sleepless nights while he vainly pursued the illusive idea, I forbore to mention how much I disliked the project. For myself I foresaw many hours of loneliness and boredom.

One afternoon in late September, then, we set off; not, from my point of view, what one might call a promising beginning. Oliver strode on rapidly, impatient to be there, scarcely noticing how I stumbled over the heathery ground. At length, after what seemed hours, we climbed a rise of the moor where beyond, in a shallow basin of desolate land, showed the shale roof of a building, its lines half obliterated in the failing light.

'Is that the place?' I asked, my heart sinking inexplicably.

Oliver ran down the curve and stopped before a broken-down gate covered with lichen.

Out of the shadows the farm arose in a chaos of neglect and decay. Hideous fungus was growing everywhere, between the chinks of the cobblestones, on the rotten and broken fences – even the walls of the farmhouse itself were smeared with curious green vegetation, while the rock-moss flourished on its roof. Trunks of old apple trees in an orchard beyond were grey with lichen and twisted by age into fantastic shapes. In the moor twilight which was creeping up cold and cheerless, with strange ominous streaks of colour where the sun had gone down, it was a dreary, desolate place.

I drew back; an indefinable fear possessed me. 'I won't go in,' I said, in a rather shaking voice.

'Rubbish, Frances; why on earth not?' demanded my husband.

He climbed determinedly over a tumbled-down wall, and stood in what had once been the farmyard, now a rat-infested wilderness. A pool to one side was green with slime, and sodden straw lay littered about in heaps. The farmhouse, a low, squat building whose ancient roof sagged and humped crazily in a last effort to avoid slipping off bodily, with its close-shut door and secretive-looking window, appeared dead and deserted amid its army of strange and hideous weeds.

[19]

I could see, as Oliver stood staring, that he was frankly revelling in it all, in its possibilities for the production of a real 'thriller'. And indeed, what with its dismal and forsaken appearance, its air of sinister and brooding quiet, its very situation, hidden away there in the fastnesses of the moor, with only the owls and the conies for any signs of life – even I, who am no dramatist, could understand the attraction it held for Oliver. Meanwhile I stood beside him, protest in every line of my body. A chilly wind sighed and whispered about our ears, and stirred the few stunted bushes growing against the crumbling walls. It was unbelievably lonely.

'There's that old harridan who's living in the place at present – what about knocking her up and getting her to show us over tonight?' Oliver proposed enthusiastically.

It was with, I knew, a mental picture of the posters outside a well-known London theatre announcing Oliver Windthrop's new success that he raised his hand and knocked loudly on the door, set so deep in a porch as to be almost invisible in the growing darkness.

The echo died away in a series of muffled responses. We waited, and five minutes passed away – ten, and still no one came. Then, just as Oliver was going away disappointed, the door silently opened the width of an inch or two. Someone made a mumbling enquiry as to what we wanted. Oliver asked, might he and his wife step in and rest for a moment, as both were tired with walking over the moors? There was no reply, but a face, white and curiously vacant, appeared round the narrow opening and peered closely into ours. Apparently satisfied with what it saw there, the door was opened a fraction wider and we were motioned to come in. We bent our heads low and entered a dark, flagged passage, then into another door which led into a black-raftered kitchen, dimly illuminated by the waning daylight that came in through the window covered with dirt and cobwebs.

Two chairs were pushed out ungraciously. We seated ourselves. I looked around uneasily, with a creeping aversion. The misshapen old creature who lived there was surely the most silent thing I had ever seen, and also the most repulsive. So bloodless, so emaciated was her face, with one shoulder held higher than the other so that her body was awry, and her gait a twisted see-sawing motion, there was something supernatural about her – something quasi-human that went with the brooding house, the lonely moor, and the night winds that swept blackly about it. She stood with a pallid watchfulness, silently waiting for us to speak.

'Do you not find life here very lonely?' I observed at length, unable to bear longer the heavy silence, the shadowy room, and the odour of damp and decay that hung clammily about it.

Her voice, a thin, bodiless whisper, replied she was never lonesome, she was one that preferred her own company.

'You live here, then, quite alone?' said my husband, rising as he spoke to put a match to the old-fashioned lamp that stood on the table, having received a nodded permission.

'Eh? Iss, quite alone, except for my thoughts – and my gert old black cat.'

She gave him a strange, unfathomable look from her sightless-looking eyes, and as she moved, so the figure of the cat sitting motionless in the gloom behind her came into view, its eyes glittering greenly. Their shadows grotesquely outlined against the wall, on a sudden rose up till they touched and spread along the ceiling, and appeared to crouch menacingly over our heads.

Nervously, I averted my gaze, but found it riveted instead on the face of the attenuated old creature standing opposite us. It was with a shock that I really saw that countenance for the first time: so fleshless the bones showed beneath its covering of skin – an expression both fixed and mask-like, a wide and lipless mouth, no eyebrows, eyes sunken in discoloured sockets, a nose with the left nostril black and closed, and one or two crooked and pointed teeth.

A tremor of repugnance shook me from head to foot. She was horrible, unnatural. It took all my will-power not to rise from my seat and run from the house there and then.

'Might I enquire why the farmhouse has been allowed to fall into its present neglected condition, which obviously is a matter of some time?' Oliver enquired at this point.

'Eh?' mumbled the old hag vaguely, as if she were a little hard of hearing. Her speech, a sequence of inarticulate sounds, was faint and difficult to understand. 'Eh, but a power o' years ago it were a proper fine farm, but they do say as how it were the scene o' terrible deeds; and now neither man or maid will come a-nigh en after the dimpse; and if it warn't for me nobody'd a-live in en.'

An eerie sound moved in her throat, which faintly resembled a chuckle. An amusement not shared by Oliver and myself; it was a sound that seemed full of a hidden meaning, and sent a cold shiver down my spine.

'"Witch's Bane" they calls the farm round these yur parts, or mebbe tes "Wolfsbane" – I disremember now – on account o' they weeds, I reckon,' she gibbered, with a silent person's garrulity; 'but, for certain sure, they'm mortal afeard to come downalong because o' thicky – but come 'long up over, and then I'll show it 'ee.'

There was something almost frightful in her smooth noiseless movements as she twisted from side to side in ceaseless contortion. So unsubstantial was she, she seemed merely the envelope that covered a thing of skin and bones. She led us upstairs first, up a rickety staircase, impossibly steep and damp, and into several empty bedrooms, all with low and sloping ceilings crossed by heavy black beams, and with the tiniest of windows that had the appearance of being sealed, so long unopened did they look. The floors, too, had a downward tilt, and sagged as one stepped upon them.

With our shadows now weirdly elongated to an exaggerated height, and now dwindling down to nothing as we wandered through the musty-smelling house – the eerie old woman like a distorted shadow herself – it was daunting to a degree. I followed shrinkingly, with a fear none the less real for being non-susceptible to definition. I could see, however, that it would be useless to appeal to Oliver: by the excited way his eyes shone he was resolved more than ever to put his crazy plan into execution. To imagine living in this ghostly place even for a day filled me with horror.

Down the stairs we creaked again, and into what once had been the farmhouse parlour. A room rather long and low, the smell of damp and mouldiness which pervaded it was made more apparent by the wooden window-shutters that were tightly shut on the outside. The ceiling, bisected by heavy oak beams, was discoloured and dropping off in places with mildew, while ancient paper hung and rotted from the walls. There was a broad window-seat, with low wide windows which, when opened, gave on to a stretch of moorland extending as far as the eye could reach; and there on the sill, grinning at me was—

I started back at once, uttering a startled exclamation. It was an object so unexpected to see there, and yet so in keeping with this room, with the strange house that lodged it.

I rubbed my hands, the slim white fingers that had touched it, with fastidious distaste. I have ever hated touching anything that is not fresh and sweet and clean – not that this thing on the windowsill was not clean: it was as clean as age and decay could make it. Yellow and smooth, it shone almost as if polished with oil: a broken, weather-beaten skull. Extremely old, it was certainly human, the forehead being very low and badly proportioned.

'O-ha-ha; her's nothin' to be afeard of – now.' Again that unpleasant

[22]

sound agitated the ancient creature's throat. 'Eh, but a famous witch she were. There's folks what do mind even now how pigs and cattle died quick and mysterious-like if her were offended, and no amount o' salt round the sties and barns would avert it, neither.'

Oliver pricked up his ears; I, too, listened with a half-willing, half-fascinated interest. This story of witchcraft of a less matter-of-fact age was strangely compelling. The odious old creature appeared to delight in it – liked to dwell on all the things that were ghoulish and horrible. The influence of the 'evil eye', the propitiating of the powers of darkness; and so forth.

'Eh, Mally Ry were her name, and her were done to death – drownded alive or sommat – in the days o' King George. But arter her were dead her wouldn't remain quiet; the most scarifying groans and screeches was heerd: her had died cursin' anyone what should berry en, and sworn that, if en warn't kep' wi'in the walls o' the house where her had lived in life, her sperrit should make it uninhabitable like fer human beings . . . Wull, in course o' time her weared away, and on'y the skull were left. But mind 'ee,' she went on with a kind of eldritch enjoyment, 'but mind 'ee, *it must never be disturbed*, for if tes, turrible sounds are a-said to be heard, and accidents, storms, fires and calamity has followed as nat'rally as sun arter rain. There were some new tenants here to once, they berried en . . . for three days. And here it has ree-mained, as tes like to do, for several more centuries.'

Delighted with this macabre recital, and more excited over his discovery of the old farm than ever, Oliver now eagerly voiced the plan he had had in view from the moment we entered the place. The ghastly old creature proving more amenable than he had hoped for (possibly the amount of the sum he offered having something to do with it), arrangements for our occupying one or two rooms were very soon completed, with satisfaction on all sides but mine. This suggested staying at the farm was a thing I dreaded beyond words. Something outside myself warned me that it was the direst folly we were contemplating. 'It is madness; nothing but disaster will come of it,' I told Oliver with the conviction of a presentiment. He, however, merely reiterated his belief that here in the old farm lay the nucleus of one of the best 'thrillers' he had yet done, that he had an idea already even, and was all impatience to be settled in and the play begun.

As the broken and lichen-grown gate closed behind us once more and we started on our homeward tramp over the now dark moors, something made me look back. The rain had ceased, and in the light of a yellow half-moon I saw the wizened figure of the old woman, the cat beside her, standing in the doorway looking after us, an evil and peculiarly malign grin twisting her lipless mouth.

At first the presence of the skull on the windowsill did not trouble me to the extent I had feared, for after all, what harm could an old broken skull do anyone? To be sure, it was not particularly pleasant; but since it was the custom, I endeavoured to conquer my nervous fears of it.

Oliver, busily at work behind a closed door, and surrounded by sheets of manuscript, was absorbed and abstracted; however, from his look of satisfaction I knew the play was shaping well. Judging from its title – 'The Death-Dealing Skull' – it promised to be all that the lovers of thrills desired.

I was almost as much startled as relieved to discover no presence of Ann Skegg (that strange personality) anywhere about; the house was left entirely to ourselves. It occurred to me that possibly she had thought better of her original intention, and had, after all, repaired to the village – if such it could be termed – until we should have departed, and her home once more be left to its former undisturbed quiet and solitude. I did, indeed, make a tentative enquiry from one or two of the cottagers there, but I was stared at so queerly with such startled attention that I didn't pursue the subject further. Beyond eliciting the information that Witch's Bane Farm hadn't been lived in for years as far as any of them knew – that the last tenant had committed suicide – and that neither love nor money would induce any of them to put so much as their noses inside it, I returned on the whole rather more perplexed than before.

Came russet October: the bare moorlands, sprent with gold and purple, bloomed anew under the spell of air crisped with the first frosts. I walked for miles each day, delighting in the exercise and the new-born beauty around me. However, the days passed; and November brought with it chill sobbing rain and empty hours. Now I was confined to the house, and the doors were shut to the wind's will, the open sunshiny air, and the blessed freedom of the moors; dank and miserable, they stretched before the farm in an endless pool-sodden waste . . . How dark it was now in the house always; even what little sun there was had no entrance; and the owls, always the owls to haunt me with a mournful crying . . .

Immersed in his work, Oliver noticed nothing of this; did not notice how slowly and imperceptibly as I passed hour upon lonely hour in the musty-smelling parlour, the sight of the skull lying there in its accustomed place began to be more than I could stand, so that I could view it only with a sense of rather absurd horror . . . How its eyeholes, inky and horrible, bored into my own, its mouth grim and awry . . . the broken, irregular teeth, the low, criminal-looking forehead . . . I both feared and loathed it. Always it appeared to grin evilly and maliciously at me, as though at some obscene jest . . .

A night came that had set in early. I was alone as if no one were in the house, so silent was the room, the farm. Outside, the wind pressed against the windows; an old tree in the yard adjoining creaked and groaned with a straining of leafless boughs, and tapped on the black panes with phantom fingers. The old parlour, seeming dingier and even more gloomy, was a place of shadows. The only light was that cast dimly by a hurricane lamp; beyond its narrow circle, into the dark corners of the room, I dared not look lest nameless things should stir and leap upon me. I trembled at every creak; awaiting with a dreadful anticipation for the very door to open silently towards me and disclose who knew what shocking spectacle; and when the long-drawn-out hoot of an owl echoed in a tree outside I sprang to my feet, shuddering violently.

In the jumping flame of the lamp, a shaft of light danced now here, now there, over the gruesome skull, lighting up the eyeholes and heightening the effect of sinister and sardonic amusement . . . I must have partially lost control of myself, or at least of my better judgment . . . Before I quite realized what I was doing, despite its alarming reputation for resenting either its removal or any indignity done to it, I had seized the loathsome thing quickly and thrust it out of sight in a dark cupboard.

That night Oliver and I were awakened by a sound of weird, unearthly screaming, that droned on and on, low, unceasing, and maddeningly monotonous. There was something terrible, something mysteriously awful in the sound, as if dead hopes and utter despair were being voiced, as if numberless souls in torment were circling in the black air above the farm and were wailing and crying their anguish through the keyholes. I listened quailing in my bed, not daring to confess what I had done. Oliver declared it was wind, for such a storm was raging, of wind and thunder, as set all the doors banging and the windows rattling. Sleep was made impossible. A little towards dawn, secretly, I restored the skull to its place. Ann Skegg, whom – strangely and unexpectedly – I encountered in one of the flagged passages, gave me a look from which I fled; there was such malevolent amusement in it.

And now, from this time, Ann Skegg never left the house. It was as though she mistrusted me – as if she feared for the safety of the skull and constituted herself its guardian. She appeared even more vague, more attenuated than before, and even more silent. A subtle difference in her both perplexed and intimidated me: her jaw was never still, her whole person shook from either old age or extreme cold, and up the front of her gown, of an outmoded fashion with which I was familiar and yet could not place, extended a curious green stain . . .

The mere sight of that twisted, contorted figure with its sideways-dipping walk, its long, lanky hands, creeping – drifting, rather – about the passages and up the stairs, sent a shuddering dread through every nerve of my body. At this time, so great was the peculiar revulsion she inspired in me, in an effort to avoid her I tramped for miles over the soaked and desolate moors. I began to entertain the most appalling notions: to question whether, like Lazarus, one who has once been dead could return alive from the grave . . . The touch of her fingers was cold and slimy, while I feared her smile more than anything in the world . . . I tried to voice my nightmare horrors to Oliver, but unfortunately, alas, he could not, or would not, understand, regarding them merely as the fancies of hysteria.

The play was almost finished . . . Triumphantly the last scene was completed. He announced his intention of going up to London with a view to its early production.

I heard him with a thrill of unreasoning terror. 'Let me come with you,' I begged. 'I cannot, and will not, stay here in this dreadful house alone!'

He demurred. 'I shan't be gone more than a few days: a week at the most,' he said. 'Now be sensible: what on earth are you so alarmed about?'

I could only stammer out something inadequate like, 'A big lonely house, the moors, and the owls, and – and Ann Skegg.'

'What has poor misshapen Ann Skegg done?' he scoffed. 'She can't help her peculiarities; the old thing is perfectly harmless, though I must admit rather a fearsome-looking object. No, no, Frances; you stay here. I'll be back in no time, and then we'll clear off – have a holiday – Switzerland, the Riviera: how about it? I feel in my bones the play will create a sensation.'

He went. In the evening a few hesitating flakes of snow hovered in the air, which before long thickened into a blizzard, continuing all night. I awoke to find the farmhouse as a beleaguered town: snowdrifts standing halfway up the doors and up to the window-ledges, the rooms filled with a strange unreal light, and the house encompassed about by that unearthly hush which snow inevitably brings. Roads – even hedges – had vanished, so that there was no means of getting out, and no possibility of holding communication with the outside world. There was only Ann Skegg for company . . . and the skull grinning eternally in its place on the windowsill.

The time went by. I became aware of a sense of evil in the farmhouse; an atmosphere so particularly strong in the dismal, mouldy-smelling parlour, that I could not only feel it but almost see it, and against which I struggled vainly and ineffectually. Dreams haunted me day and night; I grew perceptibly haggard and wild-eyed, jumping at every sound. Each day I became more terrified of the awful thing that was Ann Skegg; an aura of unspeakable malfeasance hung about her like a black cloud. I became convinced that whatever it was that animated that old wizened troll of a creature it was some unhallowed thing. A cold sweat would break upon my skin and my bones turn to water whenever she turned upon me her peculiar, flaccid-looking eyes in which gleamed a terrible and implacable hate. It was as if she resented my presence, as if she wished to be left alone with the ill-omened skull for which she appeared to cherish a ghastly affection. I would see her croon and gibber to it as if it could understand, and pass her scraggy fingers over its shiny surface almost with a caressing movement. Impossible and fantastic as it may be, it was as though there existed a secret understanding between them, an affinity . . . It made my flesh creep to watch.

Presently a horrible fascination took possession of me. I could not tear myself away from looking; I would creep along stealthily, to hold my breath in disgust and aversion.

Ann Skegg caught me thus spying upon her one night of bitter cold. She turned suddenly, the cat beside her, and saw me standing there in the doorway. The cat, its fur rising, drew back its lips and snarled hideously and noiselessly. Ann Skegg began to move and came slowly towards me with that terrible see-saw movement, her chin mim-mumbling, her head thrust forward, her baleful eyes transfixing mine – the grimmest, most ghastly thing I had ever beheld. I stood like one turned to stone, rooted there as by some strange power, incapable of moving a hand, of uttering a cry. The blood ran cold in my veins, my teeth chattered, my heart stopped beating.

Then, all at once, I shrieked. Control slipped from me. As she came slowly on, so I edged round the wall; my desperate fingers searched and found a weapon . . . Screaming wildly, with all my strength I flung the sinister skull full at the oncoming thing and its snarling beast. It fell at their feet with a dull thud and broke into several pieces.

Ann Skegg suddenly laughed – the vilest, loathsome sound.

Then, and then only, I realized what I had done. Fear held me in a remorseless grip, while a hundred and one superstitious terrors marshalled themselves before me. Instances of other happenings when the skull had been disturbed, or been made to suffer any indignity, shocking enough, rose to my mind; but I, with incredible folly, had reduced it to nothing but a heap of splintered bone. Since it had never been known to fail to punish anyone who mistreated it, I awaited in shuddering anticipation for what was coming.

That night I stayed awake, too frightened either to sleep or lie down; but inexplicably enough, there was no repetition of that low unnerving screaming for which I was waiting: only an ominous silence. (It was now I enacted that scene all over again: saw myself throw the window wide and with unnatural strength send the remains of the skull hurtling through the darkness, to fall into the frozen pond that lay beyond. I heard, and shall never cease to hear, the small sound of splintering cat-ice cut the still air.)

Yet another night passed; and on the third an indescribably dreadful shrieking and wailing began, as if maddened fiends were howling aloud in pain and derision, and were trying to force a way in from the cold and darkness outside. The terrifying noises, shrieks and groans dwindled, died down, then rose again with tenfold velocity: there was in them this time a malevolence not present upon the first occasion.

My heart thump-thumping, I sat up in bed clutching the clothes, anathematizing the wicked stupidity that had thus released this horror upon my head. Somewhere about midnight, thinking perhaps the rush of cold air might alleviate the fever of terror that alternately chilled and heated my body, I got out of bed to open the window.

I shut it with a slam, near to fainting. There in the blackness, not twenty yards from me, I heard a strange, unholy commotion going on. Wind was racketing round the four quarters of the house: owls screeched; thunder pealed. Trees, opaque shadows, swayed and groaned; a dog, far off, howled mournfully as if someone were dead; the whole world of night unusually awake and agitated. A waning moon (until then obscured) suddenly showed a wan face behind the clouds as they scurried panic-stricken across the sky, and upon this dark shadows met and parted again with an awful riot of nocturnal clamour; finally, sweeping downwards to the ebon surface of the pond which glimmered a faint silver where the moon-glints touched it, they rose with what looked like jagged pieces of bone in their hands, which they let fall again with maleficent laughter, shrieks and groans.

Suddenly, as I watched, one of the shadows that danced round and about the pool and reeled to the blattering wind and the thunder peals, detached itself and rose slowly out of the pond and, dripping, passed through the door of the farmhouse . . . With my hair rising upon my scalp, my face bedewed with cold sweat, I recognized it for the fearsome creature I had known as Ann Skegg.

I knew now with a hideous certitude that she was dead; had always been dead: that she was the terrible Mally Ry herself, who by some devilish power still walked the earth – drowned, but living. Beyond question I knew, too, that I was there alone, to pit my puny strength against the powers of darkness which my action of destroying the skull had released. Those powers which had been in abeyance so long as the sinister relic was neither moved nor harmed, now manifested themselves with tenfold force.

Nightly the uncanny shrieks and groans went on, making sleep impossible. Abating during the day, the din was merely a low monotone that droned ceaselessly and monotonously in my ears, rising to howl and batter round the house on the approach of the dusk hours. Nightly the unholy play with the broken pieces of the skull was enacted over the dark water of the pool, and ever again the old twisted corpse, which was animated by the vengeful spirit of Mally Ry, rose dripping out of the pond, and vanished into the shut door of the farmhouse.

Meanwhile the snows still held, coming on foot after foot of unbroken whiteness; the lines of the farm were obliterated, the roads impassable. There was no sun, and no ceasing of the biting chill. With every hour my soul became more benumbed by fear, the scarlet thread of my brain stretched to breaking point.

The climax came suddenly, following on the heels of Oliver's return (the snow having at length melted sufficiently to allow him to cross the moors, with great difficulty). Upon seeing him ploughing toilsomely towards the farm I tottered to the door, overcome with relief. He exclaimed aloud in shocked surprise upon seeing my altered looks, the shadow of myself that I had become; the next moment I crumpled up in a heap at his feet.

'For God's sake, what is it? What has been happening here while I have been away?' he demanded, as once more consciousness returned, and I sat up weak and shaking.

The tale was soon gasped out; he listened in growing consternation, his face paling in spite of himself. 'Perhaps it is not too late even now,' he said at length, with an uncontrollable shiver. 'The pond is not deep; I will fetch a lantern—'

He went to the door and threw it open. 'What – what are you going to do?' I started up, full of a nameless apprehension.

'Do? Why, fish the skull up again, of course! We must restore it, bind the pieces together, propitiate the powers of darkness, at once, now—'

His tongue clove to his mouth, his body stiffened as slowly, step by step, through the door came drifting the horror that had once been Ann Skegg. There IT stood, its face a cadaverous blue, its long fingers cold with the cold of death, its eyes grown empty hollows, the rank odour of stagnant water about its clothes – and on its thumb a long black hook like the hook of a bat . . .

Oliver shrieked aloud in an agony of fear. The thing smiled – the most hideous, diabolical smile, and moved soundlessly on. Upon the floor, where its feet passed, were patches of green slime . . .

As we retreated, so the thing followed, advancing with a fearful malignity on its skull-like face. Hard pressed, stark with terror, and the icy cold that radiated from it, I knew now the last scene was to be played to its appointed end.

Slowly, foot by foot, we fell before it. Oliver, lamp in hand, his expression one of frozen steadfastness, holding that terrible and basilisk gaze, was the last thing I saw before I sank down insensible for the second time . . . When I came to, the room was empty; but a rush of cold air was blowing in through the open window. I ran out into the deepening night, crying, 'Oliver! Oliver!' but there was no reply. The yard was deserted and empty; already that eldritch drone was rising and skirling round the house. Slowly I re-entered, and sat in horrible suspense awaiting his return. Several times I went to the window and gazed into the darkness; once I fancied I heard a faint cry, but attributed it to overwrought nerves . . . I moved restlessly about the room, too frightened either to stay in that haunted house or brave the unknown perils without. At last, finding the suspense unendurable, and clutching at all the remnants of my courage, I went out in search of him.

Wind, like water, swept cold and black; lightning, although it was mid-winter, cut the inky darkness of the heavens; the night was full of sound. Thunder peal upon thunder peal rumbled and rolled along the tors; the

[30]

air was close and unnaturally oppressive. I called repeatedly, with a sense of impending calamity, 'Oliver! Oh, Oliver, answer me, answer me!' but no sound of a replying voice came to my straining ears. I went on, fearful, stumbling. And then there came, borne on the wind, a piercing cry, as if someone were in deadly danger.

'OLIVER! OLIVER!' I cried again and then I saw —

I saw a sight that has seared itself indelibly upon my eyeballs. In the eerie light of the hurricane lamp that lay fallen on its side on the snowy brink of the pond, the great curtain of the night beyond, I saw Oliver – beaten back till he stood in its very water, still keeping at bay that thing of ghastly horror. My heart hammered against my ribs, my breath came and went in great gasps as I stood there staring – so fearful was the sight, so dire my foreboding. In the waving, fluttering light of the lamp I saw with dread the Thing, advancing and receding, but always coming nearer, draw close with deadly purpose, one gaunt arm outstretched; I saw Oliver's white face thrown back, his eyes almost starting out of his head with fear and loathing, staring into the eyeholes where hers had been; finally, with a despairing gesture, he threw up his arms, covered his eyes, shrieked out: 'Drown, witch, fiend, whatever you are; in the name of the Devil, drown!'

On a sudden there sprang up a moaning gust of wind; the eldritch skirling rose to a howl, the heavens opened – there came a flash of lightning, intense, blue. I saw the Horror shiver, bend, and sink down, the black water of the pool quiver. Then, even as I looked, above his head hovered something foul, something unspeakably awful, with vast leathery bar-pinions and hooked feet. Even as a cry of terror broke from me, struggling helplessly and unavailingly, he was enveloped in the shadow of the dark wings, caught up, and finally disappeared from sight into the black and howling vault above. With that, thunder crashed peal upon peal; there was a sound as of the world wailing in anguish, a sound as of demoniac laughter, triumphant and utterly vile . . .

Something shrieked – shrieked and shrieked again above the clangour. I heard it, hear it still – then blindly, I turned and ran on and on, mile upon mile over the snow-bound moors . . .

Notice having been brought to the doctor of an out-of-the-way village of a woman seen wandering about whose actions and strange appearance excited the suspicions of the villagers, I was certified and confined to an asylum as hopelessly mad. There are people who think I am still; are afraid to let me out, after having spent thirty years of my life behind high, imprisoning walls . . .

Oliver? He was found – inexplicably burnt, and almost unrecognizable, his face scarred and scarred again as with great claws ... Well, goodbye, goodbye, if you must go, thank you for coming to see an old woman like me. I'm quite sane, quite normal; only I behave strangely if I see a bat; I've forgotten why now, it's all going again ...

THE TOAD WITCH

Jessica Amanda Salmonson

Jessica Amanda Salmonson (b.1950) is one of
the busiest writers in the new generation of
American horror writers, with many short
stories, novels and award-winning anthologies to
her credit. These include *The Swordswoman, The
Golden Naginata, Ou Lu Khen and the Beautiful
Madwoman, Tales by Moonlight, Amazons I* and
II, and a definitive two-volume addition of Fitz-
James O'Brien's supernatural tales. The
following new story is a fine example of the
author's style.

I began life in 1950. Until then, everything was darkness. Afterward
was suffering and beauty. How could I not become a masochist? By
the age of four I had learned to mistrust everyone, a good
philosophy. If one expects something terrible to develop out of even
pleasant events, one may also expect consolations at moments of travail;
and even I must delude myself from time to time, succumbing to the
disease of sentiment.

People who are essentially cheerful annoy me. When they are finally
bent and deaf, they are suddenly surprised. They find out their lives were
pointless falsehoods; that it's all nearly over, and for what? When in the
end they are completely disillusioned they seek forgiveness from
everyone, for they had always been oblivious to the obvious things, to
the suffering around them. They are sorry for having insisted nothing
was ever all that bad. Destined as they are to so much disappointment,
they merit our sadness more than our disdain.

As for those of us daily anguished, we need not be pitied. The world constantly reinforces our perspective. We may nod our heads like true sages. We are impervious to disillusion, knowing as we do that worse is yet to come.

The street on which I lived as a girl was off a rural highway in western Washington. It was a dead-end street, unpaved and dusty in summer, muddy in fall. Ditches carried run-off to the end of that street, from whence the dirty water made its own route through a swamp littered by illegal dumping.

In that dark and muddy wood were two cottages. One was abandoned with the roof fallen in. I never knew who must once have lived there. Whoever it had been was long forgotten, having vanished without the least impact upon our little community of poor white trash.

The other house was a ramshackle affair surrounded by stinging nettles. An old woman lived there with a dog. Because of the nettles, we children almost never went near. I remember it being miles and miles into the forest. But it couldn't possibly have been so far or so wild as it seemed to me as a child.

The area was dangerous on account of the swamp. Children were strictly warned against playing there. Whenever we were inclined to disobey, we invariably paid with welts from briars and nettles.

We children of that back-road community devised our own mythology about the swamps, which included the sure knowledge of bottomless pools in which many a hapless child had drowned in past generations. Our own uncles and cousins, we supposed, whom we had never known, were bones in the deep black waters. Adults whispered about it when children were put to bed, for many terrible secrets, we were certain, were kept hidden by parents.

We also knew an old witch lived back there amidst the mud, litter and stickers – a witch and her skinny, weird dog.

One of us invented a story about children being turned into toads. We all came to believe it. Whenever someone caught a toad and put it in a jar, we would gather around and look at it with worried faces, wondering what child it once had been, fearful that a day would come when the old witch would cast a spell on one of us.

That same summer my brother became sick and died. He was three years older than I. I loved him a lot. Sometimes he was wicked to me, but mostly he was protective and nice. It made me bossy to other children.

I never had to threaten them with my brother, because they very well knew that I could make him do anything I wanted him to do.

The night when he was dying, he had a fever and raved about toads and witches. To me he had always seemed so much older and wiser, yet he was only a child like me. He may have been the one who made up that story about toads, but even knowing it originated in his own imagination, he believed it. And his last night on earth was filled with terror about the swamp.

I was in bed a room away, my head under the covers, tears streaming down my cheeks, biting my lower lip, listening to him rave about the witch and her assembly of toads. When he stopped raving, I heard him moaning and struggling for breath.

The doctor came. He spoke harshly to my parents. 'Why didn't you call me earlier?' He hadn't been called because our family was so poor. I got out of bed in my night gown and crept down the hall. 'We daren't move him now,' said the doctor. He and my parents built a tent over my brother, using a spare sheet with brooms and mops tied together to hold the sheet up. They started a steamer filling the tent with mist while my brother raved anew that he was trapped in a seedpod by the witch. I was whisked back to bed by my mother and told not to get up.

I finally fell asleep when my brother became silent. The last thing I remember of that night was my mother's muted weeping.

Later I blocked the funeral from my mind. I didn't believe the inert boy in the box was my brother. I believed the witch had turned him into a toad. There had to be some way to turn him back, if I could find him. So wholeheartedly did I think that this was true that even today, when I am a middle-aged woman who believes in nothing at all, I still wonder from time to time if my brother is alive in some swamp, for toads live such long lives.

From time to time I looked for him. This brought me into contact with the witch. I would put on a sweater even if it was a hot day, to protect my arms from nettles. Skirting the puddles and getting thick mud on my shoes, I often looked for the toad that was my brother. There were plenty of frogs, but toads were harder to find.

Once I saw her dog inside the cottage with its paws against the smudgy window, its blind eyes staring and staring, seeming to see something directly behind me. Another time I saw the witch gathering up sticks and taking them in her house for kindling. She and her dog were very troubling to me. They appeared in my most terrible dreams, standing outside my house in a storm.

From a vantage point amidst the bushes, I peered at the rickety house, around which were strewn hundreds of old cans and broken jars and sundry refuse. A broken rabbit hutch lay on its side. Old grey lumber was poorly stacked at the side of the house, most of it gone to rot. The witch came running out with her dog and screamed at me, 'Get away from there, scat! Scat or I'll set my dog on you!' The dog couldn't see a thing and had no teeth and woofed feebly, but to me, out there at the edge of the known world, it sounded like a monster.

I had a friend named Angeline. I told her about the monster dog with no teeth but a big slavering wormy mouth like a mudpuppy that had crawled out of the muck. We shivered with fright.

'Did you see where she keeps your brother?' asked Angeline.

'I couldn't get close enough. There are cans and jars all around her house. I'm sure she keeps him in a jar.'

Angeline nodded agreement.

She and I were in the second grade. She was a tomboy like me. Even in a flaring print dress, she could climb a tree as fast as a squirrel. Sometimes we would climb a tree together. If any boys tried to come up after us, we took off our underpants and put our feet on two branches to pee down on them. It made the boys run off. They made up a song about us, 'Angeline and Rosemary sitting in a tree! Kissing in a tree! Pissing in a tree!' They'd throw clumps of clay at us, exploding into smoky dust.

They never could make us cry. I think that's why the boys hated us. If we would only cry now and then, it would be all right. But we wouldn't. I hated them and remembered my brother, who would fix them good if I could only find him and get him changed back into himself.

I hadn't cried since the night my brother was so ill. I had somehow lost the ability. Angeline always imitated me. If she ever cried, she did it when I wasn't around, so I wouldn't know. The sound of crying was something that pulled at my heart in a way I didn't like. At the funeral, everyone had cried except me, for only I understood that my brother wasn't really dead, and therefore I had nothing to cry about. Somewhere inside me, I suppose I knew that tears meant acknowledgment. I had not acknowledged the possibility that I would never see my brother again.

One day Angeline came to the back door and asked my mother if I was home. There was something very conspiratorial about the way she was acting. We went behind an old barn and Angeline said, 'Look, I found something.'

From out of her skirt pocket she took a big, fat, bumpy toad.

'It has blue eyes,' said Angeline.

It was true. They were the colour of my brother's eyes.

'You've found him,' I whispered, cupping him tenderly in my hands.

'How can we change him back?' asked Angeline.

'I don't know.'

That night I kept him in a box beside my bed and woke up many times, checking to see that he was all right. When I looked into his toad face, it seemed to me that he was smiling impishly, in the manner of my brother.

I kept him hidden in my room and spent a lot of time catching flies from the windows of the house, ripping off one wing from each, then dropping them in the box tucked in the back of my closet. It was funny to think of my brother eating bugs and flies, but he wasn't interested in anything else I showed him.

It was the middle of summer, no school. There hadn't been much rain for weeks so the swamp was pretty dry. Angeline and I met at the end of the street where a barbed-wire fence and a warning sign blocked the way. We climbed through the fence and squatted where no one would see us. I had my brother with me and opened the cookie box for Angeline to see.

'What'll we do?' asked Angeline.

'There's only one way to stop her magic,' I said. I handed her a crinkled brown paper bag. She opened the bag and saw a can of lighter fluid and the matches.

'We have to burn her,' I said.

Angeline's brown eyes stared wide. 'Yeah?'

'That's right.'

'Are matches enough?'

'That lighter fluid can squirt real far. You run up to her and start squirting it all over her dress and dodging from side to side so she can't get you. Then I'll run up behind and throw matches on her. Witches are made out of wood. She'll go up like an old sappy stick.'

'Wow,' said Angeline.

We started through the woods toward the old woman's shack.

We skulked around the periphery of her cluttered, stickery property until we realized she wasn't home. It had never occurred to either of us that the old witch actually went anywhere, for we had never seen her out walking, never knew how she might get to a store for things she needed. After a few minutes we became bold and strode toward her house, accidentally scaring an old chicken from its hiding place. Its sudden appearance and its squawk gave us a fright, but our mission was too important, and we could not turn back with my brother unrestored.

'Watch out for her dog,' I whispered.

But the dog had apparently gone with the witch on some errand. We tried the front door and of course it wasn't locked. When I was little, almost nobody even had a lock unless they were crazies afraid someone would see what awful messes they lived in, and even they more often sealed up their doors with twisty old pieces of wire. So we went right into the witch's house.

I was surprised to see it was all rather orderly, though hardly pleasant. It smelled like an old dog – or an old woman. In her kitchen I saw a row of large dark bottles. By now my heart was tight with a sort of confused anger, and, frustrated because there was no witch to burn, I knocked several of her jars off their shelf, just to be spiteful and make a mess. The jars broke on the floor, spilling dried beans and lumpy flour.

Angeline squealed with a shocked delight, and, seeing a beautiful, fragile blue teacup on the table, she knocked it flying with a sweep of her hand. It shattered against a drawer.

I opened canisters of crusty, hardened, strange-smelling spices and dumped them on the floor. 'She probably uses these old spices in her spells,' I said. On her wood-burning stove was an old iron pot, too small to be a witch's cauldron, even though it looked like one to me. A big spider ran across the counter, and Angeline gave a shrill cry on seeing it.

'If that big ol' spider bites you,' I said, 'you'll turn into a toad just like my brother.'

She tried to find something to smash the spider, but it disappeared down a crack.

The witch's bedroom made me especially uneasy, but for reasons I hadn't expected. Against the faded wallpaper were hung framed metallic photographs so dark that the sharp-eyed people in them looked like shadows standing in darkness. The portraits were daguerreotypes, but I'd never seen one before, and I didn't know what to make of them. My first thought was that they were the perfect kind of photographs for witches, all dark and spooky. But the thing that really made me uneasy was the realization that the old witch had once had a family, that these must be photographs of her grandparents or great-grandparents, that she hadn't been conjured out of a hellish place, that she might be human after all and once might have been a child like me.

A portrait of a young woman standing beside a soldier was propped up on the cluttered dressing table. The woman wore a long, flounced white dress. The soldier wore bloomers, a broad hat, and a serious expression.

Angeline was rifling through a chest of drawers. 'Look at this!' she

[38]

exclaimed, and opened a tattered parasol, memento of the witch's youth. It had once been white but was now yellow and moth-eaten. Angeline pranced about the little bedroom and leaped upon the bed, posing with the parasol. Then she batted it to pieces on the bedstead.

'Don't do that, Angy.'

'Why not?' she said petulantly. Angeline always emulated me, always trying to please me. At that moment it was intolerable to see into such a mirror, to see what I was like as Angy tried to one-up me destroying the witch's things. She opened the brown paper sack and took out the can of lighter fluid and started squirting it on the walls. 'Let's burn down her house!' said Angy. 'Let's do it now!'

Then we heard the sound of a truck's clutch and we grew scared and quiet. Angeline left the lighter fluid can on the bed and hopped down to stand by me. We tiptoed to the cracked, sooty front-room window. Out on the rarely used driveway, a beat-up truck was bouncing toward the house. A large, ugly man was driving. I had never seen him before; he may have lived in the community the other side of the swamps. The witch was with him. When he stopped the truck, he got out and went around to help her down. He was chattering at her in a repulsively cheerful manner, saying, 'It's not that big a tragedy, Mrs Osiris. Why, I can get you a healthy little puppy for free! It's just as well that old dog was put out of his misery; cruel to let him suffer.'

'I'm all right,' said the witch in a gruff, awful manner. 'I'll be fine. Don't bring me no puppy. I don't want no other dog.'

'Well, I've got to get on home, Mrs Osiris. I'll check in on you in a day or two if you like.'

He got back in his truck and was soon gone, the clutch sounding in the distance. Angeline and I had slunk to the kitchen intending to get away by the back door. But the witch had gone around to the side of the house and we could see her. She was standing motionless by the wood pile, her head hanging low.

'Shall we burn her?' asked Angeline, breathing excitedly. 'Shall we do it now?'

I held the cookie box in front of me and pulled off the lid. The blue-eyed toad stared at me with such sad eyes, I almost thought it could hear me thinking. 'Not now,' I said. I sat the box on the table and took the toad out, holding it around the belly as its hind feet kicked and tried to find something to push against. 'Not ever,' I added.

'Why not? What about us getting your brother changed back?'

My shoe crunched on a little piece of blue glass. I was wishing I were

[39]

a toad, or that I were dead instead of my brother. Tears were streaming down my face.

'What's wrong with you, Rosemary?'

Angeline looked scared, as though she thought my incomprehensible tears were caused by an evil spell. I drew myself together in a hurry and told her, 'We've got to sneak out the front door and never come back here. We've got never to think of this place again, like it doesn't even exist. The witch's power was in that blue cup you broke. When she sees it, she's as good as dead. You ruined her for ever when you shattered it.'

We slipped away and Angeline, obedient to my commands, never went there again, never thought of it for all I know.

But I've often gone back, in my memory, where I can still see the toad witch, without wanting to do so. I see her spindly, wood-kindling body going up in flame and my brother leaping from the cookie box a laughing little boy. Then I see him as a handsome young man in soldier's bloomers, courting a beautiful woman with a flashing white parasol and a collection of daguerreotypes. I see myself playing by a wood pile with a happy, bouncing dog and calling to my best beloved grandmother at her kitchen window. I see it in every permutation I can imagine but I can never get it to come out right. I can never make the world any better than it has ever been, or ever shall be. That's the brutal fact.

CARVEN OF ONYX

Ron Weighell

Ron Weighell (b.1950) has written several short
stories and a novella (*The White Road*),
reflecting his interest in the writings of M. R.
James, Arthur Machen, de Quincey, and the
western magical tradition. 'Carven of Onyx' is a
new story, specially written for this collection.

Given clement weather, an obedient donkey or any kind of horse, the journey from Malmswell Abbey to the Priory in Longlenn could be accomplished easily in a day. The two monks had left Malmswell before dawn, but had walked their donkeys for much of the way, paused by the river in Charnwood Forest for a meal of crusty bread, cheese and home-brewed ale, and only ridden the last few miles of open moorland; so light was already fading on the low hills of Longlenn by the time they reached the Priory. Their first sight was of the spire aglow in the mellow rays of sunset. The dying light picked out the windows of the church with points of flame and a bell was tolling for vespers.

But for a deer in the forest and an unkindness of ravens over the moor, they had seen no living thing all day. Any passing stranger would have seen two men in the black habit of the Benedictine Order and given them little thought, save perhaps for the observation that the older of the two men was an individual of some bearing, slim but wiry of build, with a long, neatly bearded face that gave little away. The tight, pursed lips and lean jaw, the narrowed, searching eyes, these might have suggested a man given to keeping his own counsel. What they could not have suggested was the actual rank of this humble monk, which suited the Abbot of

[41]

Malmswell. The highways were full of brigands who would not stick at murder or ransom, and the prelate of a great religious house was reckoned a wealthy and influential prize. By travelling in so humble a fashion to Longlenn, where he acted as confessor to the Priory's forty nuns, he could dispense with pomp and protection yet remain safe from molestation. Longlenn Priory, like all the Benedictine nunneries, lay under the overall rule of the abbey, and the nearest was Malmswell. On the Abbot, then, fell the responsibility for the general running of the house. Whether the fields and forests were forbidding with chill, penetrating rain, transformed beyond recognition by a blanket of snow, or withered under the intolerable heat of high summer, he would travel at the appointed times to hear in confidence the small sins and misgivings of the Longlenn sisters.

And Heaven knew those sins were small enough to make him wonder within himself whether the work was worth the journey, for little that was disruptive to the harmony of godly living occurred there. Longlenn was not a closed order, but its isolated position naturally made it as insular and tranquil as one.

Insular and tranquil were not descriptions that could be applied to Malmswell. The Abbey stood by a great market town, and ministered to the spiritual and medical needs of a large community. For that reason, the Abbot insisted on his quiet, disguised journeys, and jealously guarded them as holy retirements in a life burdened by great responsibilities.

Longlenn had lain deserted for many years before the Order had bestowed it as the foundation for an order of nuns. The shell of the building, much dilapidated, had been allowed to degenerate still further under a succession of old and conservative prelates. The appointment of Sister Clare as Prioress had brought about a transformation, for with an enviable will she had set about rebuilding the Priory, a not unimpressive task when one considered the comparative poverty of nunneries in general. The nuns could not labour as monks – or were not generally expected to do so – and did not attract large gifts as did the monkish foundations. The Prioress had, nevertheless, instigated some extreme, though admirable, changes, encouraging the nuns to labour in the fields – by example, it had to be said – and closing the school, which had struggled to force basic lessons into a handful of children from the outlying farms for no appreciable financial return. Instead she had concentrated the efforts of the sisters on needlework and soon established a reputation for the production of the finest embroidered copes and altar cloths in the country. The ailing funds of the Priory had been steadily replenished, and in time grew great enough to allow extensive renovation of the building. Having once engaged the nearest craftsmen to repair the gutters and install a proper drainage system, the Prioress had retained them to undertake an ambitious series of extensions to the original shell, raising a finely appointed infirmary, a small guest house and new reredorter. The nuns themselves had undertaken the basic labour to avoid the expense of unskilled help.

And lately it seemed, unceasing in her determination to make Longlenn the finest religious house in the county, Sister Clare had employed a roughmason and ordered the demolition of the curious semi-circular transepts of the church in order to construct orthodox oblong structures which would produce a more fitting cruciform groundplan. No doubt, when that had been accomplished there would be some other task.

The Abbot and the novice were admitted into the cloister in time to see a group of black-habited nuns pass along the lines of carved stone pillars in the direction of the church. The Prioress herself was among them. As she saw the visitors, her full, ruddy face drew into a warm smile which the Abbot returned.

'I'm afraid we dallied on the way, Sister Clare. After so hard a winter the lure of the sunshine proved too strong.'

The Prioress nodded. 'It has been a beautiful day, Father. The new guest house is ready, so we can accommodate you properly at last.'

'Yes, I could see as we arrived that you have not been idle! Unless I am mistaken the sun is setting on new tiles; for the first time since the Priory was built, I should think.'

The Prioress flushed with a forgivable pride. '*Labore est honore*, Father. The work is progressing. I hope you can look around before you leave.'

'Of course, of course. We should be interested to see what you have done in our absence, shouldn't we, Sebastian?' The young novice stammered his agreement.

At the corner of the cloister, the Prioress opened a door and led them up a flight of winding stairs. A narrow corridor gave off into several small rooms, the first of which had been prepared for the novice. At the second door, she paused, and motioned for the Abbot to precede her. He found himself in a finely proportioned room that still smelt of planed wood and fresh plaster. The windows faced west, affording a glimpse of low hills, and a crest of trees, standing out sharply against a broad band of purple sky. Higher, the afterglow was fading gradually, into the subtle green of old copper.

The room had a narrow cot, above which the wall was decorated with a painted design of trees and flowers, encircling the Divine Lamb on a field of green.

'Quite charming!' exclaimed the Abbot.

'Sister Catherine,' said the Prioress with a smile. 'She has quite a remarkable talent.'

'Indeed she has. You seem to produce an unending supply of delicate skills and hard physical endeavour here. I confess I could not see my brothers at Malmswell, dedicated and worthy as they are, producing such diverse talents.'

'But they would not have to, Father! Malmswell is already a beautiful building in good repair. Longlenn lay deserted for many years before we came here.'

'And yet,' continued the Abbot, pressing the point, 'you are the first prioress in fourteen years to undertake any restoration work.'

The persistence of his praise threw the Prioress into a momentary confusion which she covered by saying brusquely, 'Well, there is still much to be done.'

At Longlenn two periods of rest were observed. At two in the morning the day began with matins and lauds, when the morning praises were sung. After a second period of sleep came that time of the day given over to religious duties, and it was then, at the chapter which followed mass, that the Abbot heard the confessions of the nuns. Later in the day, after dinner, came a period of recreation, during which the nuns would walk or play at ball in the garden on the north side of the church. It was then that the Abbot would compete with the Prioress at chess, a game at which she excelled. And as he moved the heavy pieces patiently on his way to customary defeat, the monk would discuss any problems raised during the chapter. On this occasion, the subject was Sister Catherine, a youngster who had but lately completed her noviciate.

'Has she shown any indiscipline with regard to her work?' he asked.

The Prioress looked distressed. 'No. In fact, she has always been such a good, hardworking child. And you have seen her work on the wall of the guest house. Her behaviour has always been exemplary.'

The Abbot nodded. 'It was for this reason that I showed leniency. But I would talk to her if I were you. She complains of disturbed sleep, bad dreams. We will always come up against this kind of problem in novices, but this girl has passed that period and should have come to terms with our life, or left us! I hope that there has been no mistake in admitting this child to our Order.'

As he said these last words, the Abbot stared pointedly at the Prioress.

'I am sure there has been no mistake, Father. She is devoted, I'm sure.'

'Her heart is not in question; it is her soul that concerns me. Is her soul troubled? Talk to her, Sister Clare.'

When such exchanges were necessary, one or the other of them could generally be relied upon to turn the conversation to lighter things, and on this occasion the Prioress raised the subject of Malmswell's massive library, which she knew to be a source of pride to the Abbot.

He, in his turn, took the opportunity to mention with enthusiasm a certain volume residing in the more modest bookroom of Longlenn. The inevitable question was asked.

'Would it trouble you to let me look at the commonplace book again, Sister Clare?'

He knew well enough what her answer would be. A slow smile spread over the nun's plump face.

'We could stop off at the cloister press on our way to look at the renovations, if you still wish to see them.'

The press, which lay in the eastern cloister, was too small to be called a room and too large to be called a cupboard. The walls were lined with rough deal planks on which stood a modest collection of books. There were the usual histories, a few standard ecclesiastical works, lives of the saints and the records of Longlenn through the previous fourteen years, written in the diverse hands of the succeeding prioresses. In this unlikely setting fate had placed a rare jewel, as rare as any that could be found among the priceless works at Malmswell.

Soon, the Abbot was opening the cover of carved ivory with trembling fingers, turning the exquisitely illumined pages with the gentlest of touches, feeling again the mingled sense of awe and exhilaration that a fine work of art never failed to produce in him.

Ironically, the volume belonged to that group of works called commonplace books, though a more uncommon book would have been difficult to imagine. On its parchment pages some monkish scribe had copied fragments of borrowed books: poetry and chronicles of war; bestiaries with their quaint amalgam of real and mythical animals; tales of strange explorations, of fabulous beasts and devils, cosmological diagrams. There was a page from an astrological manuscript showing a man with the signs of the zodiac on his body; an illustration from an early fourteenth-century French Bible *moralisée,* showing scenes from Revelations; allegorical figures of the daughter of Babylon, and Satan's dominion over the world in which the left leg, about to sever the right, was the dragon of death. The borders of every page were decorated with traceries of gold and fine images of beasts and devils. Raising his eyes at last, from a scene of the damned in Hell, the Abbot asked, 'Have you given any more thought to our offer, Sister Clare?'

The nun flushed and shook her head. 'I'm sorry, Father. The first Prioress of Staverdale wished it to come to Longlenn and remain in the keeping of the sisters. We only brought it here on that understanding.'

The Abbot nodded ruefully. 'If, for any reason, you change your mind, I would gladly purchase the book for Malmswell library.'

A bell sounded nearby. Replacing the book, the Prioress locked up the press and said, 'Well, we will see. And now, Father, would you care to look at our work on the church?'

The Abbot, gamely concealing his disappointment, suffered himself to be led towards the eastern corner of the cloister, where the assembled nuns were distributing shovels and woven baskets. As she approached, the Prioress chanted '*Eamus Ad Opus Manuum*', and led the way through the slype to the cemetery.

No stone memorials marked the graves there; simple wooden crosses had been raised over those who had died during the recent tenancy of the nuns. Of those who had worshipped at Longlenn before them, no trace remained, save for hummocks scarcely distinguishable from the grassy field itself. The sun was shining strongly, but a stiff breeze had sprung up; new-fledged clouds drifted lazily overhead, casting patches of chilly shadow upon the land.

Passing the chapterhouse, they came to what had until recently been the northern transept. All that remained was a heap of stone and a gaping hole in the church wall, covered by canvas. A mason struggling with the heaps of stone paused to greet the nuns. Without ceremony, the women set to, shifting the rubble aside in their woven baskets. Some began to dig between pegged lines, preparing the way for the new foundations.

As the Abbot stood watching, the Prioress suddenly drew him away to a space near the chapterhouse wall, where a single block of stone, some three feet high and a good fourteen inches in both width and depth, remained.

Placing her hands upon its discoloured surface, she said, 'This is something of a puzzle to us, Father. I know you have studied widely all forms of worship, godly and otherwise.'

The Abbot frowned. 'We should know our enemy, Sister Clare.'

'Of course,' she agreed quickly. 'I meant that you might help to explain the mystery. When we broke down what we thought was the only wall on this side of the transept, we came upon this space, concealed between the chapterhouse and the transept wall. The stone, as you can see, stands inside this space.'

On scanning the ground the Abbot saw that there were, indeed, two lines of foundations. The concealed space between them formed a shallow crescent of some twenty feet from tip to tip.

'A place of concealment in case of persecution?' he ventured.

'But the stone, Father. See the top of it. This is surely tallow from a candle, though it has become quite blackened with age. It must have been an altar of some kind.'

On examining the stone, the Abbot noticed that a section some nine inches square had been removed from one side, leaving a neatly carved recess. The missing section lay on the ground close by.

'There are words carved on this,' he said, brushing the block with his hand.

'Hinc – Hinc lucem something sacra. Ah, there I have it! Hinc lucem et pocula sacra. "From this source we draw light and draughts of sacred learning." Yes, it was clearly an altar!'

'Sister Catherine found the stone was loose and removed it,' offered the Prioress.

'And there was nothing inside?'

'Yes, an old silver chalice, quite tarnished.'

'I would like very much to see it.'

The Prioress called to one of the nuns and sent her back to the cloister where the chalice had been temporarily placed.

'You see why I described it as a mystery?'

This brought a smile to the Abbot's lips. Clasping his hands thoughtfully before him, he turned to her.

'Not necessarily. The building may have been constructed around the altar because it was a place of particular sanctity, a shrine of some kind. Croxbury still has the original altar from a wattle church that once stood on the site. Longlenn, I think, does stand on the foundations of an older church, I seem to remember.'

The Prioress looked greatly relieved to hear this. 'You think there is some such explanation? I had thought . . . well, no matter. Ah, here is the chalice, Father.'

The Abbot took it carefully and turned the tarnished stem in his hands. So discoloured and worn was the surface of the chalice that he could only distinguish with great difficulty the designs embossed upon it. On the stem itself, there was a rod entwined with serpents. A row of bestial faces ran around the rim.

'It is very old,' commented the Abbot. 'These twelve faces might well represent the disciples, though clumsily drawn. The snakes below them on the stem – well, perhaps the serpent over which we must all triumph.'

'It has an evil look about it to me,' ventured the Prioress.

'If it will put your mind at rest, Sister Clare, I will personally consult the histories at Malmswell and find who worshipped here before.'

'Would you, Father? I would be most grateful.'

'Very well, then. But do not worry in the meantime. I feel sure the altar was put to quite innocent use.'

So said the Abbot, though he found much to contemplate on his ride back to Malmswell the following day. The skies had grown overcast, and the wind bitterly cold, but considerations deeper than the inclemency of the sudden 'Blackthorn Winter' prompted him to forgo his customary rest beside the river in Charnwood Forest. The Abbot wished to be among books, for he knew the tallow stains upon the hidden altar were not black by age but by design, and saw more in the symbolism of the chalice than he had disclosed. Although at pains to allay the fears of the Prioress, he could guess the purpose for which they had been fashioned.

About the Priory of Longlenn there had long been something of a conspiracy of silence more damning than words. The last Benedictine Order of monks to worship there had been disbanded with indecent haste, and the general feeling seemed to be that the affair was best left to the healing hand of forgetfulness. But in blotting out the past, had the Order guessed just how far those Longlenn monks had wandered from their chosen path?

Furthermore, the discovery of the stone altar had thrown some light on another mystery, the confession of the young nun, Catherine. That once pious and gentle child had fallen prey to thoughts for which she herself could hardly find words. And in her fitful, nightmare-ridden slumbers, a feeling of growing enmity towards the Prioress had taken root. This last was the most striking of her confessions, for the impressionable young nun had previously held Sister Clare in a position dangerously close to that of a beloved saint. That Sister Catherine should have been the one to discover the hole in the altar was a remarkable coincidence, and the possible significance was not lost on the Abbot.

Had the removal of the stone released some disruptive spirit? That some influence was at work upon the young nun, he could not doubt. There was frightful power in the old worships; that the Abbot had learned in his scholarly investigations of the pagan mysteries.

At Malmswell he had access to information he sought, for at his command the rarest books and scrolls in that wealthy abbey had been rescued from the damp limbo of the cloister presses and housed in a room designated the library.

Large and lofty it was, with rough, enduring beams above and a floor of good stone flags below, and what little natural light entered fell faintly through flamboyant traceries of stained glass. Once there, he lost no time in drawing his high-backed chair of oak up to a great lectern, fashioned in a fearsome representation of the Beast of the Apocalypse. The volume supported on its carven back was huge and bound in tan leather. Around him were ranged Bibles, histories, monkish manuscripts and more – much more – for he had amassed a vast number of works on paganism and the black arts, driven by a desire to familiarize himself with all the tricks, temptations and illusory rewards to which the enemy of Christ might resort.

Thus, he could reach out and lay a hand upon *The Mysteries* of Iamblichus or the lewd and bawdy *Transformations of Lucius Apuleius of Madaura* or upon Euripides' rhythmical evocation of orgiastic rites *The Bacchae*.

In scrolls and hand-decorated folios lay fragments of alchemical works; the vivid, convoluted Latin of Ripley's *Cantilena* and the *Medulla Alchimae*: Jabir's *The Book of Furnaces* and the *Splendor Solis*, exquisitely worked on vellum and reputedly owned by Solomon Trimosin himself. Beside these could be found tomes on the art of magic and on demonology: Khalid's *The Book of Amulets*, the *Malleus Maleficarum* of Sprenger and Kramer, as well as Antonio Stampsa's *Fuga Satanae*. On a smaller reading desk behind him lay Sinistrari's *Daemonialitate; et Incubis et Succubis*.

The volume on the lectern though was somewhat more prosaic: Sterner's *History of the Religious Orders*, from which he pieced together something of the full story of Longlenn.

The existing priory had been raised on the site of a Templar monastery; so much he had surmised. But he soon found that the circular church in which the Templars worshipped had been suffered to stand, retained as the central tower of the new, so that the swelling curve of its walls formed quaint semi-circular transepts on either side of the new church. The Abbot was unable to ascertain on whose instructions such a plan had been adopted, but a more effective way of retaining, while concealing, the older worship could hardly have been found. Had the old Baphometic altar been knowingly concealed behind an innocence of new stone, or had the brothers gradually succumbed to the influence of some horrible *genius loci* and raised their own stone to the Dark One? There was no way of knowing, but what little he had learnt convinced the Abbot that the altar had been raised for ungodly purposes, and that the chalice at least was a Templar relic. The source of their 'light and learning' was clear. The voice of the Abbot broke the silence in a tone of irony and reflection.

'*Hinc Lucem et Pocula Sacra!*'

The long halls and corridors of Longlenn grew ever more cold and forbidding; the cloisters where the nuns walked and studied were immersed in grey light. Howling winds invaded the church through the canvas-covered gap in the north wall to ripple and dim the candle flames at mass. And with every rush of disturbed shadow, every howl of wind, the glowering wooden eagle that supported the brass-bound weight of the antiphoner seemed to stir its wings and cry.

Among the less hardy sisters it was a time to don again the thick woollen undergarments and fur-lined boots of winter, so recently discarded in hopeful anticipation of the sun. The night vigils in the great unshielding spaces of the church were once more cruelly cold.

Work on the reconstruction continued unabated. The mysterious altar was demolished and the first of the new, square transepts begun. And not before time, for it seemed that discord had entered with the searching spring winds. Or was it rather that the pace of work was telling on the tempers of the house? With every passing day the Prioress had been forced to deal with a growing number of minor contentions until discipline was threatened, and the rod, so long abandoned at Longlenn, was reintroduced at her command.

Amid this flurry of argument and recrimination Sister Catherine grew daily more pale and withdrawn. The Prioress, prompted as much by her own concern as any order from the Abbot, summoned Catherine to her room. The child would not admit to any conflict of faith and when she broke down wretchedly and asked what she had done wrong, the Prioress found herself at a loss to answer, for Catherine had been exemplary in the execution of her duties and denied with tears the least suggestion of personal unrest. So the Prioress could do no more than ask the girl to come to her in need, and then dismiss her. What, she reflected, has the poor child done wrong?

Into the dark, unheated dormitory, into her small cell with its hard cot and simple desk, the pale, unconnected Catherine retired and knelt wretchedly before the cross as though to pray; but in a moment she was shifting her weight from knee to knee, casting glances about her. It seemed that her devotions were so easily disrupted of late; the flimsy thread of attention broken by the creaking of a joist, the call of an owl outside in the pine tree: even by the muttering of a sister in a cell close by. She picked up her Bible and opened at a chapter of Isaiah, at certain verses which had recently done much to soothe her fears. She read quickly under her breath, her pale grey eyes flitting across the page. 'Oh thou afflicted, tossed with tempest, and not comforted, behold I will lay thy stones with fair colours, and lay thy foundations with sapphires. And I will make thy windows of agate, and thy gates of carbuncles, and all thy borders of pleasant stones.'

Thrusting the Bible aside, she drew from her habit a glazed tube of fire-hardened clay sealed with a stopper of black wax. And there she remained, clutching the tube, her eyes unfocused and afraid.

'I meant no deceit, Reverend Mother. I meant to tell you about this when I found it, but all thought of it disappeared from my mind; I found myself showing you the chalice as though it were the only thing inside the old altar. And then later I saw the light of the sunset like blood upon the lancet window, and the long pointed shape made me think of it again. I was afraid you would punish me for keeping it a secret. If I tell you now . . . The rod is cruel, Reverend Mother.'

As she whispered this, her hands were working at the stopper, reopening old cracks around the waxen seal. She emptied on to her upturned palm a piece of stone of a profound black, with faint concentric ripples of lemon–grey. Heavy and cold lay the stone against her flesh, the quaint design engraved upon its surface partly masked by encrusted smears of some yellow substance. Absent-mindedly, she rubbed the stain under her thumb, until the whole design was clear. Like a lightning flash, she thought; a lightning flash entangled in its descent with strange letters and many-pointed stars. A peculiar design indeed, but one she found soothing to look upon. When visited by pain or weakness or by anger, a moment's concentration on the stone was somehow comforting. It was as if her troubles could be poured into it, leaving her lethargic but soothed. She had poured much of herself, the turbid depths of her emotions, into it, and felt a growing gratification in return. Of late it had occurred to her – with what secret thrill of horror – that the act was like a prayer; it comforted and unburdened like a prayer. That thought itself was surely blasphemous, and yet, was the finding of comfort in a stone, the only comfort in an otherwise hard and lonely life, really a sin? Had not the Lord, according to his prophet Isaiah, promised to those 'not comforted' stones with fair colours; offered foundations and borders of pleasant stones as a refuge? And this to *release* one from terror, to establish the tempest-tossed in righteousness! If she had come to need the stone, come to long for her times of communion with it, what then? The Lord provided; but one corner of her confused mind kept crying 'Which Lord?'

Seeking further to unravel the mystery of Longlenn, the Abbot turned to a work on the heresies of the Knights Templar and discovered there, amid the familiar accusations, agonized confessions and heartless lists of 'sundry entertainments' provided for the overworked torturers, certain admissions of practices peculiar enough to nonplus even their avid enemies. Though some among the knights had broken down and admitted to the 'Worshippe of Baphomet' and to various 'obscene observances' before an idol, there was one among their number who, while stoically denying the trampling of the cross, told how the brothers had 'resorted privily to horridde incantation, an bye so doing raised an Elementarie to which ende they had employed certaine attentionnes to a stone moste strangelie fashioned'. The stone to which these strange attentions were paid had been 'given them bye the deville-worshippers of Saladin's armies'.

The demon, or 'elementarie', in question had originally become entrapped within the stone and could be released by a method which the Knight refused resolutely to divulge, even under the most atrocious suffering imaginable. Neither would he divulge the whereabouts of the stone, claiming that the 'Elementarie was more holie than our own Baphomet, being of no element known among men, neither of the earthe nor aire, nor of the fires nor waters of this worlde', for the stone had, according to its previous heathen worshippers, 'come from the stars'.

There he had it then! Surely this was the cause of the unholy influence to which the Longlenn monks had exposed themselves, unknowingly or otherwise. There they had gathered to narrow their communal will to a common devotion with so dire a result that the foundation had been dissolved and their place of worship left untenanted through years of silence, doubtless until the natural elements had swept away the odour of corruption. But the Abbot suspected from his studies that what has once been raised cannot be so easily put down. Brooding there among his books, the learned monk began to ponder on the young nun Catherine. Had she been entirely honest when recounting the contents of the hidden altar?

At that moment, the young nun was lying on the hard cot in a corner of her cell, gazing blankly into the darkness. Though her period of rest had lasted only an hour, it seemed that she had lain for days uncounted, lost in the sleepless vacuity of exhaustion. Her surroundings – her very identity – had slipped away, and something else was filling the dangerous void. She saw before her eyes the stone with its carved design, stretching above and beyond her like a great wall. The yellow smear, deposited so many centuries away in time, was gone. Why was she so irresistibly drawn to that strange design, so obsessed by it that it had become more familiar to her than the lines upon her own palm? More dear to her than the cross? She had become one with the stone, and knew within herself the true significance of the deeply incised lines upon it. They formed a kind of gateway; slots in the wall of Hell, and through them something had begun to seep. At first, an invasion indistinct and brief, it had grown strong and insistent, moving upon her ceaselessly, like a clutch of tattered darkness, locked to her flesh. Her struggles were tamed easily by rustling congeries of greasy tendrils that seemed to drain her resistance. She moaned and her mouth was at once smothered by a searching feeler as soft and noisome as mildewed cloth.

And then she knew only the grip of many limbs; so many hard, insistent surfaces that sought to penetrate and rub until despite herself, she moved with the evil rhythm of it, while the very breath was drawn from her body and the weight upon her grew.

At the tolling of the matins bell, the Prioress paused at each cell in turn, stirring the sleeper with a knock, a shake or a whispered word. Soon, small groups of nuns were shuffling along the draughty corridors by lantern light, emerging into the cold blast of the cloisters.

Having counted them into church, she paused briefly before follow-ing, to look up at the sky over the cloister garth. The clouds had passed, and the night was spattered with stars. Inside, she found the dark vault of the chancel starred too, with many tiny flames, for a candle burned beside the place of every novice who had yet to learn the psalmody.

From her place, Sister Catherine watched the service in a daze. All seemed to shift before her eyes as she glanced around the chancel. Behind the altar stood a massive reredos in the form of a triptych in oils, the central panel of which depicted the crucifixion. In the tremulous light of the candles she could see the pale, twisted body of Christ upon the cross, the noble head sagging to one side in pain, and below, the Virgin kneeling, hands clasped in despair. To gaze upon this image while the echoed chanting of the sisters swelled and eddied all about her had become the most precious of feelings, but now her hand was slipping deep into the pocket of her habit, searching out the source of an altogether stronger emotion. As her fingers closed upon the stone, she felt at once the intrusive presence darkening the air about her. Before the altar the Prioress and her obedientiaries moved like shadows.

For one second Catherine surrendered to the blissful agony erupting in her, and the church, the chanting voices, the beautiful triptych were lost. Then a part of her rebelled, she struggled through the thick, black tide, her eyes instinctively seeking the living image of her faith, as though even the painted Saviour held the power to close the gate that she had opened. But the central panel too had darkened, and the figure raised there on the cross was neither noble nor benign. The head lolling upon its sinewy shoulders was horned, dark with fur, disfigured by a leering tusked snout in which she saw grotesquely blended suggestions of a pig, an ass, an owl. A phallus, rigid as a rod, rose from the shaggy haunches. There were claws, prehensile claws, upon its threshing lower limbs and they were throttling the voluptuous, naked Virgin with her own flowing hair.

The Prioress rose to take her place in the pulpit. The *Te Deum* rolled away into silence and for one second of reverent expectation there was only the sound of canvas whipping in the wind. Then a high-pitched scream rang back from the vaulted ceiling. Amid waves of hushed whispers and turning heads, Sister Catherine was writhing. A hand reached out to support her, and the screams turned into hysterical laughter. In no time the Sub-Prioress was at her side and with the aid of another nun the girl was ushered swiftly away to the infirmary. But the echoes of that insane laughter rang through the minds of all those gathered in the chancel. Knowing this, the Prioress mounted to the pulpit swiftly and opened the Bible as though nothing had occurred. Her voice, strong and determined, drew their attention sharply back.

'Thou shalt not be afraid for the terror by night;
Nor for the arrow that flieth by day;
Nor for the pestilence that walketh in darkness.'

For all her outward calm, the Prioress was shaken by the incident. As soon as her duties were discharged she made her way to the infirmary at the south-east corner of the Priory, and found Catherine in a fever, her brow afire and running with sweat. Dismissing the Infirmarian, the Prioress sat down beside the bed, and taking up a dampened cloth, pressed it upon the young nun's face. Leaning close, she caught the words mumbled through immobile lips.

'. . . windows of Agates . . . stones of fair colours . . . I meant no wrong . . . only some . . . comfort . . .'

Turning her head towards the Prioress, Catherine opened her eyes with a look of relief.

'Help me please . . . keep it away . . .'

She closed her eyes again and the head fell back.

'It is so cold here . . .'

She began to writhe, kicking her blanket to the floor. Retrieving it the Prioress made to spread it once more over the girl, and found to her amazement that there was a second blanket gathered in a heap upon her breast. Reaching to straighten it, she felt it move under her fingers. Like a great black stain it was spreading outwards, growing, it seemed, from the prostrate body itself. One arm of darkness reached out to smother the objecting mouth and the mass began to move rhythmically upon the body of the reclining nun.

For all her numbed horror, the Prioress retained the presence of mind to draw from her pocket a phial of holy water, whispering a prayer hoarsely as she did so. No sooner had the first word been uttered than the thing paused in its unholy movements, drew up sharply and took on the tint of trodden slush. A faint smell of leaf-mould wafted across the room. Catherine squirmed again. One half-stifled moan broke from her and she fell quite still.

Tearing at the lid of her phial with trembling fingers, the Prioress emptied it out across the body and its ghastly burden. For the space of one long-drawn breath nothing moved within the room. The frantic praying apart, there was silence. Catherine – the pale, dead Catherine – and the mound of evil on her were like the painted image of a nightmare. Then the thing rose up from its anchorage on the dead loins, drawing its soft and malleable bulk into a tall, swaying column. A sluggish succession of protruberances rippled up its surface like so many flattened faces pressed against a flimsy veil, gathered half way up into one shifting lump and merged deliberately into an idiotic, distorted semblance of the dead nun's face. The Prioress stepped backwards, holding out the small cross of her rosary before her; the thing shifted off the bed and followed. There was a horrible fascination in the face, the grey rippling semblance of a face, so like and yet so unspeakably unlike Catherine. The Prioress watched spellbound as the thick, grey lips began to mumble soundlessly, then broke into a slack, toothless smile. Dragging open the door she fled into the dark corridor.

Ushered gaping into the great room of stained glass and books, the roughmason Robert handed over a folded parchment to the Abbot and stood awestruck as the grim prelate broke the seal and read, with barely controlled emotion, the pleas which it contained.

'Father, Sister Catherine died yesterday, and I have reason to believe that the opening of the concealed altar played its part. Mercifully, the other sisters have mistaken certain marks upon the body as a sign of disease only, and, may the Lord forgive me, I have not attempted to disabuse them. There is a curious stone involved, clearly fashioned for some talismanic purposes. Father, you know the methods of our Church where such practices are even suspected. My thoughts turn in desperation to you, with your deep knowledge of the Dark Arts. May I plead for your privy assistance in this matter? Had the journey to Malmswell been possible without attracting speculation this petition would have been delivered from my own lips, but alas this is not possible. Robert, the roughmason, into whose hands I entrusted this note, can be depended upon and has sworn silence.'

So, his surmise had proved correct. How wise the Prioress had been to seek his assistance privily. Turning gravely to the mason, the Abbot asked, 'Do you know what is in this letter, Robert?'

The young man shook his head emphatically. 'No, Father. I was only told to give it to you, and you alone.'

The Abbot smiled. 'Very well, then. It is enough, I think, to say that it is a matter of some urgency; a matter in which I will require your help.'

The mason fairly swelled with pride. 'I will do what I can, Father.'

'This is what I want you to do, Robert. Leave at once, and take the Charnwood road. Not far from here there is a knoll with a dead oak . . .'

'I know it, Father.'

'Good. Wait for me there but take pains to ensure that you are not seen. You will not fail me, Robert?'

The mason shook his head eagerly.

'Very well, you may go – and remember – wait at the oak.'

When he was once more alone, the Abbot sat before the carved lectern, considering the sudden turn of events. So, it was all true! The Templars had found a stone of power in the East. Taking down Khabir's *The Book of Amulets* he began to read.

It was the Abbot's duty to hear the petitions of the monks early in the evening, so little could be done before then. Afterwards, while the brothers took themselves back to the recreation room, he returned once more to the library, where he remained until the stroke of seven, when the bell rang for compline. By eight the brothers had retired and the Abbey was at rest.

At such an hour the cloisters would be locked, but, being in possession of a second key, the Abbot passed unseen into the blustery darkness.

There was a ceaseless rushing in the black spaces above, trees whipping loudly in a near gale, and when the tumbling clouds broke briefly overhead, the moon showed like a yellow talon raking at the sky. Without attempting to open the stables, he looked once at the ravaged clouds, slipped his wrist into the leather thong of a heavy walking staff and set off on foot towards Charnwood.

The night services were over, the church lay empty, and Sister Joan, the Sacrist, had only to replace the Book of Collects in the cloister aumbry to complete her duties. Alone in the echoing blackness, she felt no fear. With Sister Catherine dead and the Prioress stricken down by the same strange fever there was talk of devils and possession but Sister Joan was in complete accord with the Sub-Prioress, who had lost no time in quelling such ridiculous rumours. That talk of devils should find purchase in certain minds, however, was little wonder to the Sacrist. If the Sub-Prioress but knew what Sister Joan could tell; if she could see what Sister Joan now carried in her pocket, then her worst fears would be realized, and her hand would fall more ruthlessly on any who displayed the slightest sign of superstition. Perhaps, thought Joan, it was as well that on finding the heathen talisman upon the person of the poor Prioress I slipped it thoughtlessly into my pocket and forgot it. There was enough ill feeling in the Priory of late, Heaven knew. Had the curious stone – evidence as it assuredly was of an unbecoming idolatry – come to light, why the very name of the Prioress would have fallen into shame. And Sister Clare had done so much! No, it would not happen.

Thinking this, she slipped out through the cloister door with her awkward burden of lantern and heavy book. The wind was hissing fiercely through the covered ways, brushing like a great serpent by her legs, tugging the folds of her habit. Drawing upon the heavy studded panels of the aumbry door, she replaced the Book of Collects and locked up.

And with that duty done, she loitered a while at the edge of the pillared way, drinking in the restful outline of the slumbering Priory against a wild turmoil of moonlit cloud. She would hold her peace concerning the stone. Perhaps it was just a harmless fancy on the part of the Prioress. How cold and heavy it was though, and smooth under the fingertips.

As her thoughts ran on, she glanced across the grassy garth and discerned a figure waiting at the confluence of the southern and western walkways. Her curiosity aroused by this – for she would hardly expect anyone to walk there at such an hour – she called and received no response. Approaching, she noted that the build and bearing of the figure matched those of the Prioress, and yet poor Clare was ill in the infirmary! The thought of a sudden recovery cheered Sister Joan, but just as quickly she was visited by another, less pleasant thought. Had the poor woman wandered away, delirious, through the sleeping Priory?

She called again. The other did not respond. The posture suggested reveries too deep to be penetrated by any human call. At closer quarters, where the small circle of light from the lantern fell, the dark fabric of the habit glistened as though wringing wet. The lantern was lifted and the circle of light fell upon the face.

There was, undeniably, a certain resemblance to the Prioress in those waxy, embryonic features, but the skin of the head was only partially opaque, and flushed rhythmically with a swirl of blood-coloured tendrils moving just beneath the surface. The pale face turned magenta, and like a soft bag stretched from within by a rummaging hand, distorted, expanded, the features twisting as the whole head swelled outward and burst in a rush of soft tendrils. Sister Joan felt the unclean grip upon her and screamed, dropping the lantern. The tendrils fastened on the face and neck of the fainting nun, clung and spread while the vaguely human outline of the thing fell in, billowing and swelling; the habit-black camouflage turned livid green. Anchored upon the fallen body, the tendrils contracted and fattened as the thing began to reel itself in.

The weeks had passed quickly enough at Malmswell, for the Abbot had received a consignment of books bequeathed by a wealthy patron, and the cataloguing and arrangement consumed much time. He could have been excused for feeling somewhat frustrated when the time came to make his customary visit to Longlenn, but he dropped his task patiently and set off without complaint. Certain of his obedientaries had urged him to travel with a proper escort, for the body of a young man, battered beyond recognition, had been found beside an oak on the Charnwood road, and there was concern for the Abbot's safety. But his mind once made up could not be altered, and he refused an escort, taking only the young novice.

The day was fine and warm, a foretaste of what was to be a glorious summer, but the Abbot insisted, no doubt with their safety in mind, that they forgo their period of rest beside the river and press on to reach Longlenn by early afternoon. And that they did, arriving hot and tired but in good spirits. The Abbot had been exceptionally talkative all day, telling the novice of his own early days in the Order, and encouraging him, not altogether successfully, to talk of his own experiences. The poor youth had been too overawed by such sudden familiarity to say much.

From without, Longlenn appeared peaceful; the sun poured warmly down upon the sprawling complex of old and recent stone. They knocked for some while without reply and were at length forced to break open the door. At once they came upon a corpse lying spreadeagled in the cloister. The smell was sufficient to tell them that it had lain undisturbed for several weeks.

The Abbot at once pushed the novice out into the open, shouting into his stricken face, 'Go back to Malmswell. Tell them something has happened here!'

'But I was told to stay with you at all times, Father—'

'I will be all right, my son. Go! I will follow just as soon as I have discovered what has happened here.'

Eventually, the novice was cajoled on to his donkey and driven off towards the hills, complaining bitterly, far from convinced of the Abbot's safety. The prelate watched him out of sight before walking to his own donkey and drawing from the saddle pouch a piece of white linen and a brightly painted amulet on a chain. The cloth he tied across his nose and mouth, the chain he draped around his neck with a peculiar gesture of his right hand. Only then did he return to the cloister and begin what he guessed would be a long and unpleasant search.

The body in the cloister, though disfigured by decay, was by no means the longest dead. Certain corpses in the dormitory and the infirmary were quite putrescent. The air was fetid with the smell of them, but the abbot unflinchingly searched every one.

A year or so before, the Prioress had built a tiny chapel of the Virgin beside the church, and to it she had returned, touchingly, in death. A makeshift bier draped in black stood there with burnt-out candles at the corners. The Abbot paused there a moment, looking on the lean gargoyle that lay upon the bier, unable to equate it with the plump, smiling Prioress. It was a shame. There had been a spark in Sister Clare. He had at times thought that they were two of a kind. It was a waste of a mind of high calibre, but unavoidable. There would be no more victories at chess now, he thought, as he searched the corpse.

When at last he came upon the onyx stone, it was clasped tightly in the hand of a novice sprawled upon a bed in the second guest room. The garments of the corpse were in disarray, the body and face covered with livid marks, and a yellow stain like pus discoloured the flesh. Slipping the stone into a leather pouch at his belt, the Abbot made a repetition of the strange sign, and returned to the cloister.

With the aid of a shovel from the tool locker, he forced the press door and took up the precious ivory book. Sacrificing the protection of his mask to wrap it in clean linen, he turned to go when the glint of silver caught his eye, and he saw, with a little smile of irony, the silver chalice. One of the nuns – perhaps the unfortunate Catherine herself – had polished it, revealing clearly the raised circlet of horned heads around the rim, and a deeply embossed rod entwined with serpents and crowned with wings along the stem. This he placed, along with the ivory book, in his saddle pouch. Almost as an afterthought he took off the amulet from the book of Khabir and threw it with them. It had not been necessary after all. From the strange marks upon the corpses, he concluded that the stone had been protected by a curse of pestilence. Given enough time, it had worked itself out.

So he had the stone, the book, the chalice; and no suspicion would fall upon him. After all, what had he done? They had all come to him by *not* doing what the Prioress had asked him to do; quite literally by not doing anything.

There was undoubtedly an atmosphere, other than the obvious physical one, about the place, enough to make any man's spine crawl; but that was to be expected. Powers had been invoked here. If any magic remained in the curious stone he would control it quite satisfactorily at Malmswell. The old sorcerers could call them 'Elementaries' and give them human qualities, but the Abbot was an educated man, and he could control 'powers' easily enough. It was the application of the will in the correct quarter, merely.

The sun was touching the low western hills as he mounted. A long ride and a night in the open lay before him, but he saw no reason to tempt providence and remain at Longlenn once the sun had set.

Striking upward through the high windows, a single ray from the setting sun spread a sanguine glory across the vaultings of the church. Shadows deepened and drew in down the long aisles. And from the area of the northern transept, where the canvas flapped fitfully, an unearthly shape emerged, drifting like a half-filled sail against the intricate darkness of the rood screen. It paused, spiralling in the space below the central tower. Opaque now, with the look of substantial weight, it was fabulously rich with changing colour. As it spun, delicate red filaments trailed about it; wispy films of lace-like membrane gathered and spread upon its underside. With what unguessable sense did it discover the intruding presence moving around among the used-up husks in some far corner of the building? As the tide by the moon, it was drawn by this new satellite of flesh and blood, its movements apparently involuntary, slow and inevitable; the tide by the moon.

The intruder forced a door, rummaged among the objects within, and it was but five paces from him, separated only by thin panels of the cloister door. It waited, moving ceaselessly within its self-defined borders like some column of uneasy liquid. The man was different. There was about him some veil of protection which could not be penetrated.

Unknowing, the man walked the covered way, and it was following, just out of sight, dark and elusive among the shadowy pillars. He made as though to mount, paused to throw off some portion of himself, and the shield was gone.

As he rode towards the hills, the thing gathered itself lazily by the gate, sank to the ground and shifted smoothly through many shapes; suggestions of horns, humps and wings rose and fell on the body; beaks, snouts, featureless globes and human features passed in succession over the slowly forming head. A fleeting semblance of the Prioress, her face contorted in fear and loathing came and went, and then a thin secretive face – or something sufficiently like one – solidified above a body in which the pulsing waves of colour grew dim and darkened, until it seemed that a tall monk wrapped in hanging folds of black cloth stood there. Then, the required form achieved, the thing moved off into the gathering dusk.

Its pace was leisurely; perhaps a little faster than a trotting donkey.

FURZE HOLLOW

A. M. *Burrage*

Alfred McLelland Burrage (1889–1956) was an
amazingly prolific writer and contributor of
short stories in every conceivable genre to the
pre-war popular monthly magazines, and the
high quality of these tales was always maintained
alongside their quantity. His most controversial
novel *War is War* was published in 1930 under
the pseudonym 'Ex-Private X'. 'Furze Hollow' is
taken from his collection *Some Ghost Stories*
(1927).

Hurlow came to stay at the Walmsley Arms on the eastern border
of Jailbury Common for three reasons: he needed a country
holiday; by going to Jailbury he was breaking fresh ground; and
the inn was within walking distance of Moffat's cottage.

Moffat was a ripe scholar and a recluse, with antiquarian tastes.
Hurlow had first met him on one of his infrequent visits to London, and
had been immediately attracted to the older man. Moffat was a good
talker when he chose, and Hurlow, who worshipped intellect, and whose
lot in life was cast among dull and uninteresting people, hung upon his
words.

The liking was mutual; possibly Moffat was not adamant against
flattery which was obviously sincere. At least, he said suddenly to
Hurlow: 'If you're ever down my way, I should be glad if you would
come and see me.' This, as Hurlow learnt afterwards, was a rare remark
for him to make.

Hurlow himself was a man of forty, who worked in a city office, and was one of those reserved, ungregarious beings who find it difficult to make friends. He was a bookworm who read unintelligently; his mind was always full of undigested letterpress. Almost his only recreation besides reading was to play chess. He generally spent his annual holiday walking, with a haversack half full of books. This July, however, for the reasons already stated, he settled himself on Jailbury Common.

Moffat disappointed him. He had expected Moffat to walk miles with him every day, and show him all the places of antiquarian interest. The older man, however, could not be persuaded to stir out of doors, and although it would not be fair to call him morose, Hurlow found it difficult to get him into a talking mood. He spent most of his evenings at Moffat's cottage, and passed most of his days – they were, fortunately, fine-weather days – walking, until he knew every path and nearly every tree and furze bush on the great tract of common land. He got to know, too, several of the local peasants, whom he described as 'characters'.

There was Walters, head-keeper on the manor estate, who enjoyed telling him amusing stories about the local worthies. And there was old Granny Light, who was supposed to be well over a hundred and to possess supernatural gifts. She had not walked for years, but during the spell of hot, fine weather she was to be seen in an armchair at her granddaughter's garden gate, white as a bone, shrunken and wrinkled, and seemingly incapable of coherent speech. Her lips moved continually in a meaningless mumble, and it was seldom that even her own kith and kin heard her speak distinctly.

It happened on a certain moonless night that Hurlow left Moffat's cottage at about half-past eleven, and turned his face towards the Walmsley Arms. That night he was more tired than usual, having exceeded the average extent of his walking exercise during the day.

The inn was nearly two miles distant by road, but there was a short cut to be made by following a footpath through copses, and over part of the common through a dip called Furze Hollow. He knew the path by daylight but, his sight being poor, he had not hitherto cared to trust finding his way in the dark by this shorter route. Tonight weariness held out an extra inducement, and he took the footpath.

Hurlow found his way through the two copses without much difficulty, and eventually climbed the stile which brought him out on to the open common in the light of the night sky. The night was bright, although moonless, for the stars shone clearly out of a cloudless sky, and it was easy to follow the line of the path as it wound among furze bushes. That part of the common was always lonely, although in the early

[63]

evenings one might expect to pass one or two courting couples along the path.

Hurlow had walked only some twenty paces from the edge of the copse when his progress was arrested by a sound from the bottom of the hollow in front, low, thin, piercing, and almost startlingly sweet.

He came abruptly to a halt. He knew instinctively that these shrill, reedy notes were the music of pipes, and the environment lent magic to the sound. There in the dark, under the steadfast stars, the music shrilled and softened, and shrilled again. In such places and to such notes had Arcadian shepherds and shepherdesses danced. It was as if a poem had taken life and become tangible almost within his grasp.

But this was no lilting dance music. There was no air, only a succession of notes rising and dying away like so many separate lives, each independent of the others. Only in these thin, searching notes, there was the suggestion of one calling to another, as owl calls to owl across the dark.

All in a moment Hurlow forgot the beauty of the sounds and smelt fear. He smelt it as an animal smells it, the breath cold in his nostrils. He had read about Pan, a dead god who might safely be patronized while poring over a book in a London lodging, but here and at this hour a god not to be scorned.

The half-conscious thought was a flash which died on the instant. Pan was dead. Voices had cried his death across the Ægean Sea. This was the twentieth century. And here was he, Hurlow, afraid because somebody chose to pipe at midnight upon a common. His fear, he had to admit to himself, was incontestable; but then he was a nervous and highly strung man. In the ordinary way he would not have investigated the cause of the music, but the piper was somewhere in the hollow through which he had to pass, and to have turned back would have been a concession to the weaker side of himself. Nine men in ten would not have been nervous; Hurlow was, but he strode on all the same. There was good stuff in this highly strung, imaginative bookworm.

He had not taken half a dozen steps before the piping ceased quite suddenly, with no warning of finality in the last note. Nor, as he went on, did he know if he were glad or sorry that it was not resumed. Music or no music, he might yet meet the piper.

When, a minute or two later, he reached the lip of the hollow, he saw before him in the middle distance a flickering red light. He pressed on down the path, and presently made out in the dimness the outline of a caravan. He breathed suddenly for relief. It was only a gipsy encampment, after all, and a gipsy piper playing to the stars. He was not afraid of gipsies. They had a place of their own in romantic literature. He had read the works of George Borrow. He went forward more boldly.

At the bottom of the hollow, the drought-dried furze bushes grew sparsely, and there was ample room for a camp. Starlight and the glow of the camp-fire lit up the scene for him. Two caravans and two tents were there to leeward of the drifting wreaths of smoke; but none of the campers were astir or in sight.

Hurlow had been prepared for an exchange of civil goodnights, his nervousness gone. Now, seeing nobody, it unaccountably came upon him again. A furze bush scratched his legs as he hurried forward, lengthening his stride. If he could see nobody, he felt that others could see him – that he was watched by eyes which were neither uninquisitive nor kind. A feeling of repulsion beset him and spurred him up the further slope of the hollow away from the camp. Not once did he look back.

Later, when he had reached the edge of the sandy road, and was within a furlong of the inn, he halted to light a pipe. Then he found that his hands trembled so that seven or eight matches flickered out in quick succession.

After breakfast, on the morning following, Hurlow, lighting his first pipe of the day, stepped out of the inn door on to the sunlit road.

The sun was already strong, for he had slept later than usual. Down the road, at the door of one of the cottages which clustered around the inn at this spot, where a peninsula of cultivated land ran into the wild, Granny Light was being carried to her chair by her granddaughter and great-granddaughter.

From the other direction came Walters, the head-keeper, preceded by a mongrel, which made straight for Hurlow. The dog knew Hurlow for a friend and an occasional source of biscuits. Walters knew Hurlow for a London visitor who was generally willing to lay down the price of a pint of beer. He, therefore, gave him that salute which he normally reserved for the gentry. The head-keeper stopped to chat, first growling at his dog, which was pawing at Hurlow's coat.

'You're havin' all the fine weather, sir. If you can't say you brought it 'ere, you can say you've kept it 'ere. *Gerdairn*, Rob, will yer! Just off out for a walk, sir?'

'Yes, I expect so. Didn't know you had gipsies on the common.'

[65]

'Oh, there's always them about. It's a job to get rid of 'em so long as you don't catch 'em doing nothin'. Why, have you seen some about, sir?'

'Yes, there's a camp down in Furze Hollow.'

The keeper's black little bushy eyebrows went up. Then he laughed.

'I reckon you get some of the names a bit mixed up, sir. Furze Hollow is the one place on this common where the gippos won't go.'

Hurlow pointed.

'Don't you call that Furze Hollow over there, with a footpath running through it to White's Copse?'

'Yes, that's Furze Hollow right enough, sir. But you ain't seen no gippos there.'

'Yes, I did. At least, I walked right through their camp.'

The keeper's little beady eyes twinkled and grew smaller. Wrinkles of laughter appeared at their corners.

'And what time was this, sir?' he asked.

'Close on midnight, I should think.'

'Ah, now! Come now, sir! You've been talking to Mr Moffat, you 'ave!'

Hurlow was mystified.

'I was at his house last night,' he said. 'It was on my way home that I passed the camp.'

Walters laughed. It was the smug, triumphant laughter of a man who catches another in the act of hoaxing him.

'Yes, and a nice camp and all you passed, sir!'

'What do you mean?'

'You try them jokes on somebody else, sir,' said Walters, still laughing. 'I crossed Furze Hollow at eleven o'clock, and there weren't no camp there then. No, sir, you'll have to try me with summat else. *Kim 'ere, Rob, drat yer!* Good mornin', sir – good mornin'. See you this evenin', perhaps, sir? And don't you let Mr Moffat put you up to no more jokes, sir.'

He swung on, still laughing, leaving Hurlow mystified. He stood staring after the retreating figure with a puzzled smile. Then he walked leisurely in its wake towards the cottages.

A queer business, this, if what Walters said were true. Had the man really crossed Furze Hollow at eleven o'clock on the preceding night? Strange that the camp should have been pitched and fallen to silence, and the fire grown so mellow in that short time! And what did the fellow mean about this having been talking to Moffat, and perpetrating a joke?

He had never felt less like joking in his life, and he had certainly seen the encampment. Besides, there was the piper.

Desultory steps brought him opposite to Granny Light, who sat propped up at her door, mumbling and mouthing as usual, with a patchwork quilt wrapped around her. Only this morning there seemed more light and life in her sunken eyes. He addressed her as usual in that tone which one generally uses to beings who can neither answer nor understand.

'Good morning, Mrs Light. How are you this morning?'

Her fifty-years-old granddaughter answered for her from the doorway.

'Granny's a bit better, thank you kindly, sir. She've been talkin' plainer, and she actually wanted to get up last night. I b'lieve she was strong enough to 'ave walked if we'd ha' let her. Wonderful 'twas. Maybe though, 'tis only the last flicker of the candle.'

Hurlow listened, his gaze on the old woman's face. Her eyes met his, and it seemed to him that she was addressing him. He bent his head to listen, and, for the first time, heard coherent words from her lips.

'I heered 'ee, boy. I heered 'ee. 'Tis the time come at last, and I be ready.'

'What is she sayin', sir?' the granddaughter demanded.

Hurlow did not repeat what he had heard. A shaft of cold had struck him through the sun's heat. He wished them good morning, and set out to walk sharply to Moffat's cottage. For reasons which he did not care to analyse he did not cross Furze Hollow, but took the longer way by road.

Moffat was neither washed nor fully dressed when he arrived. The recluse performed his toilet by instalments, so that it was rarely complete before the late afternoon. He welcomed Hurlow without enthusiasm, but the story which Hurlow unfolded awoke both his interest and his activity. He began feverishly to complete his toilet.

'Apparently,' Hurlow concluded, 'there's some story I don't know. Walters was sure that I had had it from you, and was using it to poke fun at him.'

Moffat paused in the act of fastening his collar. His eyes, under bushy grey brows, were alight with excitement, but a suspicious gleam stole into them.

'My friend,' he said, 'are you sure that you did not get the story from Walters, and are using it to poke fun at me?'

'Of course not. I know no story. Besides, am I that sort of man? For heaven's sake tell me what all this mystery is about.'

[67]

'I will tell you in good time, friend Hurlow. But first let us visit Furze Hollow. If there were an encampment there last night it will either still be there, or there will be traces of it. Come!'

They set off together through the copses, Hurlow trying all the way to induce Moffat to talk, and Moffat steadfastly refraining.

On the lip of the hollow Hurlow halted and exclaimed:

'They've gone!'

Gone indeed were the caravans and tents which he had seen on the preceding night. The cup-like hollow beneath him was deserted, save for a single figure in white flannels.

'Yes, they've gone,' agreed Moffat, gnawing at his beard. 'And there's Lutford. Walters has lost no time in telling him.'

'Who's Lutford?'

'He's lord of the manor.'

'Do you know him, then?'

'I don't know anybody. I believe we nod to each other. Ah, he's seen us.'

Lutford had indeed seen them, and was making for them up the slope as fast as a pair of long legs could carry him at a walking pace. The decreasing distance revealed him as a young man with an aquiline nose, a narrow forehead, and features alike haughty and rather stupid. He nodded to Moffat when he had reached the pair, and addressed himself to Hurlow.

'Mr Hurlow, I believe?'

'That's my name.'

'Then will you have the goodness to tell me what you meant by telling my head-keeper that you saw gipsies here last night?'

'I told him that I saw a camp, and so I did.'

'Well, then, where is it? There has been no camp here. See for yourself. And in future I should be obliged if you would refrain from fabricating stories likely to disturb my tenantry.'

He brushed past them without another word, going the way they had come, leaving Hurlow too angry and amazed to speak.

Moffat laughed softly in his beard.

'There goes a superstitious man,' he said.

'Superstitious?'

'Not to believe, and still to fear; to half-believe, and scorn wholly to believe, that is to be superstitious. And now let us see if we can find any vestiges of your camp. From what Lutford said I do not think we shall.'

They searched the bottom of the hollow. There were no wheel-marks, no trodden grass, no traces of horses, no mark of tent-poles, nothing. A chill wind seemed to breathe on Hurlow. His face turned pale beneath its varnishing of sunburn.

'The camp-fire,' said Moffat; 'you say it was burning on the ground?'

'Yes.'

But they searched in vain for a burnt black patch in the open spaces among the parched, crackling furze. It might have been virgin ground, untouched since the beginning of time.

'By God!' cried Hurlow suddenly and hoarsely. 'There's something queer about this. I don't like it. What does it mean?'

'Sit down!' said Moffat, and lowered himself into a bed of dry bracken. 'Sit down and don't be afraid, and I'll tell you all that I know. It is foolish – superstitious, if you like – to be afraid, for nothing can happen against Nature. Hitherto I have kept an open mind about this matter, neither believing nor disbelieving, but admitting frankly to myself that I did not know. Now I am beginning to believe. Calm yourself, Hurlow, and remember that this old world of ours is continually making fresh discoveries and forgetting old ones. We shall never know what the denizens of the lost continent of Atlantis knew. We may never re-discover the lost arts of the Magi, among whom it is almost certain astrology – to name but one – was an exact science. Our sciences would have astonished them; theirs would equally astonish us. Only stray broken remains of the secret arts of the ancients survive. The witchcraft practised in the Middle Ages, and even in places still today, was all a blindfold stumbling after a cult at some time perfectly understood.'

He paused and Hurlow, sinking down beside him, said breathlessly:

'I don't understand you. What are you driving at? Where are you leading me?'

'I am going to tell you an old story,' said Moffat. 'It is a well-authenticated story, of which your experience may well be the sequel. A hundred years ago, or close upon it, there was a gipsy encampment in this hollow. The depredations of these people aroused the ire of the local peasantry, who accused them of witchcraft, besides stealing. The squire – a Lutford in those days – at last ordered them to move, and in revenge they are said to have compassed by witchcraft the burning of the Manor House. Certain it is that the house was gutted in about two hours one night, and the house you see standing today is not above ninety years old.

'This burning of the Manor House brought matters to a head. The villagers, led by the squire, attacked the gipsies and burned out their

[69]

camp here in this hollow. There is supposed to have been bloodshed. At least, one dying gipsy is said to have announced that they would return, and this return was naturally to be regarded as the portent of some dire happening to the Lutfords. The present-day gipsies know the story, for Furze Hollow bears an evil reputation with them, and none of them would think of camping here.

'Now, the gipsies left one girl-child behind them, who was picked up and adopted by a cottage woman who had just lost her own. And that child is Granny Light, who is still living today.'

Hurlow drew a sudden long breath.

'Good Lord!' he exclaimed. 'What are you telling me?'

'Now, this is very interesting and curious. Old Granny Light, in her day, was supposed to possess strange and unholy knowledge. She is said to have practised witchcraft, and the people about here, if you can get them to talk, will tell you of any number of miracles which she is supposed to have accomplished. Also she uttered a prophecy years ago to the effect that she would never die until her people came back for her; and you will remember that the dying gipsy had threatened their return. And here she is, still alive, perhaps a little more than a hundred years old, perhaps a little less.

'Well, there you have the story as accurately as I am able to recall it. Now you know why Walters thought you were joking, and that I had already told you all this. And you know why Lutford, whom legend threatens with a calamity, was disturbed.'

Hurlow stared at him out of eyes which had grown watery with awe.

'Granny Light! And the piper seemed to be calling some one. She was restless last night, Moffat – wanted to get up. And this morning she said quite clearly: "I heered 'ee, boy. I heered 'ee. 'Tis the time come at last, and I be ready."'

Moffat's long, thin hands were pulling a frond of bracken to shreds. 'Did she say that?' he asked jerkily. 'And she wanted to get up, eh? Let's be calm about this, Hurlow; let's be calm and try to understand. To us may be given an experience unique among living men. Let us try to be worthy of it. Granny Light is a gipsy, and these gipsies are an old people who come from the East. They have little to do with the present, so it may be reasonable to assume that shreds of the old arts and practices remain with them. The gift of prophecy and some of the arts which we ignorantly call witchcraft may yet abide with them. You and I must be here tonight, Hurlow; there may be much to see.'

Hurlow bunched his handkerchief to wipe the sweat from his brow. When he spoke, his voice was like that of a man in pain.

'You have been talking. Words, words, words – I have hardly heard them. For God's sake tell me, Moffat, what you really think.'

'What I really think?' Moffat repeated. 'Well then,' he added calmly. 'I think that Granny Light's people have come back. I think the piper called her, and I think that somehow she will join them. And after that only God knows what is to happen. You will not be afraid to come here tonight?'

Hurlow left the question unanswered.

'I will come if you do,' he said.

Moffat rolled over in the bracken, gazing out over the common from which a flickering heat-vapour ascended.

'It seems so strange to you, so impossible,' he said. 'This is daylight, and the year is 1926. In a post-office two miles away they are using the telephone and telegraph. There is a race-meeting only ten miles distant. Some people would say that the things which we find ourselves believing could not happen in such times. We can only admit the incongruity.'

He passed a hand over eyes half blinded by the sun, and said in another tone, and with seeming inconsequence:

'There will be another bad fire on this common unless we get some more rain soon, Hurlow.'

Hurlow supped with Moffat that night, and they sat talking over the empty grate until nearly half-past eleven, when they set forth together on just such a night as the previous one. The moon had risen and set, but the cloak of night was spangled with stars.

All day Hurlow had been in a state of feverish excitement, but this had slowly subsided as the time for the actual adventure drew nearer. This was partly due to the fact that the strangest experiences in life are apt to lose their effect if dwelt upon long enough, and partly due to Moffat's demeanour, which remained soberly constant. Things might interest the little, bearded, satyr-like man, but they did not disquiet him. He lent confidence to Hurlow, who would have embarked with him on this adventure sooner than with any young giant who was armed to the teeth.

Neither spoke much as they breasted the heavy darkness of the copses, but Moffat's step was resolute, even sprightly. He was the eternal student going forth to learn. He was already astride the stile separating the second copse from the open common, when he suddenly ceased moving, and squatted upright on the top bar in a listening attitude. Hurlow, a pace or two behind him, saw him framed by an arch of the branches, a faun-like silhouette with uplifted finger.

'The pipes,' said Moffat just above his breath.

Hurlow heard the notes – shrill, thrilling, and soft by turn, and calling, calling, always calling. The magic of their sweetness scarcely touched him tonight, but he marked its effect upon Moffat, who lingered astride the stile for a long minute.

At last Moffat scrambled over, and Hurlow followed and trod on his heels, desperately anxious to keep pace over the narrow path between the furze bushes. And as they hastened, again the piping died away as suddenly as if the sound were cut off by the closing of a door.

On the edge of the hollow Moffat, who had kept the lead, suddenly stopped.

'There!' he said.

Hurlow looked over his shoulder, and below them, in the cup of the hollow, he saw the ruddy light of a camp-fire. After a moment, since he already knew what to look for, he saw more than that. Starlight and the light of the fire conspired to show him dim shapes, which he recognized as tents and caravans. But down there, in that shadowland of furze and bracken, there was no movement nor any sign of life.

'What shall we do?' he whispered in Moffat's ear.

'You walked through it safely last night,' Moffat whispered without moving.

'Yes; but I couldn't tonight. Last night I didn't know.'

Moffat turned and faced him. Outwardly he was calm; his only sign of fear was that he sweated like a frightened horse. Hurlow saw moisture like dew upon his forehead.

'Nor could I,' said Moffat simply. 'I could reason soundly on the folly of fear, but I would not walk through that hollow now for all the gold in the Indies.'

Something like panic struck at Hurlow. Moffat's calm confession of fear withdrew the prop upon which he had leaned. Down there, among the motionless shadows, lurked invisible things, things that were nameless, shapeless, and malignant; things which could see without being seen. One of the long lost terrors of childhood returned to him, and like a child he put his hand into Moffat's.

'What are we to do?' he asked in a whisper, longing for Moffat to suggest that they should go.

'What can we do? It seems that we are only men and not heroes. We can only stay here and watch.'

A moment later Hurlow cried out as if a flame had scorched him. There was a sudden crackling of bracken, and a man's form appeared out of the darkness at his elbow.

'All right, sir! All right!'

It was Walters the head-keeper. His face was ghastly, and by no muscular effort could he control the chattering of his teeth.

'My dog – he ran away!' he whispered hoarsely. 'He knows! Mr Moffat, sir, for heaven's sake what does it mean?'

'I don't know.' Moffat's voice was shaken, but it sounded almost nonchalant to the other two. 'There seems to be a camp down there.'

'Yes; there was one last night, and none this morning. There was none here tonight, half an hour ago. I've been watching all day, and all this evening, and no gipsies on the move, and now – there's fire and caravans and tents. I crawled as near as I dare, but that dog of mine he howled and ran, and dogs know! I've had a scrap or two with poachers, and I've been through the war, but I'd sooner put my head in hell than go down that hollow.'

Neither Moffat nor Hurlow answered him. All three stood still, listening to the manifold little sounds which broke upon the silence of the night; the winds sighing in the feathery tops of bracken, the distant barking of a fox, the yet more distant crowing of an early cock.

'Gentlemen,' stammered Walters. 'You'll stand by me?'

'What can we do?' Hurlow growled.

'I got to warn the guv'nor that they're there. And I daren't move no more by myself. Don't stay 'ere, gentlemen. It ain't worth it. Nothin' ain't worth it.'

Moffat glanced at Hurlow.

'Let's go with him,' he whispered; 'we can return.'

Walters knew his way about the common without paths. He knew all the little open strips between the furze bushes and the gaps between clump and clump. So he led them around the edge of the hollow and out on to the road. His way lay past the inn, and, despite the lateness of the hour, the door of it was ajar, and the aperture faintly illumined by yellow candle-light. A woman, clasping a bottle, stepped back, calling out goodnight to somebody within. It was Mrs Hicket, the granddaughter of Granny Light. Hurlow stopped and asked:

'What's the matter?'

'It's granny, sir,' the woman explained. 'We've been having a trouble with her again. She've been sayin' as she must get up – her as haven't walked for ten years. I've been holdin' her, and terrible strong she've

[73]

seemed. She's quiet again now, and sleepin', but I thought it best to get brandy in case she went faint-like after it all.'

She hurried on, calling out goodnights; and the three men exchanged meaning glances.

'We need not trouble to return to the hollow tonight,' said Moffat. 'Nothing will happen now.'

All next morning the glass fell, and in the afternoon there was a marshalling of clouds in the south and west – whither the wind had veered – which slowly spread themselves across the sky. The rumble of far-off thunder, like distant guns, was heard; but the storm circled about without breaking overhead, and no rain fell.

Moffat came over to sup at the inn, and afterwards spent much time at the window of Hurlow's private sitting room, staring out into the night. Hurlow, smoking in an armchair, watched him, and presently inquired after the weather.

'I've seen lightning twice. If it would only rain!'

'Why?'

'I wish there would be a cloud-burst. I should like to see this parched land soaked and sluiced and flooded. I should like to see every ditch brimming and every pond overflowing.'

'Because the land needs it?'

'Because young Lutford needs it. My friend, we can have no doubt that unless other powers intervene there is a tragedy impending for that young man. We have seen and heard enough to assure us that old Mrs Light's people have come back. They have made good half their threat by returning from the grave, or from hell, or from where you will. The other unuttered half, they have yet to make good. We are not, thank Heaven, encompassed by only evil powers, although it would seem that to evil is given a long tether. The last tragedy was by fire. Water is the enemy of fire, and if the rain falls in time this tragedy may yet be averted. But it will be a close race. We must be out earlier tonight.'

'Where?' Hurlow asked, puffing nervously at his pipe. 'I don't – don't think I'll go to the hollow tonight.'

'Nonsense,' Moffat said gently. 'You have seen so much, and you must see the end. A storm is coming, and the storm will bring the rain. I think the end will be tonight.'

Moffat had his way, and the two set out just before eleven o'clock. And just at the junction of the footpath and the road they heard the distant sound of pipes.

'Ah!' whispered Moffat. 'As I told you. Early tonight.'

And tonight the pipes played clearly and sweetly and triumphantly on and on. Some notes broke and chuckled as with a lewd glee. And tonight the pipes called insistently, and yet played to a measure which tempted hands and feet to respond to the rhythm. Hurlow, scarcely knowing it, found himself marching springily to the beat of the tune; then came Moffat's hand on his arm, and Moffat's voice in his ear.

'For God's sake! Not this devil's dance!'

Louder, louder blew the pipes as they advanced towards the hollow. The sight of two figures ahead of them, standing on the edge of the dip, brought them to a sudden halt. Then Moffat, touching Hurlow's elbow, said:

'It is all right. They are Lutford and Walters. I know Lutford's way of leaning on his stick.'

The young squire and the keeper heard them approach, and came a little way to meet them. Lutford held out a trembling hand.

'Mr Hurlow,' he said, 'I beg your pardon for what I said to you yesterday. The unbelievable is true. It is good of you both to come tonight.'

Hurlow muttered something as the four pressed forward once more. Minute by minute the piping grew louder, more alluring, more maddening.

'Has it been like this before?' Lutford asked, between his teeth.

'No,' muttered Hurlow. 'Only a few notes. Nothing like tonight.'

On the edge of the hollow they could see the camp-fire below, but the dark around it was impenetrable. For a long minute they stood silent, listening to the strange music and the laboured sounds of one another's breathing. Lutford at last heaved a long sigh.

'I can't stand any more of this,' he whispered. 'I'm going down.'

Instantly Moffat had him by the arm, and they made a curious picture for a moment – the little, frail, bearded man clinging to the tall, wiry youth.

'No, you're not!' he cried. 'Not while there are three of us to hold you. Walters – Hurlow—'

They all seized him, and, after a moment, Lutford tacitly surrendered.

'If I were you, Mr Lutford,' said Moffat sternly, 'I should be standing by my house tonight!'

'What – at home? With all this happening here?'

'You may be wanted there. Ah!' He uttered a suppressed cry. 'Did you see?'

A jagged vein of red lightning shot down from the sky, lighting the hollow for some immeasurable fraction of time.

'I saw caravans and tents,' Lutford muttered.

'Nothing else? Listen! The piper is on the move. He is marching to and fro. You can hear. Wait for more lightning, and watch.'

As if in response to a silent request from all of them came another flash, revealing to all four pairs of eyes the cup of the hollow.

So much and so little may be seen by a flash of lightning. The eyes sees, but ere the brain can tell it what to look for the chance is gone. But what Hurlow saw will remain impressed upon his memory until the day of his death.

He saw human figures at the bottom of the hollow – perhaps a score of them – and all seemed to be swaying and gyrating to the measure of the pipes. While he still stared into the dark, Moffat clutched his arm.

'Look!' he whispered. 'That other light.'

There was another light now besides that of the camp-fire. It grew larger and larger as they stared. A tongue of flame shot up and vanished against the sky. Borne on the wind came the odour of sweet and pungent smoke.

'The furze!' cried Lutford suddenly. 'The furze is alight!'

The fire ran from bush to bush as if it followed a trail of oil. The light from a dozen blazes, which quickly merged into one crackling pool of fire, showed the smoke moving about it like a black cloak. But caravans and tents and people were gone. Only, in the midst of this sudden and growing waste of fire, the pipes played on sweetly, recklessly.

Great gusts of smoke blew into the faces of the four, but they stood watching, fascinated, unable to move, until at last Walters uttered a choking cry and pointed.

The fire had lit up all sides of the hollow, and thrown a wall of bright haze against the darkness around its edges. And as they stared, following the direction of the keeper's pointing finger with their gaze, they saw the bent figure of an old woman stumble into the radius of the light not fifty yards away.

Hurlow uttered a little gasp, and shut his eyes. He did not see what the others saw. They told him afterwards how the woman's figure, moving swiftly and resolutely, climbed down the slope and flung itself into the bath of fire, which straightway engulfed it. And on the instant the piping ceased and a blind terror came upon Walters, who uttered a sudden sobbing cry.

'Granny Light!' he cried, his voice rising to a scream. 'Granny Light! Oh, God, it was Granny Light!'

He spun about on his heels and began to run stumblingly, and this panic communicated itself to the others, so that they blundered after him. It was not until they had gained the road that Lutford regained control over himself.

'We must wake the village,' he cried. 'We must save the common if we can. Come on!'

They began again to run, and were close by the inn when a frightened woman flung herself out of a cottage gateway across their path. It was Mrs Hicket.

'Granny's dead!' she wailed. 'Granny's dead! Oh, what shall I do? Granny's dead! She wanted to get up again, and I was holding her when she died. And she shouting about the piper when the breath left her!'

A cry from the inn distracted them from the woman's half-hysterical clamouring. An upper window had been thrown open, and the landlord was leaning out and shouting at the top of his voice. He cried, 'Fire! Fire! Fire!' – the same word over and over again.

Lutford ran a few paces towards the window.

'Yes,' he shouted, 'we know. Come down, will you? The common!'

'No, not the common! Oh, look, sir!'

Away to the north they all saw another glare in the sky, and a sudden leap of flames showed them the face of a tall, long, white-fronted house.

As the old Manor House had been burned out that night nearly a hundred years before so was the new one burned tonight. And by what agency? Who shall say?

MISS CORNELIUS

W. F. Harvey

William Fryer Harvey (1885–1937), a Quaker
doctor who received the Albert Medal for
gallantry in the First World War, was a master
of the psychological horror story. In several of
these, an outwardly normal woman slowly
becomes sinister and witch-like, driving the
central character to hysteria or madness. The
most notable of these were 'Mrs Ormerod',
'Miss Avenal', and 'Miss Cornelius' (Harvey's
own favourite tale) from his celebrated
collection *The Beast With Five Fingers* (1928).

A ndrew Saxon was senior science master at Cornford School.
Cornford is a new school, re-modelled on an old foundation.
HMIs, when they can afford it, and that is not often, send their
boys there, especially if they have a bent for science. Many parents
thought that Andrew should have been head master, but he himself was
aware of his limitations. That he was more of a teacher than an
administrator, more of a stimulus than a teacher, one might guess after
reading that brilliantly disturbing book, Saxon and Butler's *Introduction
to the Principles of Organic Chemistry*.

He was known to the boys as 'Anglo-Saxon', or 'Old Alfred', and was
treated by them with an affectionate respect, which was increased by the
knowledge that he was a first-rate rifle shot, and had once been runner-
up for the King's Prize at Bisley.

Saxon had never shown any special interest in psychical research, but
when his friend Clinton, the manager of the Eastern Counties Bank,

asked him to take part in a joint investigation into what was going on in Meadowfield Terrace, he did not like to refuse. The house was occupied by Parke, a cashier in the bank, Mrs Parke and two children, a cook, who had been with Parke for five years, a rather slow-witted girl of sixteen who acted as nurse–parlourmaid, and Miss Cornelius. Saxon knew Miss Cornelius by sight as the elderly lady who lived in that rather delightful house by the Vicarage. He understood from Clinton that it was undergoing extensive renovations, and that while the plumbers and painters were about the place she had suggested lodging with the Parkes, who were always glad to receive paying guests.

The manifestations had been going on over a period of three weeks. They consisted apparently of rappings, noises like those made by the dropping of very heavy weights, unaccountable movements of tables and articles of furniture, the mysterious locking and unlocking of doors and, perhaps strangest of all, the throwing about, apart from any observed human agency, of all sorts of miscellaneous objects, ranging from chessmen and gramophone needles to lumps of coal and metal candlesticks.

'With a little luck it looks as if I should be in for an interesting evening,' said Saxon to his wife. 'If I were to hazard a guess, I should say that the servant-girl is somehow connected with it.'

Certainly the evening was interesting. In the drawing room at Meadowfield Terrace Saxon was introduced by Clinton to Parke and Mrs Parke and Miss Cornelius. At his suggestion Parke recapitulated the happenings of the last three weeks, his wife and Miss Cornelius from time to time adding or correcting details. The account was given in a straightforward manner that impressed Saxon, nor could he see in any of the three traces of hysteria. All were obviously disturbed at what they had witnessed; Mrs Parke indeed looked worn and harassed; but neither she nor Miss Cornelius had lost their sense of humour.

'Let us agree on one thing,' he said, 'before we go any further. I know very little about poltergeist manifestations – I have an open mind on the subject – but we must not presume an abnormal (I use the word in preference to supernatural) explanation, until we have excluded conscious or unconscious fraud. Apart, too, from the question of fraud, what has been seen may be connected in some way with human agency. We must all watch each other; we must even be suspicious of each other. Anything for a peaceful life. That's right, isn't it, Mrs Parke?'

They all agreed.

'What about the maids?' said Clinton.

There was no difficulty there. It was the girl's night out, and the cook had been given leave to spend the evening with a friend.

Miss Cornelius suggested that they should lock both doors, and that two of the party should make a careful search of all the rooms, to make certain that there was no one hiding to play tricks.

'You had better go with Mr Clinton,' said Mrs Parke, laughing nervously. 'I'd almost rather anything happened than find a man under my bed.'

They sat in the drawing toom while Clinton and Miss Cornelius made the round of the house. Saxon looked at his watch. 'It's just half past eight,' he said. 'And that's about the time that things begin to look lively,' said Parke. 'Listen! The rappings have begun already.'

There could be no doubt about the noises, low and muffled, as if someone were striking a rubber pad with a hammer; but it was impossible to locate them, to say whether they came from beyond the walls or the ceiling. They were quite distinct from the footsteps of Clinton and Miss Cornelius, who could be heard moving about in one of the rooms above. A minute or two later the voices of the two were heard in conversation, as they came down the stairs. Then there was a crash, and Miss Cornelius called out: 'What was that?' Parke and Saxon ran out into the hall. A wooden horse, belonging to the children, which Clinton declared that he had seen on the landing outside the nursery door, was lying with its head broken at the foot of the stairs. The evening's programme had commenced.

It was a full and varied programme, and the intervals between the items was short, filled with a tense, almost exhilarating, feeling of excitement as to what in the world would happen next. Saxon and Clinton, who had both previously agreed to take notes of what they saw, were kept busy writing. A little before half past nine there was a lull in the proceedings.

'They usually close down about now,' said Parke with a rather forced laugh. 'What about some coffee, Maisie?'

'I wonder if you would mind Mr Clinton and me running over our notes together in the dining room?' Saxon asked. 'I don't think we shall detain you very long.'

They went into the adjoining room, and Clinton noticed with surprise that his companion turned the key in the lock.

'Well, what about it?' said the bank manager. 'I confess the whole thing baffles me.'

Saxon was silent for a moment, and then broke out petulantly: 'I wish to goodness you had never brought me here, Clinton. We have got landed in the very deuce of a mess, and that is why you and I have got to come to some decision.'

'I'm afraid I don't quite follow.'

'I'll put a question to you. From what you have seen this evening do you suspect anyone?'

Clinton looked troubled and was silent.

'Parke?' went on Saxon. 'Do you suspect him?'

'No, oh, no!'

'Mrs Parke?'

'No, certainly not.'

'Miss Cornelius, then?'

'I don't think so. No.'

'You don't think so. Well, I do. Mind you, three-quarters of what I have seen I can't account for at present. Why the rocking-chair should go on moving as it did, for example. I searched in vain for a thread of black cotton – I even looked for a hair. On the other hand, when that lump of coal flew across the room, I am almost positive that it came from the hand of Miss Cornelius. She had been standing by the coal-box only a minute before. If you noticed, she was constantly fidgeting with different articles on the table and mantelpiece. Her hands were never still. It seemed almost that she had to hold her itching fingers down. I did see – and that I am prepared to swear to – her throw the pen that stuck in the ceiling. The whole thing was suspicious. It's unusual, to say the least of it, to find pens lying about on the mantelpiece. There is one in this room, you will notice; put there, I suggest, by Miss Cornelius to await the opportune moment. In the case I'm speaking of she held it in her hand behind her back, and gave it a curious little flick with her thumb. I believe with practice I could do the same myself.'

He took the pen from the mantelpiece and repeated the action he had described.

'There!' he cried triumphantly, 'I told you it could be done. It's stuck in the sofa cushion instead of the ceiling, for which I was aiming; but you must admit that my hand was behind my back for not more than a fraction of a second. Why did you hesitate when I mentioned Miss Cornelius's name, when you were emphatic in denying that you suspected the Parkes?'

'A good many of the objects certainly seemed to come from her direction,' said Clinton slowly, 'and it struck me that once or twice she called attention to them almost too soon. You know the quick, startled way she had of exclaiming: 'What's that?' so that all of us looked in the

[81]

direction she was looking in. Well, it struck me as a bit fishy – that was all.'

'Look at your notes a minute,' Saxon went on. 'Things have happened this evening on the stairs, in this room, and in the drawing room; while we have been sitting all together, and while some of us have been here and some in the drawing room; but you will notice that the manifestations other than the noises and rappings only took place in the presence of Miss Cornelius.'

'And you suggest—?'

'That the sole invariable antecedent is probably the cause.'

'Then what the deuce are we to do about it?'

'The only thing we can do,' said Saxon – 'I say we, but I mean I, because I don't see why you need be dragged into it – is to go into that other room and be perfectly frank with them. These things have got to stop. Apart altogether from the strain on Mrs Parke, there are the children to be considered. There will be an unholy row, possibly sleepless nights for some of us, but we've got to take the bull by the horns. Let's go in and get it over. It's like striking an old woman,' he added, after a pause. 'My God! Clinton, I wish you had never brought me here.'

'And what do you make of it all?' asked Miss Cornelius with a smile, when they were all assembled in the drawing room. 'I do so hope you are going to set our fears at rest.'

Saxon looked her straight in the face. He saw the false fringe, the wrinkles, and the eyes, dark and challenging, in which cruelty lurked.

'Mrs Parke,' he began, 'I am more sorry than I can say, and I hate what I am going to say, but I believe that Miss Cornelius is closely concerned with what we have witnessed tonight. Miss Cornelius, won't you be frank with us? What is said now need go no farther than this room.'

They were all looking at her. Her face was the colour of old ivory.

'Maisie,' she said, 'this is an outrage! What right has this man, who has been talking to me this evening as if he were my friend, to turn suddenly round and try to blacken my character in the presence of people whom I have known intimately for years? I know nothing of what he has been saying. I am as guiltless of fraud or trickery as those two little children asleep upstairs.'

'Excuse me,' Saxon interrupted, 'it is only fair to remind you all that we *did* agree to see this matter through and to disregard the personal factor. I said I was going to be suspicious of everyone, and I have been.'

'That's right,' said Parke, reluctantly. 'But what is it you accuse Miss Cornelius of?'

'I don't accuse her of anything. But I do say that I saw her throw a pen; on several occasions I almost saw objects leaving her hand; and that the phenomena we have witnessed this evening – I should be the first to admit that I cannot at present explain them all – have always occurred in her presence. One word more and I have done. I want to be charitable in what I say and think. I do not say that Miss Cornelius has consciously deceived us. I think that probably unknown to herself she has developed unusual powers of legerdemain, and that she has used it to foster that extraordinary, exhilarating feeling of excitement and suspense which we have been conscious of this evening. And now I think I will go.'

'He thinks he will go!' said Miss Cornelius, speaking with pent-up fury. 'He sprinkles me with pitch and then he thinks he can clear off. But let me tell you, Mr Saxon, an old woman speaking to a comparatively young man, that you will live to be sorry for this day. You will know what it is to pray that your tongue might have withered at its roots rather than it should have said the things it has tonight.'

'I may have been too abrupt,' said Saxon, as he walked back home with Clinton. 'My wife tells me that I have no tact; but it struck me that the only thing to do was to cut quickly and deeply and not waste time over the anaesthetic.'

'The fault is mine,' the other replied, 'in having dragged you into it. Though I'm sorry for the Parkes, I'm almost more sorry for you. I think you did the right thing, and I don't mind telling you that it's more than I could have done.'

Saxon found his wife sitting up for him. 'Were the spooks genuine after all?' she said. 'I'm longing to hear all about it.'

'I think I'd rather leave it over until tomorrow. It's not been exactly a pleasant evening, and I am afraid I have made one enemy for life – Miss Cornelius.'

He told her all about it next morning at breakfast.

'I don't know whom to pity most,' she said, 'you or the poor old lady. I've always thought of her as one of those quiet, inoffensive old dears, that give the atmosphere to the drawing rooms of South Coast boarding-establishments. Anyhow, I'm not going to have you worried about it. Why not get off to Flinton for a long weekend of golf? You were going to some time during the holidays, you know.'

Saxon hummed and hawed, and raked about half-heartedly for

excuses, but she could see that the idea appealed to him, and by noon she had seen him off.

That was on a Friday afternoon. It was certainly very jolly down at Flinton. They were an unusually congenial little party at the Dormie House. MacAllister of Trinity was there with a young biochemist from King's, with whom he crossed swords to good purpose in the evenings. And he was on top of his form as well. Monday morning brought a long letter from his wife.

Dear old Alfred [she wrote], I'm quite sure you did the right thing in getting away. The clouds – metaphorical – are blowing over. You'll hardly believe me when I tell you what I've done. I've bearded the lion and taken the bull by the horns. In other words, I've seen and spoken with Miss Cornelius. Now don't call me rash or foolish, until you hear how it all came about. Somehow I didn't feel like going to church this morning – the new half-warmed fish curate was preaching – and went for a walk instead down by the river. I saw Miss Cornelius in the distance, sitting on a seat, and looking lonely and withered, and to cut a long story short, I went up to her and told her how sorry I was that all this should have happened. At first I could see that she did not quite know what to make of me, but she soon began, if not to blossom out, at least to burgeon, and was really very kind. She admitted that she was inexcusably rude to you, but thought you would understand that the provocation was great. She says that she is entirely innocent of any attempt at deceit, and if she did throw the pen, that she knew nothing about it. She still believes that the manifestations are the work of some Poltergeist – I don't know if that's the way you spell it – and the utmost she will admit is that there is an element of infection about these things and that, unknown to herself, she may have got infected. I gather that the Parkes were very nice about it all, and that, as her house was practically finished apart from the outside painting, they mutually agreed – is that a right use of the word mutual, you old pedant? – that she should go back there. And there she is: and that's that.

There was a postscript too:

Don't come back until Wednesday, and get all the golf and exercise you can. In fact, you can't very well come back before then, because I have decided to spring clean the study. It ought to have been done at Easter. I'll take care of your papers.

'Molly at her best,' thought Saxon, with affectionate pride, 'clearing up her husband's messes without his leave and making no fuss about it.'

When, after enjoying his days of grace to the full, he returned home on the Wednesday, the events of the previous week appeared strangely remote. It seemed indeed that, whatever his relations with Miss Cornelius were to be in the future, his wife had gained from his encounter a new acquaintance.

'Not only did I beard the lion, as I told you in my letter,' said Molly, 'but since then I have braved the lion, or rather lioness, in her den. And it really is the most charming old house, Andrew. I'd no idea Cornford could boast such a place. I've got some photographs somewhere that Miss Cornelius gave me. They make you quite covetous and uncharitable, like the illustrated advertisements of houses for sale in *Country Life*.'

The week that followed passed without incident. Miss Cornelius called one afternoon when he was out, and brought with her a new stereoscopic camera to show his wife. The old lady, curiously enough, was an ardent photographer – Saxon already had revised Molly's South Coast boarding-house picture of her – and offered to take some views of the house. Mrs Saxon jumped at the proposal. They would be just the thing to send to her sister in New Zealand, with the vivacious Molly in the foreground.

The prints were excellent.

'Now, if only you had married an actress, Old Alfred,' she said, 'we could turn an honest penny by making this into an illustrated article. Me in the garden – yes, I adore flowers; me in the study – I don't know what I should do without my books; me in the kitchen – I always make my own omelettes; me in my boudoir – yes, I picked up that old mirror in Spain.'

'My dear,' said Saxon, 'it's really wonderful the amount of unmitigated nonsense you can talk.'

Miss Cornelius sent, too, a few photographs of the interior of her own house. No one would have taken them for the work of an amateur, and when seen through the stereoscope an impression of solidity and depth was obtained, 'as if,' Mrs Saxon said, 'you were really inside the rooms.'

Then, as August drew to a close in a week of sultry heat and thunder, things began to happen, strange and purposeless things, that brought into the little house an atmosphere of tension that was completely foreign to it. At first they laughed, when they found the toast rack lying at the top of the stairs. Then one evening Molly's bedroom slippers moved across the room and landed neatly together in the empty fire-grate. On another occasion Saxon's pyjamas disappeared from underneath his pillow and, after a long search, were found tightly knotted together on the top of the wardrobe. The papers in his study were disarranged. One morning a jumper Molly had been knitting lay in the coalbox, unravelled, the wool wound in inextricable tangles around the legs of the table and chairs. They could make nothing of it.

'It almost looks,' said Molly, with a forced laugh, 'as if the spooks were trying to convince us that we had been too hasty in our judgment of Miss Cornelius.'

'Don't be foolish, my dear,' replied Saxon, testily. 'It's far more likely that that woman has been getting at the maids. My advice for the moment is to keep our eyes open and to say nothing about it.'

But he himself was deeply disturbed. Though professing an open mind on matters supernatural, he was hardly prepared for this cold and most unpleasant draught of doubt. He found himself thinking, more often than he liked to acknowledge, of Miss Cornelius and that venomous outburst of hate. What if she— But of course there must be some natural explanation. And so the week dragged by.

It was Sunday morning. They had finished their breakfast and Saxon, rising from the table, stood looking out of the window, when, turning round suddenly, he saw his wife fingering the handle of the breadknife. Next moment it flashed through the air and knocked over a vase on the mantelpiece.

'Andrew!' she cried. 'Wherever did that come from? Oh, I can't bear it. Andrew, don't you realize it might have hit me? Don't! Don't!'

He ran to her and put his arms round her. 'Molly, darling, it's all right. You mustn't be alarmed. We must pull ourselves together and not allow our nerves to get on edge. Let's go into the garden. We can talk better there.'

He hardly knew what he was saying, for his heart was torn with pity. He had longed for a natural explanation, never guessing that it would be one so terrible as this. He could see it all now. He had been far too graphic in his description of what had happened that evening at the Parkes'. She had evidently been fascinated by the story – fascinated by the abnormal in Miss Cornelius – until, unconsciously, she herself had been infected by this vile lust of deception and trickery, that turned folly into terror. These were the thoughts that jostled each other on the threshold of consciousness while he tried to comfort his wife.

'We have both of us been brooding on this too much,' he said. 'My suggestion is that we get out of the groove of the last week and adopt a new routine. We'll go in for picnic lunches.'

'Things are pretty serious when Old Alfred suggests that,' said Molly, with a wintry smile.

'But not if we can laugh about it. You shall have all the picnic lunches that you want, and we'll sit in a cold wood on damp stones and eat sardine sandwiches. And then each day we'll have some people in for tea or supper. And I'll go to the cinema.'

Molly kissed him. 'I think your suggestions are very sensible. And now for mine. I believe we were wrong in not speaking of this to anyone. We've been too bottled up. I think we should each confide in someone. And, because you are a secretive old scientist, I want you to let me choose who your father confessor shall be.'

'I draw the line at Miss Cornelius and parsons.'

'No, it's Dr Luttrell. I'll ask him to tea tomorrow. You know you like him, and though we haven't seen much of him lately, I can never forget how good he was to us that winter two years ago.'

'All right,' said Saxon, after a pause. 'I agree. And now for your confidante. Not the vicar, and certainly not Mrs Saunderson. I've got it! The very thing; and we shall kill two birds with one stone. Your cousin, Alice. Write and get her to stay a few days with us. She herself suggested a visit.'

Molly's face brightened.

'I believe she would come,' she said. 'I know you don't like missionaries; but she is a medical missionary, and I think you would get on very well together. I'll write to her today.'

As he listened to her talking, as he heard the old note of eager gaiety echoing again in her voice, Saxon found himself asking if he could not have been mistaken in what he had seen. If only he could believe that his senses had deceived him! If only he could persuade himself that there was something wrong with his eyes! If Luttrell came, he would get him to test his sight.

Molly went round with a note to the doctor that afternoon. He came next day a little later than they had expected. Saxon was working over in the laboratory, and when he got back to the house, he found Luttrell talking with Molly in the drawing room. As soon as tea was over – he remembered afterwards the rather forced vivacity of his wife's conversation – Andrew suggested that they should stroll over to his room in the science block, where they could talk and smoke undisturbed.

'I shall come for you in half an hour then,' said Molly, 'because Dr Luttrell has promised to advise me on the rock garden before he goes.'

Andrew got a great deal into those thirty minutes. Luttrell made a good listener, and only interrupted him now and then with a question. He examined his eyes too.

'And if you find my vision wholly defective, if you tell me that I can't trust my sense of sight, God knows, doctor, that you will have taken an unbearable weight off my mind.'

'As a matter of fact,' said Luttrell, when he had finished his examination, 'your vision isn't exactly normal.'

'Then what do you make of the whole confounded business? You've heard the plain, unvarnished facts, and remember that I'm not imaginative or given to overstatement. I'm a trained scientific observer.'

Luttrell rubbed a long forefinger thoughtfully over his gaunt cheek.

'There are two things that arise out of what you have told me. The first is what do I think of it? I'm not prepared at present to say. I should like myself to witness the phenomena you have described. The second and more important point relates to the immediate present and to Mrs Saxon. You are rightly anxious about her. I think you ought to have someone in the house whom you can trust. Not a nurse. I don't suggest that for a moment, but a cheerful companion.'

Saxon told him of the invitation that had been sent to Miss Hordern, the medical missionary, who was a cousin of his wife.

'Excellent!' he said; 'an admirable person to have with you at this juncture. When she comes, I should very much like to have a talk with her.'

Their conversation was brought to an end by the entrance of Mrs Saxon, who reminded Luttrell that he must not go without seeing her garden.

'And what about the new addition to my 'lab'?' said Andrew. 'We'll go back that way. It won't take us more than a few minutes.'

The minutes, however, lengthened out, as Andrew dilated on the beauties of his new equipment, half-forgetful in his enthusiasm of the dark cloud which hung over him. He was busy explaining a rather complicated piece of apparatus to Luttrell, when they were startled by the noise of something falling and the sound of broken glass.

'I'm awfully sorry, my dear fellow,' said Luttrell. 'It was inexcusably clumsy of me. I knocked it off the bench in turning.'

'Richard,' shouted Saxon, and there was something curiously hard in his voice, 'leave that job you are doing at once, and come and clear up this mess. A bottle of sulphuric acid was broken on the floor. Molly, dear, you go on. We'll be with you in a minute. I just want to see that the boy knows what to do.'

'Luttrell,' he said, when they were alone, 'You lied like a gentleman. But *she* threw that vitriol. You couldn't see her from where you were, but I could. The bottle came from there,' and he pointed to an empty place in the shelf at the farther end of the bench where they were standing. 'We must get her out of this, Luttrell; you must get her out of it, or I shall go mad myself.'

'It's more serious than I thought,' said the doctor. 'Has she a mother she could go to for a few days?'

'Yes, but she lives up in town – a kind, fussy woman, not the sort of person who would be much help in an emergency.'

'Never mind! She's her mother. Your wife must go off tonight. I give you my most solemn assurance that away from this place she will be all right. I can't explain now, but I'm absolutely sure of it. She can pack her bag at once, and I'll see her to the station and into the 6.20. No, I wouldn't come with her, if I were you. It might only disturb her. You can write out a telegram to her mother and I'll send it off on my way back, because I'm coming back to see you. I shall bring you a stiff sleeping draught. You've had about as much as a man can stand. Leave me to settle things with Mrs Saxon. And mind, she shall come back as soon as that missionary cousin of hers can come and stay with you.'

'Luttrell, you're a true friend,' said Saxon with emotion. 'I don't know what—'

'Pooh! my dear fellow, you would do the same for me, if I were in your place. It's all in a day's work. Just leave it all to Mrs Saxon and me.'

Saxon went to bed that night with a feeling of relief. Decisions, and wise decisions too, had been made for him, and in the making of them he was conscious of events being controlled by one in whom he could put implicit trust. He drank his sleeping-draught, nor had he long to wait before the kindly mists of oblivion blotted out the memories of that eventful day.

Mrs Saxon was away for nearly a week. She wrote nearly every day, long and cheerful letters, which Andrew only half succeeded in answering in the same spirit. He spent the hours of daylight in the laboratory, trying to forget himself in the completion of a long-delayed piece of research work. But at night he found it impossible to concentrate, and paced the garden for hours together, hoping that the tired body would lull to rest the tired mind. He looked back at that fatal evening with horror. If only he had never met Miss Cornelius, had never crossed her path! He had not seen her since his visit to the Parkes'; but one afternoon when he was out she called and left a card. The idea of anything approaching intimacy between her and Molly filled him with loathing, but, unwilling to risk an open rupture, he contented himself by writing a formal note, explaining that his wife was away from home and that the date of her return was uncertain.

One step he took in Molly's absence after long consideration, and that was to write to Bestwick whom he had known at Oxford, and who was now second-in-command at the Raddlebarn Asylum, asking him if in his opinion Molly should undergo psychoanalysis. The reply he received – he locked the letter in a drawer in his desk – asked for further particulars, and suggested that Bestwick should be put in touch with their private practitioner.

Molly came on the same day that Alice Hordern arrived. His first impression of Molly's cousin was of a sad-faced woman of about fifty, with an attractive smile. She was silent and reserved, but the two felt in her presence the spirit of peace that had for so long eluded them.

There had been no outward cause of alarm since the happenings which Luttrell had witnessed in the laboratory, and Saxon had almost begun to hope that they were waking from a ghastly dream, when Miss Cornelius again called at the house and spent an hour or more alone with Molly.

'I didn't invite her, and I didn't want her,' she said, when Saxon asked her about it, 'but I couldn't tell her so. I had to be civil.'

'There's no need to go stroking vipers,' he broke out excitedly. 'All our troubles are due to that woman. You had better write to her and tell her that her acquaintance is not desired.'

'I shall do no such thing, Andrew. How can you be so foolish? She's more to be pitied than anything else. But for heaven's sake don't let's wrangle about it. It's not worth it.'

No, they were too tired to quarrel; too tired, rather, to go through all the emotion-wearying processes of reconciliation that would be bound to follow. Saxon, however, had made his decision. On the following afternoon, without saying anything to Molly about it, he called on Miss Cornelius.

'I rather expected that you would be coming to see me, Mr Saxon,' she said, when he was shown into the drawing room. 'Pray sit down.'

'I am afraid—' he began.

Miss Cornelius laughed.

'That's quite obvious; you are horribly afraid of *me*. But I interrupt.'

'What I came to say,' Andrew went on, 'was to—'

'Was to ask me not to call and to drop your wife's acquaintance. That was the sum and substance of it, wasn't it? And why, may I ask, should a request from you carry any weight?'

He hesitated for a moment, not knowing what to reply.

'Your difficulty,' she went on, 'and part of your fear too, is that you don't know what to make of me. A fortnight ago I was a poor old lady of the boarding-house type, with itching fingers and a passion for creating interesting situations. Now you are not quite so sure. But cheer up, Mr Saxon. We live in a rational world. There is not the slightest need for you to suppose that I am a witch. Telepathy will explain most things, and I don't see why the things that have been troubling you recently should not be explained on those lines. I can well understand what a relief it would be to have those troubles explained away. But if I were you, I should write to some psychoanalyst and suggest that he should treat your wife. There is a man at the Raddlebarn Asylum, I think, who goes in for that sort of thing.'

Saxon sat staring at her with horror-struck eyes.

'Yes, it must be fearfully confusing to you,' she went on. 'I know just what you must feel like, and the dilemma is awful. Either I have an altogether uncanny power of reading your thoughts, Mr Saxon, and of knowing what passes in your house, or else your good little wife has played false to you and has rifled the drawer of your desk, read that letter, and betrayed its contents to your enemy. No wonder you hardly know what to think.

'And the dilemma is even worse than I suppose it to be,' she went on, 'because, granted you have the courage to ask Mrs Saxon if she broke into that locked drawer, and granted that she indignantly declares that she has done no such thing, in view of what has happened in the last fortnight, you will never absolutely be certain that she is not lying.'

Miss Cornelius burst into a fit of laughter.

'What the devil do you mean by all this?' he cried, in a transport of fury.

She rang the bell.

'Chalmers,' she said to the maid, 'show Mr Saxon out, and please remember that when he calls again I am not at home.'

Saxon said nothing to his wife about that visit. He was haunted by the weary look in her eyes and the forced gaiety of her smile. She had more than she could bear already. But on the following evening, when Molly had gone to bed, he had a long talk with Alice Hordern. The evening was chilly and the fire which had been lighted in the study invited confidence. Miss Hordern, who neither knitted nor sewed embroidery, echoed the invitation by asking Saxon if he had such a thing as a cigarette.

'I beg pardon,' he said with a smile, 'I am afraid I never associated women medical missionaries with tobacco.'

'You do quite right, Andrew, but I'm a woman first, doctor second, and missionary third; and number three, you must remember, is on furlough. You look worried. It's not Molly, is it? Because I don't think you have any immediate cause to be worried about her. Tell me about it.'

And so he told her everything, while his wife's cousin looked at him through the blue cigarette smoke with wise and kindly eyes.

'And so, you see, it's no use your telling me not to mind,' he said, when he finished. 'Black hate like this, that strikes at you through the one you love, is devilish. You've got to mind.'

'Granted, though, that Miss Cornelius is all that you think she is—'

'I daren't think what she is,' he groaned; but Alice Hordern took no notice of the interruption.

'Surely you only play her game by reciprocating her black hatred.'

'It's the missionary who is speaking now, I suppose,' he said bitterly.

'No, it's just me. You can't hate a person without always thinking of them. Hatred is like love in that. People use the expression to forget and forgive; but they put the cart before the horse. Until you have forgiven, you cannot forget. It is necessary for your peace of mind to forget Miss Cornelius. And so you must forgive her.'

'It could only be juggling with words. How can I, when I know what she has done and is doing? And what right have I to forgive, when it is not me she is injuring so much as Molly?'

'I am not sure of that,' said Miss Hordern. 'You can but try. Remember this, though. If you ask Molly whether she opened that drawer and read that letter and she says no, believe her. Not even Miss Cornelius can break the truth in Molly. She cannot touch you there.'

The clock had struck eleven when they rose to go to bed. They went upstairs together, but on the landing Saxon stopped for a minute to close the window.

'Good God!' he exclaimed. 'She's there in the garden, standing in the shadow of the yew tree, looking up at the house.'

Miss Hordern hurried to his side.

'Where?' she said. 'I don't see anyone.'

'She's gone now, but she was there a moment ago. I saw her face.'

'Come with me,' said Miss Hordern. 'We'll go into the garden. If Miss Cornelius is indeed there, it is a matter for the police.'

But they searched the garden in vain.

'My fancy, I suppose,' said Saxon wearily, 'my cursed fancy. Unless,' he added as an afterthought, 'it was an example of the attractive power of hate.'

Once more and once only was he to see Miss Cornelius before that fatal motor accident liberated him by her death from a life of daily torture and nightly despair.

Dr Luttrell, at Saxon's request, had written to Bestwick, who in his reply fixed a date for an interview with Molly. Luttrell himself was unable to go with the Saxons, but he arranged for his car to take them over, and Miss Hordern came with them for the sake of the ride. He was grateful for the consideration which made her choose the seat by the driver, for he could see that Molly was depressed and in no mood to introduce the countryside to her guest. He did his best to comfort her, explaining how a frank talk with Bestwick might help them both to see things in proper perspective, and assuring her that she would find him an easy man to get on with.

As they drew near their destination, he saw that she was crying.

'Andrew,' she said, 'dear Old Alfred, you do trust me, don't you? You'll never believe that I ever plotted against you or did anything to hurt or injure you? Promise me that.'

'Of course I trust you, my darling. I trust you implicitly and always will do.'

'And I'd like Alice to be with me when I talk to Dr Bestwick. You don't mind, do you? You see, she's been my father confessor and knows all about it.'

'I think it is an excellent idea,' he said. 'I have a very high opinion of your cousin.'

And so, when they had met and shaken hands with Bestwick, Saxon was left in a rather sombre reception room, while the doctor took the two ladies off to his study for a preliminary talk. After ten minutes he returned alone.

'And now,' he said, 'I want to hear your statement of things from the beginning. Don't hurry. Take your time over it, but tell me everything, however trivial it may seem.'

'Saxon,' he said, when Andrew had finished. 'I am afraid what I am going to say to you will come as a great shock. But you can set your mind at rest over one thing, and I believe that for you it is the most important thing. There is nothing the matter with your wife. There is no need to examine *her*.'

[93]

The slight emphasis that he placed on the last word startled Saxon. 'What do you mean?' he said.

'You've passed through a most upsetting experience, that came on the top of a hard term's work when you were completely tired out. That first meeting with Miss Cornelius, and all that you went through then, threw you temporarily off your balance. Your natural anxiety for your wife's safety made matters worse.'

'You mean – you mean,' said Saxon slowly, 'that I'm mad.'

'The word means so many things. But you were not your normal self when you threw the breadknife, or when Luttrell saw you throw the vitriol. You were not your normal self when you thought you saw the figure of Miss Cornelius from the landing window. And remember this, Saxon, your friends may have deceived you for your own good, but I speak now in absolute sincerity. I see no reason why you should not recover. You may only be here for a comparatively short time. But until you have recovered – you see I am speaking to you as if you were your old self, and that surely should give you hope – we must think of the safety of your wife. She has done what many a woman could never do; she has faced danger and misunderstanding with courage and devotion. It was I who persuaded her that it was best for her and for you not to say good bye. She will be seeing you again in a few weeks' time, I expect.'

'But Miss Cornelius,' Saxon gasped. 'Miss Cornelius! What about her?'

'Miss Cornelius,' said the other, 'is a vicious and cruel woman. I think that your original judgment of her was correct. She has probably dabbled in Spiritualism, and together with abnormal powers she has very likely developed a habit of unconscious trickery and legerdemain. Many genuine mediums are wholly untrustworthy. But Miss Cornelius is the occasion, not the cause, of your trouble.'

'Then what is she doing there?' cried Saxon suddenly. He had sprung to his feet, and was pointing wildly out of the window. 'That closed car that is passing down the road now! Quick! She has lowered the window and is waving her hand to me.'

Bestwick caught a glimpse of a car and a hand waving.

'It may or may not be Miss Cornelius,' he said, 'but come with me and I will show you your room.'

ONE REMAINED
BEHIND

Marjorie Bowen

Marjorie Bowen (1886–1952) was an amazingly
prolific author with nearly 200 novels,
biographies and short story collections to her
credit, including a large variety of supernatural
'twilight tales'. Her first historical novel,
The Viper of Milan, inspired Graham Greene
to become a novelist.
'One Remained Behind', subtitled a *'Romance à
la mode Gothique'*, originally appeared in the
Help Yourself! Annual (1936), a fund-raising
publication which raised large amounts of
money for charity.

R udolph quarrelled fiercely with M. Dufours, the antique dealer,
but in low tones so as not to be overheard in the street.

'If you do not sell it to me – and cheaply – I shall report you
to the police,' he whispered, firmly clasping the large book bound in
wood and brass that he had found on a top shelf in the little room at the
back of the shop.

'I do not think, M. Rudolph, that you would care to go to the police,'
retorted the old man, sucking in his toothless mouth with fury. 'I would
not part with the *grimoire*, no, not for fifty thousand francs.'

'You will, however,' sneered Rudolph, 'sell it to me for fifty francs. I
have no objection to informing the police that you are a receiver of stolen
goods, a moneylender at an exorbitant rate of interest, a dealer in
dangerous drugs, charms and black magic—'

'Ah, indeed,' replied the shopkeeper, trying to be sarcastic but really rather uneasy. 'And pray what are *you*, M. Rudolph? Unless I am very much mistaken *your* reputation is none too pure.'

'Bah! What does it matter about my reputation? The police have nothing against me. I am a poor student, a poet, a philosopher, and I intend to have this treasure that I have discovered on your shelf.'

'You admit that it is a treasure!' raged the old man. 'And yet you offer me a miserable fifty francs for it!'

'It is no treasure for you,' replied Rudolph scornfully. 'You are a pitiful dabbler in the black arts. You would never have the courage to proceed far along this dangerous, fascinating road! You do not even understand the secrets concealed here!' He tapped with elegant soiled white fingers the cover of the disputed book. 'I doubt if you can even read the title.'

Overcome by curiosity, the old man asked:

'What is this volume that you think so highly of, M. Rudolph?'

'Ha! ha! And just now you said you wanted fifty thousand francs for it!'

'Well, I know that it is an ancient *grimoire*, and therefore valuable.'

'It is,' sneered the student. 'The *Grimoriam Veram*, written by Alibeck the Egyptian and printed at Memphis in 1517 – together with this are bound several other treatises exceedingly rare.'

'What do you want with these things?' demanded the antique dealer suspiciously. 'You have no skill to interpret those signs and wonders—'

'Nor have you, or you would not be living here in this shabby shop, existing by petty crimes!'

'I might say the same of you, M. Rudolph! It is obvious that the study of black magic has not done you much good – your shirt is darned, your coat shiny at the elbows, your trousers are ragged round the hems, and one of your shoes is split!'

The student's eyes gleamed with malice.

'Nevertheless, perhaps I might surprise you, sordid old miser that you are! Please have the goodness to look into this!'

Still retaining the *grimoire* under his arm, the young man whipped out a small mirror that seemed to be of polished metal from his breast and flashed it in front of the reluctant gaze of M. Dufours.

He found, however, that it was impossible to avoid the metallic disc; his bleary eyes, worn by age and counting over the contents of his money-bags, stared, without his volition, into the magic mirror.

On the surface of this appeared a little cloudy figure, curled up like a bird in the nest, that gazed back at the old man with small black eyes that glittered vindictively.

'There is nothing in my shop,' muttered the curio dealer drowsily, 'like that; what can it be a reflection of?'

The student laughed and the little figure flew out of the mirror and hung between it and the frightened face of M. Dufours; then, with a buzz like that of an angry insect, it rushed at the curio dealer's nose and pinched it violently until the old man howled with fear and pain. Rudolph laughed and returned the metal disc to his pocket, upon which the spirit vanished.

'It was some wasp or bee flew in,' muttered M. Dufours, rubbing his red, smarting nose.

'Was it?' sneered the student. 'Kindly look round your filthy shop.'

The old man obeyed, fascinated by the brilliant black eyes, pallid face and mocking lips of M. Rudolph.

His jaw dropped and a trembling ran through all his shrunken limbs at what he saw – every object in his shop was transformed into something devilish. The old coats on their pegs waved their sleeves at him; the pawned trousers kicked as if prancing in a polka; grimacing faces peered from the blotched, cracked mirrors, the cupidons on the tarnished candelabra that hung from the cobwebbed rafters began to fly about like pigeons, and a lady in a very bad portrait by Legros, the art student, winked rudely at M. Dufours and shook at him her bouquet of miserably drawn roses which really resembled pickled onions.

M. Dufours rubbed his eyes and when he looked round again everything was normal.

'You see,' remarked Rudolph, 'that I know a few tricks. I shall keep the *grimoire* and owe you the fifty francs.'

With an air of disdain he picked up his dusty, frayed beaver hat, that he thrust on the side of his head jauntily above his long jet-black locks, and strode into the street; M. Dufours shook a lean fist after him, but dare not raise a hue and cry. There was really something Satanic about M. Rudolph – that nip on the nose, now, surely he had not imagined that!

The student went gloomily along the street, the *grimoire* clasped tightly under his arm; the sky was a pale violet colour above the roofs that were shining wet from a shower of rain, and a delicate breeze from the hills beyond the town stirred the rubbish in the gutter.

Outside the wineshop several students were sitting over their pints of claret, discussing their work and love affairs, joyously speculating as to

[97]

their chances of prizes, of kisses, of distinction, and of monies that might be sent from their relatives.

As Rudolph strode past without taking any notice of them, they fell into a silence and stared after him. How poor and proud he was! No one knew much about him and everyone was slightly afraid of him; he was morose, haughty and had no friends – how was it that he could afford to pay for the course at the University?

He was brilliant at his work, but was not likely, the professors said, to be successful, for he attended so few of the lectures.

How did he spend his time?

The students often asked one another this question and were afraid to answer it; the rumour was that Rudolph wasted his days and imperilled his soul by studying the forbidden arts.

They craned their necks after him in awe and admiration; he was so handsome with his high brow, black hair and cavernous eyes; every Fifi and Mimi in the town was in love with him and he never as much as glanced at any of them.

The other students admired his courage, too; he never concerned himself with any kind of civility and they were envious of his top hat – that *chapeau en haute forme* that he wore instead of the usual college cap.

True, this fashionable headgear was old and had probably been bought secondhand *chez Dufours*, but it had the address of a maker in the *rue St Honoré* inside the brim and was undoubtedly elegant.

Sourly gratified by these admiring glances that he affected not to notice, Rudolph proceeded to his poor lodgings, which were in an inconvenient part of the town, a long way from the University.

Not only poverty, however, persuaded Rudolph to live in this remote quarter; he liked the solitude of the deserted street where the tumble-down houses huddled beneath the broken walls of the town, where at night it was silent save for the hoot of an owl or so that strayed in from the woods and brooded on the roof-tops, and dark save for the yellow spurts of light from the dirty street lamps.

Holding the *grimoire* tightly, he mounted the twisting staircase to his attic; he was the sole lodger in the ancient house. An old woman and her grandchild owned the crazy building and dwelt on the ground floor.

Rudolph locked his door (he had fashioned the lock himself and carefully fixed it in place of the rude latch), and seating himself by the window in the lean-to roof, began to read his book eagerly.

There were many curious objects in the attic, stacked away in dark corners and under the dusty chairs and truckle-bed; on a bare table stood a lamp, a desk, on a shelf was a row of books; there were hanging cupboards, pegs for clothes and a number of boxes.

Rudolph read long in the *grimoire*, until the sun declined behind the roofs of the town, dusk filled his garret, and Jeanette, the landlady's grandchild, knocked at the door, crying out, in her thin, piping voice, that she had brought up the supper.

Rudolph, startled from his self-absorption, whispered a malediction, tossed the tangled hair from his eyes, rose and unlocked the door.

The little tin lamp on the stairs had been lit; this feeble light showed the broken banister rails, rotting floor boards and dust everywhere.

Jeanette, who looked like a white rat, hurried timidly into the room and placed Rudolph's supper on the table – a pint of wine, two slices of black bread, a dish of salted ham and pickled onions, and a withering apple; she then lit his lamp.

'Ha, little misery!' exclaimed the student wildly. 'How is it that thou canst continue this wretched existence, unworthy of a human being who owns a mortal soul?'

'Indeed, Monsieur, I don't know,' stammered the girl, trying to drop a curtsey; her skirts were so scanty that she could not achieve much elegance, and when she bent her knee it stuck through a hole in her rags. 'Grandmother says that if you could pay the rent—'

'Begone,' scowled Rudolph, waving his elegant hand. 'I have my studies awaiting me.'

Jeanette hurried away, glad to escape, and Rudolph pondered deeply on what he had read in the *grimoire*.

It certainly was a treasure, that book! It contained secrets that he had long been seeking to discover and directions for conjurations and divinations that he longed to try immediately. Unfortunately all these required expensive materials, new-born infants, kids, black or white cocks, costly drugs, shew stones, tables of sweet-wood and squares of undyed wool taken from a spotless lamb and woven by a maiden.

Rudolph knew a great deal about black magic, but he had never made any money from either that or the poetry which stood in dusty stacks against the walls; indeed, most of his meagre substance had gone in buying ingredients or articles for his forbidden studies.

He frowned gloomily, staring with disgust at the coarse food on the table. How he longed for luxury, a splendid castle, troops of liveried servants, a carriage with six white horses, a superb mistress clad in Venetian velvet!

Again he opened the *grimoire* and carefully re-read something that had

[99]

greatly taken his fancy. As he perused the badly printed page his pallid face gradually assumed a diabolical expression, for Rudolph wished evil to all mankind, and all his experiments – mostly taken from the *Clavicle of King Ptolomeus* – had been of the following kinds: 'Of hatred and destruction' – 'Of mocks and gainful seeking' – 'Of experiments extraordinary that be forbidden of good men.'

What fascinated him now was the description of certain rites whereby four strangers could be brought to the celebrant's room and one of them forced to do his will – even to the revealing of hidden treasure, the gift of luck at cards and success in a chosen career.

Rudolph nibbled an onion and brooded over this prospect; he decided at once on three of the people whom he would summon in this manner, so humiliating to them and so gratifying to himself.

First he would force Saint-Luc, the arrogant young aristocrat who had so often sneered at him and whom he so greatly detested, to appear in his wretched garret; second he would bring the vicious old professor, Maître Lachaud, who had so often told him, Rudolph, that he was idle, stubborn and a disgrace to the University; and third he would drag along by his magic spells M. Lecoine, the fat banker who had laughed in his, Rudolph's face, when he had asked for a loan.

But here again expensive materials were required, and the experiment might fail and all the money and effort be wasted.

Rudolph ate his bread and ham, then went to the window and glared out at the sky from which all daylight had now receded. A full moon was appearing above the house-tops and a few dark clouds that might have been witches impatiently flying off for nocturnal delights showed beneath it. As Rudolph gazed a great longing took possession of him to make the experiment of which he had read in the *grimoire*; not only did he earnestly desire to vex and terrify three people whom he detested, he was dazzled by the hope of luck in cards, in his career, and the finding of a hidden treasure.

'I shall be the greatest poet in the world and I shall have more money than any man ever had before.'

Such a prospect was worth a large sacrifice.

Rudolph turned back into the room and dragged an ancient carpet-bag from under his bed; he opened it, unfastening the cumbrous lock, while he sighed deeply and from swathes of old silk rags he took out a large golden ring set with a pale stone that gave out more light than the dirty lamp fed by cheap oil.

This jewel had been given to Rudolph by his great-grandfather with strict charges never to part with it –'except from the purest motives' the old man had said. He had been a famous roué in his time and had squandered all the family fortune on English jockeys, boxers and Italian dancers.

Rudolph disliked the thought of parting with the ring because the possession of such a gem increased his self-esteem and also because he was afraid of his great-grandfather's curse; he decided, however, to do so, and thrusting the ring in his bosom left the attic and turned to the fashionable part of the town beyond the University buildings that, rising directly in front of the moon, looked as if they were cut out of black paper.

The shutters were just being put up in front of the shop of M. Colcombet, the jeweller, but Rudolph dashed through the door and laid his ring on the counter, on the length of black velvet that covered the glass that contained flashing parures in heart-shaped boxes lined with satin.

'This is a family piece,' said the student haughtily. 'It is worth a good sum.'

M. Colcombet was doubtful, however, both of the ring and the customer; he peered suspiciously, first at the sardonic young man, then at the white jewel which was brighter than any diamond in the shop.

'It is a beryl,' he remarked.

'Not an ordinary beryl,' replied Rudolph, contemptuously flashing the ring about in his hand so that in the light of the well-trimmed silver lamp the stone cast out flames of blue, green and crimson.

'Well,' admitted M. Colcombet, who seemed fascinated by the stone, 'I daresay the Comtesse Louise would like it for her wedding *toilette.*'

'Ha, is the Comtesse Louise to be married?' asked Rudolph, who remembered with anger this haughty beauty who had stared through him when her carriage had passed him in the street, covering him with mud.

'Yes, to the Prince de C—. It is to be a splendid affair,' gossiped the jeweller. 'At her father's château, you know – the chapel is hung with cloth of gold and there is to be a festival for all the neighbourhood. Many of the students have had cards of invitation, and some of them have been in here to buy their presents – M. le Marquis de Saint-Luc, for instance. You perhaps yourself, Monsieur?' he added with an inquisitive glance at Rudolph's shabby clothes.

'What do you offer for the ring?' demanded the student fiercely.

'It is white,' said the jeweller, 'but not, I am sure, a diamond; reset it would look very handsome, perhaps in the centre of a tiara or on a corsage ornament—'

'How much? I am in a hurry.'

M. Colcombet, who felt rather embarrassed and confused, stammered:

'Two thousand francs, Monsieur.'

'It is worth far more, but I was not born to bargain – give me the money.'

As Rudolph flung down the ring he disarranged the black cloth over the show case and revealed a set of pearl and diamond ornaments in cases of pale blue satin.

'It is the wedding parure of the Comtesse Louise,' said M. Colcombet as he counted out the notes from his pocket-book; Rudolph took up the money and passed out into the street that, when the shutters were all up in front of the shops, was lit only by the light of the rising moon; the small dark clouds had now disappeared and the sky was pale and pure.

The student returned in a melancholy, bitter mood to his lodgings; although he had two thousand francs in his pocket he felt poorer than when he had been in possession of the beryl ring.

The mention of the Comtesse Louise had considerably vexed him; how he detested that proud girl with her little sneering mouth and large, slightly prominent blue eyes! He had several times seen her driving in the town, and once he had come face to face with her in a bookshop where she was buying foolish novels and he was trying to sell some Aldine volumes with superb sepia-coloured initials; on that occasion he had held open the door for her, and she had passed him with the most icy of unspoken rebukes in her lofty carriage and set sweetness of glance.

He had, however, seen her leaning on the arm of Saint-Luc, that ostentatious dandy who spent more in a year on his trousers and *gilets* than the whole of Rudolph's annual income.

Hatred and another dark emotion that was almost despair inspired the student with a diabolic pain; absenting himself from all classes and lectures he devoted all his time to carrying out precisely the instructions in the *grimoire* published at Memphis in 1517.

He made his plans carefully and arranged for his great experiment to take place on the evening of the wedding day of the Comtesse Louise and Prince de C—.

First he provided himself with a magic wand by going into the woods and cutting two twigs, one of hazel and one of elder, from trees that had never borne fruit; at the end of these he placed steel caps magnetized with a lodestone; then he took from the carpet-bag some ink made from sprigs of fern gathered on St John's Eve and vine twigs cut in the March full moon which had been ground to powder and mingled with river water in a fair glazed earthen pot; this mixture had been boiled up over a fire of virgin paper.

Rudolph also possessed a phial of pigeon's blood and a male goose quill and a bloodstone which possessed the virtue of protecting the wearer from evil spirits; he had always found this a very necessary precaution.

On the third day of the new moon Rudolph purchased a black cock and a white cock from the market place and kept them in his garret until nightfall; he then put the birds in a wicker cage, his paraphernalia in the carpet-bag, and set out beyond the town, beyond the woods until he came to an open space that surrounded the ruins of an Abbey reputed to be haunted by the spirits of monks who had been unfaithful to their vows.

Here the grass was short and scarred by stones and rocks; an ancient thorn tree, sacred to heathen deities, stood bleak and twisted by a small pool. The Gothic windows of the Abbey showed a black framework against the luminous sky; the bats flew in and out of the crisp, dark ivy; several noxious fungi grew round the pool, which was covered by a dull red floating weed so that it did not reflect any light.

Rudolph had often visited this place before; it was exactly what the *grimoires* said was required for infernal rites – 'a desolate spot free from interruptions'.

With mutterings to himself, while the sweat gathered on his high, pallid brow, the student made the grand Kabbalistic circle. From his carpet-bag he took out his rods, a goatskin, two garlands of Vervain, two candles of virgin wax made by a virgin – Jeanette whose meagre charms guaranteed her chastity – a sword of blue steel, two candlesticks of massive silver, two flints, tinder, a flask of *eau-de-vie*, some camphor, incense, and four nails from the coffin of a child – which last item Rudolph had paid Pierre, the coffin-maker, very highly for, for it had been necessary to go to the burial vaults of Saint Jean to obtain them.

With this material Rudolph made his grand circle of goatskin, sprinkling the incense and camphor in a wheel shape and kindling his fire of wood (that he fed with the cognac) in the centre, then, with his right arm bared to the shoulder, he sacrificed the two cocks, burning them on the fire while he muttered his evocations.

The bats and owls fled from the ruins, the moon veiled in the sky, the earth shook, the red scum of weeds on the lake became agitated; Rudolph pressed the bloodstone to his cheek and muttered an even more powerful spell.

The water was troubled furiously and a lovely boy rose to the surface of the lake and in a pleasant voice demanded of the student what he wished.

Rudolph was not deceived by this civility; he knew that the apparition was Lucifer himself, the most violent of the evil spirits who would tear the celebrant to pieces if he were to step out of the circle or to drop his bloodstone. Astaroth came, Rudolph was well aware, in the shape of a black and white ass, Beelzebub in hideous disguises, Belial seated in a flaming chariot, and Beleth on a white horse preceded by a company of musicians.

'What is your will?' asked Lucifer gently, but puffing out his red cheeks with rage.

'Monsieur,' said the student respectfully, 'I am about – at the end of the month, to be exact – to make a great experiment, that described on page twenty-three of the *Grimoire* of Alibeck the magician, published at Memphis in 1517.'

'A rare edition,' remarked Lucifer. 'You were fortunate to find it.'

While he spoke he was carefully watching to see if the student made the least mistake, so that he might seize him and pull him to shreds, but Rudolph was prudent and kept well within the centre of the magic circle with the bloodstone pressed to his cheek.

'I want to know, Monsieur, if you will assure me that the experiment will be successful?'

'You seem to know a few tricks,' smiled the fiend. 'No doubt, if you will fulfil all the requirements given in the *grimoire*, the experiment will be successful. You will take the consequences, of course.'

'If I can have four strangers in my room to do my bidding, discover a hidden treasure, become a famous poet and lucky at cards, I shall require nothing more,' sneered Rudolph, who even when talking to a devil could not for long maintain a submissive tone.

'All that you shall have,' promised the lovely child in a sweet voice, but his pretty little eyes were sparkling with fury at this insolence.

'I ask no more!' cried Rudolph, shaking his magic hazel wand at the lake. 'Foul fiend begone!'

With a dreadful hiss the boy sank into the lake, the red weed closed over the place where he had been, the moon came to a standstill in the sky, the bats and owls flew back to the ruins, and the student stepped out of the magic circle and began to pack away his materials into the carpet-bag.

When he returned through the town he heard the violinists above the music shop of M. Kuhn practising for the wedding festivities of the Comtesse Louise.

As the time drew near for the great experiment Rudolph made his final preparations; these had cost him nearly all the money he had received for the beryl ring and the suspicious looks of his fellow students.

He had paid his rent and given Jeanette a present to bribe her to sweep and clean out his chamber so that no dirt remained anywhere; he had then perfumed it with mastic and aloes and hung clean white curtains at the window, furnished the bed with fair linen, woollen coverlets and a mattress of goose-down.

He bought also a table and four chairs of plain white wood, four platters of white damask. To rid himself of the curiosity of Jeanette he declared that these preparations were for a visit from his mother and two sisters that he was expecting.

For three days before the date fixed for the wedding of the Comtesse Louise, Rudolph fasted and looked to his room, making sure that there were no hangings, nor indeed any objects, set crosswise, that no clothes were on pegs, that there was not a bird-cage in any corner of the room, and that everything was scrupulously clean.

On the evening of the great day itself the student set his four chairs round his table, placed out on the fair damask cloth the four platters with a wheaten loaf on each, and the four glass beakers full of clear water. Beside his bed he set his old armchair, and the windows he opened wide onto the moonlit night.

In the centre of the table he placed a shaker of goatskin, three black and one white bean, then, everything being in readiness, he cast himself on his knees and uttered the powerful conjuration given in page twenty-three of the *grimoire* of Alibeck. Then he lay down on his bed, wearing a handsome chamber-robe that he had bought for the occasion.

He heard the church clock strike midnight, and then the moonlight in the attic began to quiver a little and Professor Lachaud floated in through the open window, not moving his feet nor looking to right nor left, but stiffly passing alone; taking no heed of Rudolph, the dry little *savant* seated himself at the table and gazed in front of him through his silver-rimmed spectacles.

The next arrival was the banker, M. Lecoine; with an expression of surprise on his chubby face he floated in from the outer moonlight, a table napkin tucked under his chin and a pen in his hand; without speaking he seated himself opposite Lachaud. Almost at once the window was darkened again as M. Saint-Luc appeared wearing a fashionable evening costume with a superb *gilet* of sky-blue *moiré anglaise*; in silence he occupied the third place at the table.

Rudolph felt ill with excitement; the white curtains blew out in the moonlight and a lady all in white entered – the Comtesse Louise, or rather the Princess de C—, in her bridal gown of silver and satin with her wreath of myrtle and her parure of diamonds and pearls; on the thumb of her right hand was the beryl ring.

She took the fourth place at the table and the four strangers began to eat and drink; their movements were stiff and jerky like those of automata, and they were silent, without seeming to notice anything.

'One remains behind,' whispered Rudolph from the bed. 'One remains behind.'

The four strangers ate the wheaten loaves to the last crumb and drank the crystal water to the last drop; then the professor took up the goatskin shaker and put inside it the three black and one white bean, so that they might draw lots as to who should stay behind.

It was the lady who took out the white bean; the three men then rose and, still in silence, floated out of the window one after the other, the professor's robe, the youth's *frac* coat and the banker's napkin fluttering for a second in the night breeze as they disappeared into the moonlight.

The Comtesse Louise then rose, and crossing the room without moving her feet, seated herself in the armchair beside Rudolph's bed.

There were many things that the student would have liked to have asked the bride, but he remembered the danger of deviating from the formula of Alibeck, so he said:

'Confer on me luck at cards.'

She slipped the beryl ring off her thumb, handed it to him and replied:

'As long as you wear this you shall have luck at cards.'

'Confer on me the gift of fame.'

'You shall be the most famous poet alive.'

The lady answered clearly and promptly, but she ignored Rudolph as utterly as she had ignored him when she had met him in the bookshop or the street; this angered him and he made his third demand very haughtily:

'Reveal to me some hidden treasure.'

She rose.

'Come with me.'

The student left his bed and followed her out of the window, walking on the air as if it had been curdling foam with firm sand beneath it. They passed over the house-tops, Rudolph in his bedgown that floated out behind him and his pearl-grey trousers, the lady in her bridal dress and the long veil that billowed into the moonlight until it seemed part of the silver vapour of night.

When they reached the market square the lady descended like a ray of light and paused before the great iron-studded door of the Church; when she saw that Rudolph was behind her, she passed through the door, and the student found no difficulty in doing the same.

The Church was cold and dim; as these two entered all the lamps before the shrines burnt very low, but the spell held.

The Comtesse Louise paused on a gravestone in the chancel; it sunk beneath her, and Rudolph, who was close behind, descended with her to the vaults.

Here the only light was that which emanated from the brilliant figure of the bride, who hovered over the rows of coffins like a will-o'-the-wisp.

Over one of these that was covered with a rotting pall cloth she hung motionless, and her voice, hollow as an echo in a shell, broke the silence of the vault.

'Here is your treasure.'

Rudolph wrenched at the wooden coffin lid, then at the leaden shell beneath, and found that both came away like paper in his hands; the supernatural light cast by the Comtesse Louise enabled him to see a skeleton, livid with the hues of decay, lying in a tattered shroud; under the skull was a cluster of diamonds and sapphires arranged like a pillow; these had been enclosed in a silken case which had frayed to a few faded threads.

The student despoiled the coffin, filling the pockets of his *robe de chambre*, of his waistcoat and trousers with the gems. When he had grabbed up the last of the jewels he harshly told the lady to lead him back to his garret.

She instantly rose through the stone floor of the Church and passed down the aisle, through the wooden door and into the public square; without moving her feet, without speaking, with glancing to right or left, she led him over the roofs to his garret.

Rudolph did not think of her at all until he had packed all the jewels into his carpet-bag and hair-cord trunk; then he looked at her standing immobile in her wedding splendour, gazing in front of her with her blue, slightly prominent eyes, and he felt a twinge of compassion for her.

'You may return to your bridegroom,' he said disdainfully.

She did not, however, move, and Rudolph could not recall what the formula of dismissal was in this conjuration.

He searched in the *grimoire* and could find nothing on this point: 'One remains behind' was all that was written in the instructions.

The student did not greatly concern himself about this, however; he felt very drowsy and cast himself on his bed. 'No doubt she will be gone in the morning.'

When Rudolph awoke the sun was bright in his room and Jeanette was at his bedside with coffee and rolls; on the tray was a letter with the Parisian postmark.

The student tore the envelope open and found inside an enthusiastic letter from a publisher to whom he had submitted his poems a year ago. This gentleman had, it seemed, printed the poems without telling the author, and the thin volume had been a *succès fou* . . . 'You are acclaimed as the greatest poet of the century, far beyond Lamartine or Byron.'

Rudolph sprang out of bed in an excess of joy, which was checked however when he saw the bride still standing where he had left her last night, erect by the table staring in front of her with her blue, slightly prominent eyes.

He now perceived that she was as transparent as the lace that she wore and that she looked as if sketched with white chalk on the dark background of the room; he saw also that she was perceptible to himself only, since Jeanette had not only taken no notice of her, but, in leaving the room, had walked right through her. Rudolph then realized that the four strangers had been spectres or phantoms, not, as he had thought, the human beings themselves.

He felt that he had humiliated the lady sufficiently – besides, he was becoming bored with her company; so he again commanded her to depart, and, when she took no heed of him, he once more consulted the *grimoire*. This authorative work, however, had one serious defect – it offered no advice on how to be rid of spirits, ghosts, wraiths or supernatural appearances that had outstayed their welcome.

Rudolph was however too excited and too anxious to put his good fortune to the test to concern himself very much about the phantasm that had already done him such a good service.

'Pray please yourself, Madame la Princesse,' he said with a sarcastic bow, and hastened into the street, the lady floating behind him with feet that were motionless and with a fixed gaze.

As he passed the University the student saw a knot of his fellows gathered round the steps. One of them hailed him:

'Rudolph, have you heard the news?'

'About the success of my poems?' asked the student haughtily.

'Your poems? No, indeed – poor Professor Lachaud died suddenly last night. He was shut up in his library to study as usual, and this morning he was found stiff in his chair!'

Rudolph passed on in silence; he felt rather disturbed.

M. Colcombet and some friends were gossiping outside his shop.

'Oh, M. Rudolph, have you heard, what a dreadful tragedy? Last night, just as the bride – the Comtesse Louise – was being conducted to the bridal chamber, she fell down dead! Yes, dead as a stone! And what do you think, at the same moment one of the guests, M. Saint-Luc, had a stroke of apoplexy, and he too fell dead, with a glass of champagne in his hand!'

Rudolph looked over his shoulder at the phantom, that gazed ahead serenely; he thought . . . 'the *grimoire* did not state that the spell would cause the death of the four strangers. But perhaps if it had I should not have hesitated.'

As he passed the Bank he saw the black shutters being put up; in the doorway were clerks fastening black bands to their arms.

'Someone dead?' asked Rudolph drily.

'M. Lecoine himself! He retired to his counting-house, as he always does on Friday evenings, at ten minutes to twelve – old Auguste took him in his cup of soup, and he was alive then – this morning he was dead in his chair, with his napkin under his chin and his empty cup on his desk!'

'What a number of deaths in this town!' remarked Rudolph sarcastically. 'I hope that it isn't the plague!'

Although at first he had been shocked to learn of the dreadful results of his spell, he soon consoled himself; the four dead people were all detestable – perhaps one might be a little sorry for the bride, until one remembered how cold and haughty she had been, how insulting with her icy looks.

No, everything was as it should be; the only difficulty was how to be rid of this phantom that followed him so closely . . . 'One remains behind.'

'Eh, well,' thought Rudolph, 'no one can see her but myself, and no doubt she will soon tire of following me about or I shall be able to find a spell to dismiss her.'

So, being strong-minded as well as hard-hearted, he contrived to forget the filmy-white shape that was the dead bride, and that never left him, day or night. Everywhere that he went she accompanied him, and when he returned home in the evenings she seated herself by his bed in the worn armchair.

The phantom was the last thing he saw at night, the first thing he saw in the morning, and though he searched his whole library through he could not discover any spell to be rid of her; he was also debarred from any magical ceremonies, divinations or conjurations, for it is well-known that the company of a ghost is fatal on these occasions.

His good fortune, however, prevented him from troubling much about this inconvenience; not only had he the treasure taken from the vaults of Saint Jean, but his fame as a poet spread over the entire country, and he found that whenever he played at cards, when wearing the beryl ring he was lucky, so that his winnings at play afforded him a considerable income.

He soon moved to Paris, where he became the centre of a crowd of admirers; all the ladies were singing his verses to harps or guitars, all the gentlemen copied his waistcoats and the manner in which he tossed his long black hair off his pallid brow.

The student now enjoyed almost everything that he had ever wished for; he had a handsome apartment, liveried servants, a smart *phaeton* – but he had no mistress.

All the women adored him, but if he tried to make love to any one of them, she seemed repelled, frightened, and always ended up by running away.

Rudolph cursed and wished that he had asked for luck in love instead of luck in cards, for the sale of the treasure trove would supply him with all the money he needed. He knew why the women avoided even the slightest intimacy with him – they could not perceive the ghost of the bride, but they felt it, a miasma of death that killed their rising passion, a bitter chill that cooled their warm hearts and withered the kisses on their lips.

The student used all the arts at his command in the hope of destroying the phantom, but nothing was of any avail; sometimes she was so pale as to be scarcely visible, sometimes she was as solid as a living woman; but she was always there and Rudolph's nerves began to quiver every time he looked over his shoulder ... 'One remains behind' he would mutter, gazing up into her glassy eyes. He tried to argue out the matter with her, to appeal to her compassion, even to make love to her, but she never took any more notice of him than she had taken when she had passed him in the bookshop or in the street of the University town.

There were other flaws in the student's good fortune; his publisher continually implored him to write some more poems.

'You know there are only ten poems in that little volume, and everyone in France knows them by heart! Soon people will begin to say that you are incapable of writing anything else!'

This was precisely what had happened; whenever Rudolph sat down to write, the spectre of the bride glided round to the other side of the table, and seated there, stared at him with her blue, slightly prominent eyes, and while she gazed at him he found it impossible to compose a single line.

With relief he remembered the sheaves of paper, all covered by verses that he had, in his excitement, left behind in his garret, so he wrote to Jeanette telling her to send them at once. The girl had, however, used the papers to light the kitchen fire, and the student uttered a bitter malediction when he received the ill-spelt letter in which she gave him this news.

Gradually his popularity waned; the Parisians became tired of his ten poems, of his gloomy, preoccupied airs, and began to laugh at his failures in love. He was too successful at cards, and so found himself avoided, not only at the gambling parties in private houses, but even at the halls in the *Palais Royal*.

One morning he was seated over his coffee pondering how he should be rid of the phantom when his eye caught a line in the *Gazette* that his English valet had left on the table beside his service of coffee, rolls and fruit.

In the University town of S— a horrible outrage had been discovered; a sacrilegious robbery had been committed in the Church of Saint Jean – a tomb had been broken open and a vast treasure was stolen.

The student read this account with a good deal of interest.

'I never heard any of this,' he commented bitterly, 'when I was in that detestable town.'

The ancient Church, it seemed, possessed a vast treasure, largely consisting of offerings at the miraculous shrine of Ste Pelagie, which had been hidden in the coffin of that saint during the dangers of the late revolutions; all record of this had been lost, and for a generation people had searched in vain for the hidden treasure; then a paper found in the sacristy had given them the clue and the coffin with the gems had been discovered.

They had been left there while the Bishop was consulted as to the propriety of moving them; His Grace had not only given his consent to this, but had come in person to see this remarkable discovery – only to learn that the jewels had been stolen by thieves who had broken into the vault. At first the police had kept the matter hushed up in order that they might pursue their investigations more at ease, now they decided to make the matter public.

'Ah, Madame!' cried Rudolph, addressing the phantom that hovered over his breakfast table. 'You have deceived me grossly!'

He morosely decided to leave Paris. The jewels might be traced and he did not dare to try to sell those that he had left; on consulting with his major-domo he found that he was short of money – he had been living most extravagantly, spending thousands of francs on horses, dogs, furniture, pictures and other things that he did not care for in the least.

So in order to raise the money for his travelling expenses, he put on the beryl ring and went to one of the worst gambling dives in Paris where accomplished gamblers nightly stripped newcomers to the capital.

Rudolph entered his den of vice. As he threw off his long black cloak there was a murmur of admiration for his superb blue *gilet* in *moiré anglaise*.

He was not, however, very welcome even in that dreadful place, for even these hardened gamblers, coarsened by debauchery, felt uneasy in his presence; the phantom spread a chill about her that surrounded Rudolph like a cold sea mist and caused those who came near him to shiver. These scoundrels, however, could not for long resist the lure of the piles of gold that the student flung down on the long green baize table – these represented the last remnants of his ready money, the rest of his fortune was contained in the stolen treasure that he dare not dispose of in France.

When he had been playing and winning for an hour, a huge pile of gold pieces was amassed in front of him, and hellish looks of black hatred were cast on him by the *habitués* of the gambling dive.

Rudolph felt depressed and took little pleasure in his fortune, that was more than sufficient to take him to Vienna or Rome or some other city where he could sell the stolen gems; his head ached and the flames of the ring of candles above the table seemed to penetrate his brain like hot nails, all the vicious, greedy faces sneering about him seemed to float detached from their bodies in the thick, foul air.

The phantom of the bride had become quite solid; it seemed impossible to Rudolph that she was invisible to the company as she hovered over the piles of dirty cards, her wedding splendour floating about her like a cloud of moonshine.

'Madame,' he said between his teeth, 'have the goodness to leave me – this is not a fit place for a gentlewoman. But, if you do not cease plaguing me, I shall take you to worse—'

'What are you muttering?' asked his companion, a stout man whose face was covered by carbuncles and whose breath was hot as flame.

'Oh, nothing, I was merely counting my winnings,' sneered Rudolph with his hands over the pile of gold.

'Pray,' said he of the carbuncles, 'have another cast of the dice with this young gentleman,' and he nudged the student in the ribs to let him know that here was another pigeon to be plucked.

Rudolph saw a spruce youth with a baby face bowing before him, and he thought: 'This is a fool fresh from college, he reminds me of Saint-Luc. I may as well have his money.'

So he agreed to play with the young stranger, who had a pleasant lisping voice, a cheek as smooth as a girl's and slightly reddened eyes.

'Surely,' thought the student, 'I have seen him before.' He was tormented by this likeness to someone whom he had once known and so did not observe that the bride had made a movement for the first time since she had followed him; always she had moved through the air in one piece, like a floating statue, now she leaned forward and drew from his finger the beryl ring.

The student played carelessly, certain of his luck, and lost all his winnings to the youth with the baby face.

'Ah!' he shrieked, 'I have been deceived!'

He stared closer at the young man who was gathering up the gold; now he recognized him – it was Lucifer who had appeared to him on the weed-covered pond outside the ruined abbey.

With a yell, echoed in the mocking laughter of the gamblers, Rudolph rushed into the street, the bride floating after him, the great beryl flittering on her pale finger.

When the student reached his luxurious apartment he found that the police were in possession; the stolen jewels had been traced to him. His publisher was also waiting for him in the antechamber.

'You are a cheat as well as thief, M. Rudolph,' he declared severely. 'I do not believe that you wrote those poems, or you would be able to write others. Ah, he who could rob a church, the dead, is capable of anything!

[113]

Tomorrow I shall publish a statement in the *Gazette* to the effect that you are not the author of the poems, and you will be the laughing stock of Paris!'

Rudolph did not stay to hear these indignant words; he fled out into the night with the *agents de police* lumbering after him, and reeling along under the moon that shone over the house-tops, reached the river that dark as ink flowed between houses white as paper.

The phantom pressed close to the student, like a cold fog in his lungs. For the first time she spoke:

'You cannot complain. All the promises in the *grimoire* have been fulfilled.'

'Do not let us, Madame, waste words,' replied Rudolph. 'Will you return me my beryl ring?'

'Never!'

'Will you leave me?'

'Never! One remains behind!'

The student then perceived that he had come to the end of his story; he jumped into the river. As he sank he raised his top hat and said politely:

'Goodbye, Madame la Princesse de C—'

The phantom remained hovering over the spot where he had disappeared, then slowly dissolved into air, her pearls and diamonds turning into drops of rain, her veils and laces into wisps of vapour, the beryl ring being caught up into a shaft of moonshine.

This romantic suicide made Rudolph very popular again in Paris; it was believed that he had written the poems after all, and the fashionable colour for that season became a faded green named *vert Rudolph*. The police became disliked for their hasty action in raiding the apartments of the sensitive poet, for it was discovered that the so-called gems in his possession were mere paste and had nothing to do with the treasure trove in the vaults of Saint Jean.

M. Dufours travelled to Paris and bought back the *grimoire* from the sale of Rudolph's effects and returned it to the shelf at the back of his shop where it soon became again covered with dust.

CATNIP

Robert Bloch

Robert Bloch (b. 1917) is one of America's
best-known writers of horror stories, a worthy
successor to Edgar Allan Poe and H. P.
Lovecraft. Since 1935 he has written hundreds
of short stories for a large number of magazines
and anthologies, while among his novels are
American Gothic, *Night-World*, and the immortal
Psycho, filmed by Alfred Hitchcock. Many of his
stories are noted for their unexpected twists and
verbal puns, and the unforgettable 'Catnip'
(from *Weird Tales*, March 1948) is no
exception!

Ronnie Shires stood before the mirror and slicked back his hair.
He straightened his new sweater and stuck out his chest. Sharp!
Had to watch the way he looked, with graduation only a few
weeks away and that election for class president coming up. If he could
get to be president then, next year in high school he'd be a real wheel. Go
out for second team or something. But he had to watch the angles—

'Ronnie! Better hurry or you'll be late.'

Ma came out of the kitchen, carrying his lunch. Ronnie wiped the grin
off his face. She walked up behind him and put her arms around his
waist.

'Hon, I only wish your father were here to see you—'

Ronnie wriggled free. 'Yeah, sure. Say, Ma.'

'Yes?'

'How's about some loot, huh? I got to get some things today.'

'Well, I suppose. But try to make it last, son. This graduation costs a lot of money, seems to me.'

'I'll pay you back some day.' He watched her as she fumbled in her apron pocket and produced a wadded-up dollar bill.

'Thanks. See you.' He picked up his lunch and ran outside. He walked along, smiling and whistling, knowing Ma was watching him from the window. She was always watching him, and it was a real drag.

Then he turned the corner, halted under a tree, and fished out a cigarette. He lit it and sauntered slowly across the street, puffing deeply. Out of the corner of his eye he watched the Ogden house just ahead.

Sure enough, the front screen door banged and Marvin Ogden came down the steps. Marvin was fifteen, one year older than Ronnie, but smaller and skinnier. He wore glasses and stuttered when he got excited, but he was valedictorian of the graduating class.

Ronnie came up behind him, walking fast.

'Hello, Snot-face!'

Marvin wheeled. He avoided Ronnie's glare, but smiled weakly at the pavement.

'I said hello, Snot-face! What's the matter, don't you know your own name, jerk?'

'Hello – Ronnie.'

'How's old Snot-face today?'

'Aw, gee, Ronnie. Why do you have to talk like that? I never did anything to you, did I?'

Ronnie spit in the direction of Marvin's shoes. 'I'd like to see you just try doing something to me, you four-eyed little—'

Marvin began to walk away, but Ronnie kept pace.

'Slow down, jag. I wanna talk to you.'

'Wh–what is it, Ronnie? I don't want to be late.'

'Shut your yap.'

'But—'

'Listen, you. What was the big idea in History exam yesterday when you pulled your paper away?'

'You know, Ronnie. You aren't supposed to copy somebody else's answers.'

'You trying to tell me what to do, square?'

'N–no. I mean, I only want to keep you out of trouble. What if Miss Sanders found out, and you want to be elected class president? Why, if anybody knew—'

Ronnie put his hand on Marvin's shoulder. He smiled. 'You wouldn't ever tell her about it, would you, Snot-face?' he murmured.

'Of course not! Cross my heart!'

Ronnie continued to smile. He dug his fingers into Marvin's shoulder. With his other hand he swept Marvin's books to the ground. As Marvin bent forward to pick them up, he kicked Marvin as hard as he could, bringing his knee up fast. Marvin sprawled on the sidewalk. He began to cry. Ronnie watched him as he attempted to rise.

'This is just a sample of what you get coming if you squeal,' he said. He stepped on the fingers of Marvin's left hand. 'Creep!'

Marvin's snivelling faded from his ears as he turned the corner at the end of the block. Mary June was waiting for him under the trees. He came up behind her and slapped her, hard.

'Hello, you!' he said.

Mary June jumped about a foot, her curls bouncing on her shoulders. Then she turned and saw who it was.

'Oh, Ronnie! You oughtn't to—'

'Shut up. I'm in a hurry. Can't be late the day before election. You lining up the chicks?'

'Sure, Ronnie. You know, I promised. I had Ellen and Vicky over at the house last night and they said they'd vote for you for sure. All the girls are gonna vote for you.'

'Well, they better.' Ronnie threw his cigarette butt against a rosebush in the Elsners' yard.

'Ronnie – you be careful – want to start a fire?'

'Quit bossing me.' He scowled.

'I'm not trying to boss you, Ronnie. Only—'

'Aw, you make me sick!' He quickened his pace, and the girl bit her lip as she endeavoured to keep step with him. 'Ronnie, wait for me!'

'Wait for me!' he mocked her. 'What's the matter, you afraid you'll get lost or something?'

'No. *You* know. I don't like to pass that old Mrs Mingle's place. She always stares at me and makes faces.'

'She's nuts!'

'I'm scared of her, Ronnie. Aren't you?'

'Me scared of that old bat? She can go take a flying leap!'

'Don't talk so loud, she'll hear you.'

'Who cares?'

Ronnie marched boldly past the tree-shadowed cottage behind the rusted iron fence. He stared insolently at the girl, who made herself small

[117]

against his shoulder, eyes averted from the ramshackle edifice. He deliberately slackened his pace as they passed the cottage, with its boarded-up windows, screened-in porch and general air of withdrawal from the world.

Mrs Mingle herself was not in evidence today. Usually she could be seen in the weed-infested garden at the side of the cottage; a tiny, dried-up old woman, bending over her vines and plants, mumbling incessantly to herself or to the raddled black tomcat which served as her constant companion.

'Old prune-face ain't around!' Ronnie observed, loudly. 'Must be off someplace on her broomstick.'

'Ronnie – please!'

'Who cares?' Ronnie pulled Mary June's curls. 'You dames are scared of everything, ain't you?'

'*Aren't*, Ronnie.'

'Don't tell *me* how to talk!' Ronnie's gaze shifted to the silent house, huddled in the shadows. A segment of shadow at the side of the cottage seemed to be moving. A black blur detached itself from the end of the porch. Ronnie recognized Mrs Mingle's cat. It minced down the path towards the gate.

Quickly, Ronnie stooped and found a rock. He grasped it, rose, aimed, and hurled the missile in one continuous movement.

The cat hissed, then squawled in pain as the rock grazed its ribs.

'Oh, Ronnie!'

'Come on, let's run before she sees us!'

They flew down the street. The school bell drowned out the cat-yowl.

'Here we go,' said Ronnie. 'You do my homework for me? Good. Give it here at once.'

He snatched the papers from Mary June's hand and sprinted ahead. The girl stood watching him, smiling her admiration. From behind the fence the cat watched, too, and licked its jaws.

It happened that afternoon, after school. Ronnie and Joe Gordan and Seymour Higgins were futzing around with a baseball and he was talking about the outfit Ma promised to buy him this summer if the dressmaking business picked up. Only he made it sound as if he was getting the outfit for sure, and that they could all use the mask and mitt. It didn't hurt to build it up a little, with election tomorrow. He had to stand in good with the whole gang.

He knew if he hung around the school yard much longer, Mary June would come out and want him to walk her home. He was sick of her. Oh, she was all right for homework and such stuff, but these guys would just laugh at him if he went off with a dame.

So he said how about going down the street to in front of the pool hall and maybe hang around to see if somebody would shoot a game? He'd pay. Besides, they could smoke.

Ronnie knew that these guys didn't smoke, but it sounded cool and that's what he wanted. They all followed him down the street, pounding their cleats on the sidewalk. It made a lot of noise, because everything was so quiet.

All Ronnie could hear was the cat. They were passing Mrs Mingle's and there was this cat, rolling around in the garden on its back and on its stomach, playing with some kind of ball. It purred and meeowed and whined.

'Look!' yelled Joe Gordan. 'Dizzy cat's havin' a fit 'r something, huh?'

'Lice,' said Ronnie. 'Damned mangy old thing's fulla lice and fleas and stuff. I socked it a good one this morning?'

'Ya did?'

'Sure. With a rock. This big, too.' He made a watermelon with his hands.

'Weren't you afraid of old lady Mingle?'

'Afraid? Why, that dried-up old—'

'Catnip,' said Seymour Higgins. 'That's what he's got. Ball of catnip. Old Mingle buys it for him. My old man says she buys everything for that cat; special food and sardines. Treats it like a baby. Ever see them walk down the street together?'

'Catnip, huh?' Joe peered through the fence. 'Wonder why they like it so much. Gets 'em wild, doesn't it? Cat's'll do anything for catnip.'

The cat squealed, sniffing and clawing at the ball. Ronnie scowled at it. 'I hate cats. Somebody oughta drowned that damn thing.'

'Better not let Mrs Mingle hear you talk like that,' Seymour cautioned. 'She'll put the evil eye on you.'

'Bull!'

'Well, she grows them herbs and stuff and my old lady says—'

'Bull!'

'All right. But I wouldn't go monkeying around her or her old cat, either.'

'I'll show you.'

Before he knew it, Ronnie was opening the gate. He advanced towards the black tomcat as the boys gaped.

The cat crouched over the catnip, ears flattened against a velveteen skull. Ronnie hesitated a moment, gauging the glitter of claws, the glare of agate eyes. But the gang was watching—

'Scat!' he shouted. He advanced, waving his arms. The cat sidled backwards. Ronnie feinted with his hand and scooped up the catnip ball.

'See? I got it, you guys. I got—'

'*Put that down!*'

He didn't see the door open. He didn't see her walk down the steps. But suddenly she was there. Leaning on her cane, wearing a black dress that fitted tightly over her tiny frame, she seemed hardly any bigger than the cat which crouched at her side. Her hair was grey and wrinkled and dead, her face was grey and wrinkled and dead, but her eyes—

They were agate eyes, like the cat's. They glowed. And when she talked, she spit the way the cat did.

'*Put that down, young man!*'

Ronnie began to shake. It was only a chill, everybody gets chills now and then, and could he help it if he shook so hard the catnip just fell out of his hand?

He wasn't scared. He had to show the gang he wasn't scared of this skinny little dried-up old woman. It was hard to breathe, he was shaking so, but he managed. He filled his lungs and opened his mouth.

'You – you old witch!' he yelled.

The agate eyes widened. They were bigger than she was. All he could see were the eyes. Witch eyes. Now that he had said it, he knew it was true. Witch. She was a witch.

'*You insolent puppy. I've a good mind to cut out your lying tongue!*'

Geez, she wasn't kidding!

Now she was coming closer, and the cat was inching up on him, and then she raised the cane in the air, she was going to hit him, the witch was after him, oh Ma, no, don't oh—

Ronnie ran.

Could he help it? Geez, the guys ran too. They'd run before he did, even. He had to run, the old bat was crazy, anybody could see that. Besides, if he'd stayed she'd of tried to hit him and maybe he'd let her have it. He was only trying to keep out of trouble. That was all.

Ronnie told it to himself over and over at supper time. But that didn't do any good, telling it to himself. It was the guys he had to tell it to, and fast. He had to explain it before election tomorrow—

'Ronnie. What's the matter? You sick?'

'No, Ma.'

'Then why don't you answer a person? I declare, you haven't said ten words since you came in the house. And you aren't eating your supper.'

'Not hungry.'

'Something bothering you, son?'

'No. Leave me alone.'

'It's that election tomorrow, isn't it?'

'Leave me alone.' Ronnie rose. 'I'm goin' out.'

'Ronnie!'

'I got to see Joe. Important.'

'Back by nine, remember.'

'Yeah. Sure.'

He went outside. The night was cool. Windy for this time of year. Ronnie shivered a little as he turned the corner. Maybe a cigarette—

He lit a match and a shower of sparks spiralled to the sky. Ronnie began to walk, puffing nervously. He had to see Joe and the others and explain. Yeah, right now, too. If they told anybody else—

It was dark. The light on the corner was out, and the Ogdens weren't home. That made it darker, because Mrs Mingle never showed a light in her cottage.

Mrs Mingle. Her cottage was up ahead. He'd better cross the street.

What was the matter with him? Was he getting chicken-guts? Afraid of that damned old woman, that old witch! He puffed, gulped, expanded his chest. Just let her try anything. Just let her be hiding under the trees waiting to grab out at him with her big claws and hiss – what was he talking about, anyway? That was the cat. Nuts to her cat, and her too. He'd show them!

Ronnie walked past the dark shadow where Mrs Mingle dwelt. He whistled defiance, and emphasized it by shooting his cigarette butt across the fence. Sparks flew and were swallowed by the mouth of the night.

Ronnie paused and peered over the fence. Everything was black and still. There was nothing to be afraid of. Everything was black—

Everything except that flicker. It came from up the path, under the porch. He could see the porch now because there was a light. Not a steady light; a wavering light. Like a fire. A fire – where his cigarette had landed! The cottage was beginning to burn!

Ronnie gulped and clung to the fence. Yes, it was on fire all right. Mrs Mingle would come out and the firemen would come and they'd find the butt and see him and then—

He fled down the street. The wind cat howled behind him, the wind that fanned the flames that burned the cottage—

Ma was in bed. He managed to slow down and walk softly as he slipped into the house, up the stairs. He undressed in the dark and sought the white womb between the bedsheets. When he got the covers over his head he had another chill. Lying there, trembling, not daring to look out of the window and see the flare from the other side of the block, Ronnie's teeth chattered. He knew he was going to pass out in a minute.

Then he heard the screaming from far away. Fire-engines. Somebody had called them. He needn't worry now. Why should the sound frighten him? It was only a siren, it wasn't Mrs Mingle screaming, it couldn't be. She was all right. He was all right. Nobody knew . . .

Ronnie fell asleep with the wind and the siren wailing in his ears. His slumber was deep and only once was there an interruption. That was along towards morning, when he thought he heard a noise at the window. It was a scraping sound. The wind, of course. And it must have been the wind, too, that sobbed and whined and whimpered beneath the windowsill at dawn. It was only Ronnie's imagination, Ronnie's conscience, that transformed the sound into the wailing of a cat . . .

'Ronnie!'

It wasn't the wind, it wasn't a cat. Ma was calling him.

'Ronnie! Oh, Ronnie!'

He opened his eyes, shielding them from the sunshafts.

'I declare, you might answer a person.' He heard her grumbling to herself downstairs. Then she called again.

'Ronnie!'

'I'm coming, Ma.'

He got out of bed, went to the bathroom, and dressed. She was waiting for him in the kitchen.

'Land sakes, you sure slept sound last night. Didn't you hear the fire-engines?'

Ronnie dropped a slice of toast. 'What engines?'

Ma's voice rose. 'Don't you know? Why boy, it was just awful – Mrs Mingle's cottage burned down.'

'Yeah?' He had trouble picking up the toast again.

'The poor old lady – just think of it – trapped in there—'

He had to shut her up. He couldn't stand what was coming next. But what could he say, how could he stop her?

'Burned alive. The whole place was on fire when they got there. The

Ogdens saw it when they came home and Mr Ogden called the firemen, but it was too late. When I think of that old lady it just makes me—'

Without a word, Ronnie rose from the table and left the room. He didn't wait for his lunch. He didn't bother to examine himself in the mirror. He went outside, before he cried, or screamed, or hauled off and hit Ma in the puss.

The puss—

It was waiting for him on the front walk. The black bundle with the agate eyes. The cat.

Mrs Mingle's cat, waiting for him to come out.

Ronnie took a deep breath before he opened the gate. The cat didn't make a sound, didn't stir. It just hunched up on the sidewalk and stared at him.

He watched it for a moment, then cast about for a stick. There was a hunk of lath near the porch. He picked it up and swung it. Then he opened the gate.

'Scat!' he said.

The cat retreated. Ronnie walked away. The cat moved after him. Ronnie wheeled, brandishing the stick.

'Scram before I let you have it!'

The cat stood still.

Ronnie stared at it. Why hadn't the damn thing burned up in the fire? And what was it doing here?

He gripped the lath. It felt good between his fingers, splinters and all. Just let that mangy tom cat start anything—

He walked along, not looking back. What was the matter with him? Suppose the cat did follow him. It couldn't hurt him any. Neither could old Mingle. She was dead. The dirty witch. Talking about cutting his tongue out. Well, she got what was coming to her, all right. Too bad her scroungy cat was still around. If it didn't watch out, he'd fix it, too. He should worry now.

Nobody was going to find out about that cigarette. Mrs Mingle was dead. He ought to be glad, everything was all right, sure, he felt great.

The shadow followed him down the street.

'Get out of here!'

Ronnie turned and heaved the lath at the cat. It hissed. Ronnie heard the wind hiss, heard his cigarette butt hiss, heard Mrs Mingle hiss.

He began to run. The cat ran after him.

'Hey, Ronnie!'

Marvin Ogden was calling him. He couldn't stop now, not even to hit the punk. He ran on. The cat kept pace.

Then he was winded and he slowed down. It was just in time, too. Up ahead was a crowd of kids, standing on the sidewalk in front of a heap of charred, smoking boards.

They were looking at Mingle's cottage—

Ronnie closed his eyes and darted back up the street. The cat followed.

He had to get rid of it before he went to school. What if people saw him with her cat? Maybe they'd start to talk. He had to get rid of it—

Ronnie ran clear down to Sinclair Street. The cat was right behind him. On the corner he picked up a stone and let fly. The cat dodged. Then it sat down on the sidewalk and looked at him. Just looked.

Ronnie couldn't take his eyes off the cat. It stared so. Mrs Mingle had stared too. But she was dead. And this was only a cat. A cat he had to get away from, fast.

The streetcar came down Sinclair Street. Ronnie found a dime in his pocket and boarded the car. The cat didn't move. He stood on the platform as the car pulled away and looked back at the cat. It just sat there.

Ronnie rode around the loop, then transferred to the Hollis Avenue bus. It brought him over to the school, ten minutes late. He got off and started to hurry across the street.

A shadow crossed the entrance to the building.

Ronnie saw the cat. It squatted there, waiting.

He ran.

That's all Ronnie remembered of the rest of the morning. He ran. He ran, and the cat followed. He couldn't go to school, he couldn't be there for the election, he couldn't get rid of the cat. He ran.

Up and down the streets, back and forth, all over the whole neighbourhood; stopping and dodging and throwing stones and swearing and panting and sweating. But always the running, and always the cat right behind him. Once it started to chase him and before he knew it he was heading straight for the place where the burned smell filled the air, straight for the ruins of Mrs Mingle's cottage. The cat wanted him to go there, wanted him to see—

Ronnie began to cry. He sobbed and panted all the way home. The cat didn't make a sound. It followed him. All right, let it. He'd fix it. He'd tell Ma. Ma would get rid of it for him. Ma.

'Ma!'

He yelled as he ran up the steps.

No answer. She was out. Marketing.

And the cat crept up the steps behind him.

Ronnie slammed the door, locked it. Ma had her key. He was safe now. Safe at home. Safe in bed – he wanted to go to bed and pull the covers over his head, wait for Ma to come and make everything all right.

There was a scratching at the door.

'Ma!' His scream echoed through the empty house.

He ran upstairs. The scratching died away.

And then he heard the footsteps on the porch, the slow footsteps; he heard the rattling and turning of the doorknob. It was old lady Mingle, coming from the grave. It was the witch, coming to get him. It was—

'Ma!'

'Ronnie, what's the matter? What you doing home from school?'

He heard her. It was all right. Just in time, Ronnie closed his mouth. He couldn't tell her about the cat. He mustn't ever tell her. Then everything would come out. He had to be careful what he said.

'I got sick to my stomach,' he said. 'Miss Sanders said I should come home and lay down.'

Then Ma was up the stairs, helping him undress, asking should she get the doctor, fussing over him and putting him to bed. And he could cry and she didn't know it wasn't from a gutache. What she didn't know wouldn't hurt her. It was all right.

Yes, it was all right now and he was in bed. Ma brought him some soup for lunch. He wanted to ask her about the cat, but he didn't dare. Besides, he couldn't hear it scratching. Must have run away when Ma came home.

Ronnie lay in bed and dozed as the afternoon shadows ran in long black ribbons across the bedroom floor. He smiled to himself. What a sucker he was! Afraid of a cat. Maybe there wasn't even a cat – all in his mind. Dope!

'Ronnie – you all right?' Ma called up from the foot of the stairs.

'Yes, Ma. I feel lots better.'

Sure, he felt better. He could get up now and eat supper if he wanted. In just a minute he'd put his clothes on and go downstairs. He started to push the sheets off. It was dark in the room, now. Just about suppertime—

Then Ronnie heard it. A scratching. A scurrying. From the hall? No. It couldn't be the hall. Then where?

The window. It was open. And the scratching came from the ledge outside. He had to close it, fast. Ronnie jumped out of bed, barking his shin against a chair as he groped through the dusk. Then he was at the window, slamming it down, tight.

He heard the scratching.

And it came from *inside the room*!

Ronnie hurled himself upon the bed, clawing the covers up to his chin. His eyes bulged against the darkness.

Where was it?

He saw nothing but shadows. Which shadow moved?

Where was it?

Why didn't it yowl so he could locate it? Why didn't it make a noise? Yes, and why was it here? Why did it follow him? What was it trying to do to him?

Ronnie didn't know. All he knew was that he lay in bed, waiting, thinking of Mrs Mingle and her cat and how she was a witch and died because he'd killed her. Or had he killed her? He was all mixed up, he couldn't remember, he didn't even know what was real and what wasn't real any more. He couldn't tell which shadow would move next.

And then he could.

The round shadow was moving. The round black ball was inching across the floor from beneath the window. It was the cat, all right, because shadows don't have claws that scrape. Shadows don't leap through the air and perch on the bedpost, grinning at you with yellow eyes and yellow teeth – grinning the way Mrs Mingle grinned.

The cat was big. Its eyes were big. Its teeth were big, too.

Ronnie opened his mouth to scream.

Then the shadow was sailing through the air, springing at his face, at his open mouth. The claws fastened in his cheeks, forcing his jaws apart, and the head dipped down—

Far away, under the pain, someone was calling.

'Ronnie! Oh, Ronnie! What's the matter with you?'

Everything was fire and he lashed out and suddenly the shadow went away and he was sitting bolt upright in bed. His mouth worked but no sound came out. Nothing came out except that gushing red wetness.

'Ronnie! Why don't you answer me?'

A guttural sound came from deep within Ronnie's throat, but no words. There would never be any words.

'Ronnie – what's the matter? Has the cat got your tongue?'

THE YEW TREE

Shamus Frazer

Shamus Frazer (1912–66) began his career as a
highly acclaimed novelist while still completing
his studies at Oxford University. His first novel
Acorned Hog (1933) was published by Chapman
& Hall, Evelyn Waugh's publisher, and many
critics (including Howard Spring) immediately
declared Frazer to be alongside Waugh 'at a
single stride'. His second novel *Porcelain People*
(1934) quickly followed and later novels
include the antediluvian fantasy *Blow, Blow Your
Trumpets (1945)*.
'Mr Frazer has a freshness, wit, a spirit all his
own', wrote Cyril Connolly in the *New
Statesman and Nation*; and Ralph Straus (in the
Sunday Times) called him 'an imaginative writer
of no little distinction'.
Frazer spent most of his later years working in
Singapore, and at his death left several
unpublished works: some excellent children's
stories, poetry, and a collection of 'tales of the
Dead and the Undead' entitled *Where Human
Pathways End*. Unfortunately this book has
never been published in its entirety, though
some of the best tales (including 'Florinda' in
Chillers for Christmas) have appeared in
magazines and anthologies. Another story, 'The
Tune in Dan's Café', was televised in the
American 'Night Gallery' series in 1971.

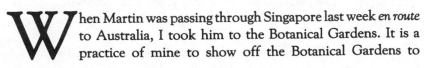

When Martin was passing through Singapore last week *en route*
to Australia, I took him to the Botanical Gardens. It is a
practice of mine to show off the Botanical Gardens to

visitors from England; they feel at home there. It is Kew all over again without the glass.

But in Martin's case our visit was very far from being a success. At first I put his queer behaviour down to fear of snakes. When we were skirting the top end of the lake he kept to the centre of the narrow path, glancing uneasily at the great tongues of foliage that fringe the borders and treading as delicately as Agag. Once he shied at a root that lay twisted like a snake across his path.

'I've been here a hundred times,' I said, 'and I've never seen a snake yet. It's as safe as Ireland.' He pulled himself together and stepped over the root, but I noticed his hands were shaking and his face had the look of a cheap soap-stone carving – a greenish pallor on which the features seemed tenuously and grotesquely scratched.

You know that great banyan tree by the wooden bridge at the farther end of the lake – a grotto of knolled roots and python thick columns formed by the fibres coiling down from the branches like Rapunzel's hair to root in the soil? Well, nothing could induce Martin to go past that tree. He stuck on the edge of the lake, looking ghastly. We had in the end to retrace our steps.

If only I'd not thought of bringing him up by the terraced pergola, the evening might have ended less embarrassingly for us both – but at the same time I should possibly have missed a very strange story.

We were going up the steps under the arch of creepers when I heard a gasp from Martin. 'Good God!' he cried. 'Don't tell me there are yew trees in Malaya.' He was looking at a tree on the terrace a few yards to our left – a tree which does, in fact, bear some resemblance to the yew.

'I think that's a *sintada*,' I said. 'There's certainly a likeness . . .' Then I noticed Martin's expression. He was staring in horror at that *sintada* tree, and he was positively tottering on the edge of the steps as if he were going to faint. I caught him by the arm, helped him down the last flight of steps and steered him to the car. He was pale and dazed as a zombie, and I half feared he was suffering from heatstroke.

By the time we reached home he had recovered – more or less; but his teeth clinked like ice against the rim of the tumbler as he drank off the double whisky I poured for him.

'I'm sorry,' he said at last. 'I made an awful ass of myself just now. I ought never to have gone into the beastly place. But I didn't expect . . . You see, though it happened a good many years ago, I suppose I've not got over it yet. I wonder if I ever shall.'

'Don't tell me if it'll upset you again,' I said with revolting hypocrisy

– for I am curious by nature, and nothing is more distasteful to me than unresolved mysteries.

He was silent for a while, and I thought he was going to take me at my word. I poured him a stiffer drink.

'They do say these things are sometimes better for a father confessor,' I said. A sudden sigh of wind stirred a rustling from the trees in the garden, and Martin shivered and pulled his chair round with a creak to face the sound.

'You won't believe the tale,' he said; 'nobody does. Sometimes I try to kid myself it was a dream. But that's no use. It wasn't, you see.' He hesitated again. Then he asked, 'Do you know Darkshire?'

'I stayed near Doomchester once. It's a pretty place.'

'If you like trees ...' he said, without any particular expression, 'there's the remains of Robin's forest, and those great feudal estates, the Princedoms.'

'All sold up now,' I said.

'I used to spend holidays there when I was a child,' said Martin. 'I loved the place. Trees, too. But I didn't know the western side until a few years ago, when I was sent up there on a job. Do you know that side at all?'

'Vaguely. Bleak and hilly – full of limestone caverns and lead-workings and streams spilling over boulders.'

'It's an evil place,' he said, and relapsed into silence.

'But there are few *trees*, Martin,' I said, keeping him to the point.

'Oh, the forest creeps up into those Pennine valleys. The hills are bare enough, but you get those beastly secretive valleys. Like Hallowvale, for instance.'

'Never been there.'

'You can be thankful you won't have a chance. It lies under several million gallons of water now. I was sent up to report on the place. You know that group of great reservoirs there that feed Sheffield and several of the Yorkshire industrial towns? Well, they were planning an extension of the Tarnthorpe Reservoir, and Hallowvale seemed a likely place to meet requirements. For one thing, no one lived there. No one had lived there for well over a hundred years. So I was sent off to make a preliminary survey.

'I put up first at Baronsbridge – a pleasant pub there; but it was rather far from the valley, and as the work progressed I looked around for some place nearer at hand.

'There was a deserted farm cottage overlooking the western end of

Hallowvale, and the firm had it put in order for me. My early reports had convinced them that the Hallowvale plan was feasible, and they decided I should stay and hunt around for snags, especially over the winter months. Snow and winter rains can upset the finest paper calculations as far as my survey work is concerned.

'Well, the cottage was snug enough: a honeymooner's dream but lonely for a bachelor. A path led from it round the neighbouring hill and so descended abruptly into Baronsbridge on the other side. This was the path I liked to take, especially as the evenings were drawing in. There was another path which led into Hallowvale itself – through the woods – but I didn't much care for it. It was gloomy and dark, and about a quarter of a mile beyond the cottage you passed the skeletons of a church and some derelict cottages, all that was left of the old village of Hallowvale. I'm not ... I wasn't anyway a very imaginative sort of person, but there was a kind of desolate knowingness about the place, and I avoided this path when I could.

'Blasting had begun in the eastern end of the valley, and an army of woodcutters was at work cutting down the fir and sycamore plantations, under the stern eye of old Wyke who had sold us the valley but kept a retainer on the timber. My work, now that winter was setting in, consisted of checking and revising my earlier calculations, and it involved a good deal of field-work, wriggling down potholes, plumbing underground waterways, testing the altered direction of streams with fluorescein powder and so on. Often I didn't get back till nightfall, and I found it sometimes convenient to take the path through the woods and past the old village of Hallowvale. I never enjoyed the walk, though. The plantation stopped before you got to the village – but there was a lot of undergrowth among the ruins ... and ... and things on the path, brambles, I suppose, that caught the ankles and made walking difficult. The ruined church tower made ... made noises in the moonlight ... Owls I imagined ... Then about a hundred yards on there was a kind of ... of open place ... *beastly* ... a sort of crossroads with the roads vanished, if you see what I mean. And the path sloping up very steeply to my own cottage below the brow of the ridge. It was this open place I loathed in the daylight and could hardly bring myself to pass at night. You see, there was growing there ... a yew tree.'

That soap-stone look again. I pushed him over another drink.

'A yew tree,' he repeated, 'largish, black as a hearse-plume, and in winter dotted all over with blood-drops of berry. Perhaps it had been clipped by a topiarist a century or more ago – but whatever shape it had once was lost. It had the suggestion of some kind of bird, though; yes, an owl or a bat, some flying nocturnal thing with ragged wings and a shapeless, swollen body. I thought it might have marked the limit of an old graveyard – but it would have to have been a very spacious graveyard, and would have needed to fill it more dead than even the hamlet of Hallowvale could have provided in a thousand years, I should have thought. Perhaps it may have belonged to the garden of a long vanished house – but whoever lived in that house must have been damnably wicked, I felt.

'I asked old Wyke about the place once, and he wasn't reassuring. "When you wanted the cottage, I told you as you'd be happier below in Baronsbridge," he said. "Don't say I didn't warn you. What've you been hearing, lad? About something that flies in the night, I know. Them's all old wives' tales, but I won't say but it's lonesome up here."

'I'd heard nothing about the place, and Wyke couldn't be persuaded to say another thing. But after he'd gone I thought over that phrase of his about something that flew in the night. During the autumn gales I had often fancied I'd heard a sound like beating wings, a flapping below in the valley as if some gigantic thing had gone to roost there. I had put it down to the wind playing tricks in the broken plantations at the foot of the valley. On one very gusty night the flapping had seemed to sound just outside the walls of the cottage, and I was woken from sleep by a slithering and tapping at the cottage door and a scratching at the shutters.

'One late November day my work took me to a cavern on the northern ridge of the valley; a matter of testing how much strengthening would be needed there if the waters of the proposed reservoir reached a certain level. I'd taken a haversack lunch with me; but the job took longer than I'd thought, and the winter sun was flattening itself like a great red leech among the peaks beyond my distant cottage when I set off on my return journey. It was quickest to return by the valley – though I could not hope to make the cottage before nightfall.

'At first it was easy going. Soon I reached the bulldozer, its silhouette like an antediluvian monster's in the dusk. It marked the limit of the woodcutters' work for the day. One of the men – a little grey-haired chap called Whittaker from Sheffield – gave me good night; he'd evidently stayed behind to set rabbit snares, for wires were dangling from his pockets, and he stuffed something inside his jacket and was pretending to adjust the set of his red bandana neckerchief as I approached. I think I must have taken a wrong path in the steep plantation beyond, for by the time I reached the first of the ruined houses of Hallowvale there was a bright frosty moon which made indescribably horrible the gaping window sockets and the leprous tuft-eared church tower.

'The brambles were particularly obstructive after I'd passed the church, and once or twice I fell headlong in the path. When I reached that open space, the crossroads you know . . . well, the yew tree wasn't there. I mean simply that. It just wasn't there. There was a great hole, like an open grave ragged at the edges where it had stood – but not a sign of the tree. I told myself that the woodcutters must have uprooted it with the winch – though there was no evidence of any such activity: only that great crumbling gap in the soil. It was a horrible tree, and I should have been glad it had gone, if only the hole it had left behind were not inexpressibly worse, a horror of horrors. I thought I saw something white at the bottom of the pit, and was just stepping forward to the brink when I heard again that monstrous flapping in the valley behind me and, it seemed, a thin, inhuman, far-off cry. I didn't stay to hear more, but set off almost at a run on the last breathless climb to my cottage.

'I made up a roaring fire and toasted cheese at it, and after supper read until eleven. I don't think I concentrated much on my thriller. I was straining my ears into the silence for that monstrous sound of wings. Once or twice I thought I heard it – but it might have been a falling branch.

'I slept that night uneasily. About two I was woken by a rattling and shaking of the cottage door. The wind, I thought; yet when I sat up in bed I realized it could not have been so: the night was quite still.

'There was a rustling flap, like an enormous bird settling itself on its perch: the sound you hear when you pass a fowl-house at night, but grotesquely magnified. I lit the lamp at my bedside and waited. There was the familiar slithering sound; it seemed this time to come from above me, from the roof. Then I heard a sliding in the chimney, and I saw something snakelike writhing in the grate, something yellowish moving across the floor to my bed. It stopped half-way, writhing frustratedly, trying to flatten itself a little further, trying to gain an extra inch. The thing was a tree root – a root with the earth still clinging to it. The whole room stank of the graveyard. For a moment the tip of the root quivered and writhed and beckoned; then it was slowly withdrawn, and I heard it coiling itself back up the chimney.

'After that I just went out like a blown match.

'I'd have thought it a dream in the morning – but the lamp had burnt itself out at my bedside, and there were bits of earth in the grate and on the hearth-rug.

'There was a hard frost outside, and there were strange marks in the silver as though snakes had drawn themselves over the turf. On my doorstep there was a scattering of scarlet berries – and a sprig, I'd almost said a feather, of yew.

'The sound of woodcutting came from farther down the valley. I wanted human company desperately just then, so I set off the shortest way. And there was no gap at the crossroad place; the yew tree stood where it had always been, black and secretive and malignant.

'I found Wyke with the group of men round the bulldozer. He was in a growling rage.

' "One of the fellows has cleared off. Whittaker, the chap who's the best hand at the winching. You can't rely on these Sheffield chaps. Just taken his hook and gone. But it's causing no end of trouble with the men here. They been listening to stories, too. Want to knock off an hour early."

'I said I sympathized with them, and I suggested they should start the morning's work on the yew tree at the head of the valley.

'The men murmured among themselves, and "Yew tree, indeed!" said Wyke. "Pack of old-wives' tales."

' "Old-wives' tales or not, Mr Wyke," I said, "I'll bet you ten guineas you wouldn't spend tonight in that cottage with me."

'Wyke loved guineas – but he hesitated and tried to bluff it out.

' "It's all stuff. And I won't have you upsetting my men with your tales, neither."

'But the men were on my side. "It's a fair wager, Mr Wyke."

' "Ten guineas," I said, "take it or leave it. If you come, bring one of those axes with you. I'll borrow this one if I may. We can start work on the yew tree tomorrow!"

'When Wyke came to my cottage at about four in the afternoon, he brought the axe and a clergyman with him. Mr Veering, the rector of Baronsbridge, was a white-haired man with a thin, intelligent face and pleasant manners.

' "Rector's interested in these tales, so I've brought him, too."

' "Hallowvale used to be a part of the parish of All Souls, Baronsbridge, Mr Keith. I have at home a journal kept by one of my predecessors, a Mr Endor. He was rector here forty years – and died in 1810. Hallowvale was abandoned at the end of the eighteenth century, and Mr Endor's account of what caused it . . . well, he was an old man, and it is charitable to suppose that his wits were beginning to wander."

'I told them what I had seen and heard during the night. Veering

[133]

looked at me sharply once or twice, and Wyke muttered uneasily, "He's been listening to gossips' tales, rector, that's what it is."

' "The last rector did, I believe, rather indiscreetly speak about the . . . matters contained in Endor's journal."

' "The only gossip I've heard has come from Wyke," I said; "about something that flies in the night."

' "Quite, quite. Well, we shall see."

'We did. The Thing came flapping about the cottage just after midnight. This time it tried out new tactics. It loosened a couple of tiles, and the roots came coiling down like snakes through the gap and gripped Wyke by the ankle. He yelled fearfully, while Veering and I slashed at the tentacles that held him with our axes. They were horribly tough, and when we had cut through them, the severed tendrils writhed like worms on the floor. The weight on the roof shifted, and we heard it flapping off dismally into the valley.

' "It'll come back again," Wyke cried hoarsely. "It'll come back and widen that hole."

' "The Thing keeps to the valley," said the rector. "Endor said it kept to the valley. It came like this, and people disappeared from their homes."

' "It'll come again," Wyke wailed, "once it's found a way in it'll come again."

' "We could get to the top of the ridge," I said, "and over it to Baronsbridge."

' "It'll swoop on us before ever we can get to the top. We're done for."

' "I don't relish the idea of waiting for it to come back," said Veering. "Outside the valley, we are in God's hands. Here . . . we can pray at least."

' "And then make a dash for it," I said.

'The valley was quite silent. We knelt – keeping as far as possible from those still writhing root tips on the floor – while Mr Veering prayed that we might be delivered from the Powers of Darkness. Then we let ourselves out of the back door and scrambled up the hill. The Thing scented us and came hawking after us. We heard it flapping behind us, and sometimes glimpsed a shape like a huge bird with ropes instead of talons circling over the tree tops or sprawling ungainly on the valley slope. We kept as best we could to cover, but the trees thinned out as we neared the summit of the ridge, and in our last wild scramble to the top it sighted us. I heard a whistling noise as it swooped and a cry from

Veering. He had tripped and fallen, and behind him I could make out a great dim mass, slithering and moving over the turn.

'At first I thought him lost; the Thing had only to pounce again and . . . and then I understood. It *could* fly no higher: it was caged in its evil valley; it had come to roost below the ridge, and was sending up those long yellow tentacles of roots to take its prey.

'"Get up!" I shouted. "For God's sake, Veering. A few more steps and you're safe."

'Already a thin loop had coiled round one foot, and thicker coils wriggled obscenely towards him over the grass.

'"Use your axe, parson," cried Wyke. "Your axe."

'"Veering heard us: there was a thud, an angry whistling, and the next moment we had pulled him to safety beside us.

'For a while we lay all three exhausted on the ridge path, listening to the slithering of those roots as they sought blindly the victim that had escaped them. Then we turned our backs on Hallowvale, and took the steep path down the other side to Baronsbridge.

'When we reached the rectory, Mr Veering handed me a quarto volume bound in green morocco leather, and I sat up all the night reading old Endor's spidery script in the faded sepia ink; while Wyke huddled in a seat by the fire with a Bible on his knees. The trouble, according to Endor's account, had begun when the yew tree bore its first berries. There was a legend current in his day that in the early seventeenth century a woman from Hallowvale was hanged for witchcraft, and was buried at the crossroads with a stake, a yew stake, through her heart. On the scaffold she vowed that she would come back, flying in the night, and exterminate the village. The last words she spoke before the hangman pulled the noose were: "When the first drop of blood shall be sprinkled on his feathers the owl will go a-mousing."

'In the morning we brought several cans of petrol and a stick or two of gelignite to that yew tree above the ruined village of Hallowvale, and we blew the accursed thing up. It screamed as it fell.

'There were things tangled among its roots, skulls and bones, a rusted sword, an old flint-lock pistol and a gold chain – some rabbit snares, too, and a red bandana handkerchief quite unrotted. But the most awful thing was a great pink slug, cocooned in grey hair – a palpitating, bloated thing that suggested a woman hideously swollen with a dropsy. We poured petrol among the roots and into that vile pit, and set fire to it. The fire burnt all day – and not much remained of the tree or the things . . . the Thing in its roots.

'When I last looked down into Hallowvale, it was a great tarnished-looking glass of water. All the same, when the firm offered me a job boring for water in the great Dust Bowl of Australia, I jumped at it. You can travel for miles, they tell me, without seeing a single tree.'

GRAMMA

Stephen King

Stephen King (b. 1947), today's unrivalled monarch of the macabre, has a growing list of international blockbusters to his credit, including *Carrie, Firestarter, The Shining, Salem's Lot, Misery* and *The Dead Zone*. 'Gramma', his best short story dealing with the subject of witchcraft, first appeared in *Weird Book* magazine (1984) and was reprinted in his bumper collection *Skeleton Crew* (1985).

George's mother went to the door, hesitated there, came back, and tousled George's hair. 'I don't want you to worry,' she said. 'You'll be all right. Gramma, too.'

'Sure, I'll be okay. Tell Buddy to lay chilly.'

'Pardon me?'

George smiled. 'To stay cool.'

'Oh. Very funny.' She smiled back at him, a distracted, going-in-six-directions-at-once smile. 'George, are you sure—'

'I'll be *fine*.'

Are you sure what? Are you sure you're not scared to be alone with Gramma? Was that what she was going to ask?

If it was the answer is no. After all, it wasn't like he was six any more, when they had first come here to Maine to take care of Gramma, and he had cried with terror whenever Gramma held out her heavy arms toward him from her white vinyl chair that always smelled of the poached eggs she ate and the sweet bland powder George's mom rubbed into her flabby wrinkled skin; she held out her white-elephant arms, wanting him

[137]

to come to her and be hugged to that huge and heavy old white-elephant body. Buddy had gone to her, had been enfolded in Gramma's blind embrace, and Buddy had come out alive . . . but Buddy was two years older.

Now Buddy had broken his leg and was at the CMG Hospital in Lewiston.

'You've got the doctor's number if something *should* go wrong. Which it won't. Right?'

'Sure,' he said, and swallowed something dry in his throat. He smiled. Did the smile look okay? Sure. Sure it did. He wasn't scared of Gramma anymore. After all, he wasn't *six* anymore. Mom was going up to the hospital to see Buddy and he was going to stay here and lay chilly. Hang out with Gramma awhile. No problem.

Mom went to the door again, hesitated again, and came back again, smiling that distracted, going-six-ways-at-once smile. 'If she wakes up and calls for her tea—'

'I know,' George said, seeing how scared and worried she was underneath that distracted smile. She was worried about Buddy, Buddy and his dumb *Pony League*, the coach had called and said Buddy had been hurt in a play at the plate, and the first George had known of it (he was just home from school and sitting at the table eating some cookies and having a glass of Nestlé's Quik) was when his mother gave a funny little gasp and said, *Hurt? Buddy? How bad?*

'I know *all* that stuff, Mom. I got it knocked. Negative perspiration. Go on, now.'

'You're a good boy, George. Don't be scared. You're not scared of Gramma anymore, are you?'

'Huh-uh,' George said. He smiled. The smile felt pretty good; the smile of a fellow who was laying chilly with negative perspiration on his brow, the smile of a fellow who Had It Knocked, the smile of a fellow who was most definitely not six anymore. He swallowed. It was a great smile, but beyond it, down in the darkness behind his smile, was one very dry throat. It felt as if his throat was lined with mitten-wool. 'Tell Buddy I'm sorry he broke his leg.'

'I will,' she said, and went to the door again. Four o'clock sunshine slanted in through the window. 'Thank God we took the sports insurance, Georgie. I don't know what we'd do if we didn't have it.'

'Tell him I hope he tagged the sucker out.'

She smiled her distracted smile, a woman of just past fifty with two late sons, one thirteen, one eleven, and no man. This time she opened the door, and a cool whisper of October came in through the sheds.

'And remember, Dr Arlinder—'

'Sure,' he said. 'You better go or his leg'll be fixed by the time you get there.'

'She'll probably sleep the whole time,' Mom said. 'I love you, Georgie. You're a good son.' She closed the door on that.

George went to the window and watched her hurry to the old '69 Dodge that burned too much gas and oil, digging the keys from her purse. Now that she was out of the house and didn't know George was looking at her, the distracted smile fell away and she only looked distracted – distracted and sick with worry about Buddy. George felt bad for her. He didn't waste any similar feelings about Buddy, who liked to get him down and sit on top of him with a knee on each of George's shoulders and tap a spoon in the middle of George's forehead until he just about went crazy (Buddy called it the Spoon Torture of the Heathen Chinee and laughed like a madman and sometimes went on doing it until George cried), Buddy who sometimes gave him the Indian Rope Burn so hard that little drops of blood would appear on George's forearm, sitting on top of the pores like dew on blades of grass at dawn, Buddy who had listened so sympathetically when George had one night whispered in the dark of their bedroom that he liked Heather MacArdle and who the next morning ran across the schoolyard screaming GEORGE AND HEATHER UP IN A TREE, KAY-EYE-ESS-ESS-EYE-EN-GEE! FIRSE COMES LOVE AND THEN COMES MARRITCH! HERE COMES HEATHER WITH A BABY CARRITCH! like a runaway fire engine. Broken legs did not keep older brothers like Buddy down for long, but George was rather looking forward to the quiet as long as this one did. Let's see you give me the Spoon Torture of the Heathen Chinee with your leg in a cast, Buddy. Sure, Kid – EVERY day.

The Dodge backed out of the driveway and paused while his mother looked both ways, although nothing would be coming; nothing ever was. His mother would have a two-mile ride over washboards and ruts before she even got to tar, and it was nineteen miles to Lewiston after that.

She backed all the way out and drove away. For a moment dust hung in the bright October afternoon air, and then it began to settle.

He was alone in the house.

With Gramma.

He swallowed.

Hey! Negative perspiration! Just lay chilly, right?

'Right,' George said in a low voice, and walked across the small, sunwashed kitchen. He was a towheaded, good-looking boy with a spray of freckles across his nose and cheeks and a look of good humour in his darkish grey eyes.

Buddy's accident had occurred while he had been playing in the Pony League championship game this October 5th. George's Pee Wee League team, the Tigers, had been knocked out of their tournament on the first day, two Saturdays ago (*What a bunch of babies!* Buddy had exulted as George walked tearfully off the field. *What a bunch of PUSSIES!*) . . . and now Buddy had broken his leg. If Mom wasn't so worried and scared, George would have been almost happy.

There was a phone on the wall, and next to it was a note-minder board with a grease pencil hanging beside it. In the upper corner of the board was a cheerful country Gramma, her cheeks rosy, her white hair done up in a bun; a cartoon Gramma who was pointing at the board. There was a comic-strip balloon coming out of the cheerful country Gramma's mouth and she was saying, 'REMEMBER *THIS* SONNY!' Written on the board in his mother's sprawling hand was *Dr Arlinder*, 681-4330. Mom hadn't written the number there just today, because she had to go to Buddy; it had been there almost three weeks now, because Gramma was having her 'bad spells' again.

George picked up the phone and listened.

'—so I told her, I said, "Mabel, if he treats you like that—"'

He put it down again. Henrietta Dodd. Henrietta was always on the phone, and if it was in the afternoon you could always hear the soap opera stories going on in the background. One night after she had a glass of wine with Gramma (since she started having the 'bad spells' again, Dr Arlinder said Gramma couldn't have the wine with her supper, so Mom didn't either – George was sorry, because the wine made Mom sort of giggly and she would tell stories about her girlhood), Mom had said that every time Henrietta Dodd opened her mouth, all her guts fell out. Buddy and George laughed wildly, and Mom put a hand to her mouth and said *Don't you EVER tell anyone I said that*, and then *she* began to laugh too, all three of them sitting at the supper table laughing, and at last the racket had awakened Gramma, who slept more and more, and she began to cry *Ruth! Ruth! ROO-OOOTH!* in that high, querulous voice of hers, and Mom had stopped laughing and went into her room.

Today Henrietta Dodd could talk all she wanted, as far as George was concerned. He just wanted to make sure the phone was working. Two weeks ago there had been a bad storm, and since then it went out sometimes.

He found himself looking at the cheery cartoon Gramma again, and wondered what it would be like to have a Gramma like that. *His* Gramma was huge and fat and blind; the hypertension had made her senile as well. Sometimes, when she had her 'bad spells', she would (as Mom put it) 'act out the Tartar', calling for people who weren't there, holding conversations with total emptiness, mumbling strange words that made no sense. On one occasion when she was doing this last, Mom had turned white and had gone in and told her to shut up, shut up, *shut up!* George remembered that occasion very well, not only because it was the only time Mom had ever actually *yelled* at Gramma, but because it was the next day that someone discovered that the Birches cemetery out on the Maple Sugar Road had been vandalized – gravestones knocked over, the old nineteenth-century gates pulled down, and one or two of the graves actually dug up – or something. *Desecrated* was the word Mr Burdon, the principal, had used the next day when he convened all eight grades for Assembly and lectured the whole school on Malicious Mischief and how some things Just Weren't Funny. Going home that night, George had asked Buddy what *desecrated* meant, and Buddy said it meant digging up graves and pissing on the coffins, but George didn't believe that . . . unless it was late. And dark.

Gramma was noisy when she had 'bad spells', but mostly she just lay in the bed she had taken to three years before, a fat slug wearing rubber pants and diapers under her flannel nightgown, her face runnelled with cracks and wrinkles, her eyes empty and blind – faded blue irises floating atop yellowed corneas.

At first Gramma hadn't been totally blind. But she had been *going* blind, and she had to have a person at each elbow to help her totter from her white vinyl egg-and-baby-powder-smelling chair to her bed or the bathroom. In those days, five years ago, Gramma had weighed well over two hundred pounds.

She had held out her arms and Buddy, then eight, had gone to her. George had hung back. And cried.

But I'm not scared now, he told himself, moving across the kitchen in his Keds. *Not a bit. She's just an old lady who has 'bad spells' sometimes.*

He filled the teakettle with water and put it on a cold burner. He got a teacup and put one of Gramma's special herb tea bags into it. In case she should wake up and want a cup. He hoped like mad that she wouldn't, because then he would have to crank up the hospital bed and sit next to her and give the tea a sip at a time, watching the toothless mouth fold itself over the rim of the cup, and listen to the slurping sounds as she took the tea into her dank, dying guts. Sometimes she slipped sideways on the bed and you had to pull her back over and her flesh was *soft*, kind of *jiggly*, as if it was filled with hot water, and her blind eyes would look at you . . .

George licked his lips and walked toward the kitchen table again. His last cookie and half a glass of Quik still stood there, but he didn't want them anymore. He looked at his schoolbooks, covered with Castle Rock Cougars bookcovers, without enthusiasm.

He ought to go in and check on her.

He didn't want to.

He swallowed and his throat still felt as if it was lined with mitten-wool.

I'm not afraid of Gramma, he thought. *If she held out her arms I'd go right to her and let her hug me because she's just an old lady. She's senile and that's why she has 'bad spells'. That's all. Let her hug me and not cry. Just like Buddy.*

He crossed the short entryway to Gramma's room, face set as if for bad medicine, lips pressed together so tightly they were white. He looked in, and there lay Gramma, her yellow-white hair spread around her in a corona, sleeping, her toothless mouth hung open, chest rising under the coverlet so slowly you almost couldn't see it, so slowly that you had to look at her for a while just to make sure she wasn't dead.

Oh God, what if she dies on me while Mom's up to the hospital?

She won't. She won't.

Yeah, but what if she does?

She won't, so stop being a pussy.

One of Gramma's yellow, melted-looking hands moved slowly on the coverlet: her long nails dragged across the sheet and made a minute scratching sound. George drew back quickly, his heart pounding.

Cool as a moose, numbhead, see? Laying chilly.

He went back into the kitchen to see if his mother had been gone only an hour, or perhaps an hour and a half – if the latter, he could start reasonably waiting for her to come back. He looked at the clock and was astounded to see that not even twenty minutes had passed. Mom wouldn't even be *into* the city yet, let alone on her way back out of it! He stood still, listening to the silence. Faintly, he could hear the hum of the refrigerator and the electric clock. The snuffle of the afternoon breeze around the corners of the little house. And then – at the very edge of audibility – the faint, rasping susurrus of skin over cloth . . . Gramma's wrinkled, tallowy hand moving on the coverlet.

He prayed in a single gust of mental breath:

PleaseGoddon'tletherwakeupuntilMomcomeshomeforJesus'sakeAmen.

He sat down and finished his cookie, drank his Quik. He thought of turning on the TV and watching something, but he was afraid the sound would wake up Gramma and that high, querulous, not-to-be-denied voice would begin calling Roo-OOTH! RUTH! BRING ME M'TEA! TEA! ROOO-OOOOOTH!

He slicked his dry tongue over his drier lips and told himself not to be such a pussy. She was an old lady stuck in bed, it wasn't as if she could get up and hurt him, and she was eighty-three years old, she wasn't going to die this afternoon.

George walked over and picked up the phone again.

'—that same day! and she even *knew* he was married! Gorry, I hate these cheap little corner-walkers that think they're so smart! So at Grange I said—'

George guessed that Henrietta was on the phone with Cora Simard. Henrietta hung on the phone most afternoons from one until six with first *Ryan's Hope* and then *One Life to Live* and then *All My Children* and then *As the World Turns* and then *Search for Tomorrow* and then God knew what other ones playing in the background, and Cora Simard was one of her most faithful telephone correspondents, and a lot of what they talked about was 1) who was going to be having a Tupperware party or an Amway party and what the refreshments were apt to be, 2) cheap little corner-walkers, and 3) what they had said to various people at 3-a) the Grange, 3-b) the monthly church fair, or 3-c) K of P Hall Beano.

'—that if I ever saw her up that way again, I guess I could be a good citizen and call—'

He put the phone back in its cradle. He and Buddy made fun of Cora when they went past her house just like all the other kids – she was fat and sloppy and gossipy and they would chant, *Cora-Cora from Bora-Bora, ate a dog turd and wanted more-a!* and Mom would have killed them *both* if she had known that, but now George was glad she and Henrietta Dodd were on the phone. They could talk all afternoon, for all George cared. He didn't mind Cora, anyway. Once he had fallen down in front of her house and scraped his knee – Buddy had been chasing him – and Cora had put a Band-Aid on the scrape and gave them each a cookie, talking all the time. George had felt ashamed for all the times he had said the rhyme about the dog turd and the rest of it.

George crossed to the sideboard and took down his reading book. He felt it for a moment, then put it back. He had read all the stories in it already, although school had only been going for a month. He read better than Buddy, although Buddy was better at sports. *Won't be better for a while*, he thought with momentary good cheer, *not with a broken leg*.

He took down his history book, sat down at the kitchen table, and began to read about how Cornwallis had surrendered up his sword at Yorktown. His thoughts wouldn't stay on it. He got up, went through the entryway again. The yellow hand was still. Gramma slept, her face a grey, sagging circle against the pillow, a dying sun surrounded by the wild yellowish-white corona of her hair. To George she didn't look anything like people who were getting old and getting ready to die were supposed to look. She didn't look peaceful, like a sunset. She looked crazy and . . .

(and dangerous)

. . . yes, okay, and *dangerous* – like an ancient she-bear that might have one more good swipe left in her claws.

George remembered well enough how they had come to Castle Rock to take care of Gramma when Granpa died. Until then Mom had been working in the Stratford Laundry in Stratford, Connecticut. Granpa was three or four years younger than Gramma, a carpenter by trade, and he had worked right up until the day of his death. It had been a heart attack.

Even then Gramma had been getting senile, having her 'bad spells'. She had always been a trial to her family, Gramma had. She was a volcanic woman who had taught school for fifteen years, between having babies and getting in fights with the Congregational Church she and Granpa and their nine children went to. Mom said that Granpa and Gramma quit the Congregational Church in Scarborough at the same time Gramma decided to quit teaching, but once, about a year ago, when Aunt Flo was up for a visit from her home in Salt Lake City, George and Buddy, listening at the register as Mom and her sister sat up late, talking, heard quite a different story. Granpa and Gramma had been kicked out of the church and Gramma had been fired off her job because she did something wrong. It was something about *books*. Why or how someone could get fired from their job and kicked out of the church just because of *books*, George didn't understand, and when he and Buddy crawled back into their twin beds under the eave, George asked.

There's all kinds of books, Señor El-Stupido, Buddy whispered.

Yeah, but what kind?

How should I know? Go to sleep!

Silence. George thought it through.

Buddy?

What? An irritated hiss.

Why did Mom tell us Gramma quit the church and her job?

Because it's a skeleton in the closet, that's why! Now go to sleep!

But he hadn't gone to sleep, not for a long time. His eyes kept straying to the closet door, dimly outlined in moonlight, and he kept wondering what he would do if the door swung open, revealing a skeleton inside, all grinning tombstone teeth and cistern eye sockets and parrot-cage ribs; white moonlight skating delirious and almost blue on whiter bone. Would he scream? What had Buddy meant, *a skeleton in the closet*? What did skeletons have to do with books? At last he had slipped into sleep without even knowing it and had dreamed he was six again, and Gramma was holding out her arms, her blind eyes searching for him; Gramma's reedy, querulous voice was saying, *Where's the little one, Ruth? Why's he crying? I only want to put him in the closet . . . with the skeleton.*

George had puzzled over these matters long and long, and finally, about a month after Aunt Flo had departed, he went to his mother and told her he had heard her and Aunt Flo talking. He knew what a skeleton in the closet meant by then, because he had asked Mrs Redenbacher at school. She said it meant having a scandal in the family, and a scandal was something that made people talk a lot. *Like Cora Simard talks a lot?* George had asked Mrs Redenbacher, and Mrs Redenbacher's face had worked strangely and her lips had quivered and she had said, *That's not nice, George, but . . . yes, something like that.*

When he asked Mom, her face had gotten very still, and her hands had paused over the solitaire clockface of cards she had been laying out.

Do you think that's a good thing for you to be doing, Georgie? Do you and your brother make a habit of eavesdropping over the register?

George, then only nine, had hung his head.

We like Aunt Flo, Mom. We wanted to listen to her a little longer.

This was the truth.

Was it Buddy's idea?

It had been, but George wasn't going to tell her *that*. He didn't want to go walking around with his head on backwards, which might happen if Buddy found out he had tattled.

No, mine.

Mom had sat silent for a long time, and then she slowly began laying her cards out again. *Maybe it's time you did know*, she had said. *Lying's worse than eavesdropping, I guess, and we all lie to our children about Gramma. And we lie to ourselves too, I guess. Most of the time, we do. And*

[145]

then she spoke with a sudden, vicious bitterness that was like acid squirting out between her front teeth – he felt that her words were so hot they would have burned his face if he hadn't recoiled. *Except for me. I have to live with her, and I can no longer afford the luxury of lies.*

So his Mom had told him that after Granpa and Gramma had gotten married, they had had a baby that was born dead, and a year later they had another baby, and *that* was born dead too, and the doctor told Gramma she would never be able to carry a child to term and all she could do was keep on having babies that were dead or babies that died as soon as they sucked air. That would go on, he said, until one of them died inside her too long before her body could shove it out and it would rot in there and kill her, too.

The doctor told her that.

Not long after, the *books* began.

Books about how to have babies?

But Mom didn't – or wouldn't – say what kind of books they were, or where Gramma got them, or how she *knew* to get them. Gramma got pregnant again, and this time the baby wasn't born dead and the baby didn't die after a breath or two; this time the baby was fine, and that was George's Uncle Larson. And after that, Gramma kept getting pregnant and having babies. Once, Mom said, Granpa had tried to make her get rid of the books to see if they could do it without them (or even if they couldn't, maybe Granpa figured they had enough yowwens by then so it wouldn't matter) and Gramma wouldn't. George asked his mother why and she said: 'I think that by then having the books was as important to her as having the babies.'

'I don't get it,' George said.

'Well,' George's mother said, 'I'm not sure I do, either . . . I was very small, remember. All I know for sure is that those books got a hold over her. She said there would be no more talk about it and there wasn't, either. Because Gramma wore the pants in our family.'

George closed his history book with a snap. He looked at the clock and saw that it was nearly five o'clock. His stomach was grumbling softly. He realized suddenly, and with something very like horror, that if Mom wasn't home by six or so, Gramma would wake up and start hollering for her supper. Mom had forgotten to give him instructions about that, probably because she was so upset about Buddy's leg. He supposed he could make Gramma one of her special frozen dinners. They were special because Gramma was on a salt-free diet. She also had about a thousand different kinds of pills.

As for himself, he could heat up what was left of last night's macaroni and cheese. If he poured a lot of catsup on it, it would be pretty good.

He got the macaroni and cheese out of the fridge, spooned it into a pan, and put the pan on the burner next to the teakettle, which was still waiting in case Gramma woke up and wanted what she sometimes called 'a cuppa cheer'. George started to get himself a glass of milk, paused, and picked up the telephone again.

'—and I couldn't even believe my eyes when . . .' Henrietta Dodd's voice broke off and then rose shrilly: 'Who keeps listening in on this line, I'd like to know!'

George put the phone back on the hook in a hurry, his face burning. *She doesn't know it's you, stupe. There's six parties on the line!*

All the same, it was wrong to eavesdrop, even if it was just to hear another voice when you were alone in the house, alone except for Gramma, the fat thing sleeping in the hospital bed in the other room; even when it seemed almost *necessary* to hear another human voice because your Mom was in Lewiston and it was going to be dark soon and Gramma was in the other room and Gramma looked like

(yes oh yes she did)

a she-bear that might have just one more murderous swipe left in her old clotted claws.

George went and got the milk.

Mom herself had been born in 1930, followed by Aunt Flo in 1932 and then Uncle Franklin in 1934. Uncle Franklin had died in 1948, of a burst appendix, and Mom sometimes still got teary about that, and carried his picture. She had liked Frank the best of all her brothers and sisters, and she said there was no need for him to die that way, of peritonitis. She said God had played dirty when He took Frank.

George looked out the window over the sink. The light was more golden now, low over the hill. The shadow of their back shed stretched all the way across the lawn. If Buddy hadn't broken his dumb *leg*, Mom would be here now, making chilli or something (plus Gramma's salt-free dinner), and they would all be talking and laughing and maybe they'd play some gin rummy later on.

George flicked on the kitchen light, even though it really wasn't dark enough for it yet. Then he turned on LO HEAT under his macaroni. His thoughts kept returning to Gramma, sitting in her white vinyl chair like a big fat worm in a dress, her corona of hair every crazy whichway on the shoulders of her pink rayon robe, holding out her arms for him to come, him shrinking back against his Mom, bawling.

Send him to me, Ruth. I want to hug him.

He's a little frightened, Momma. He'll come in time. But his mother sounded frightened, too.

Frightened? Mom?

George stopped, thinking. Was that true? Buddy said your memory could play tricks on you. Had she really sounded frightened?

Yes. She had.

Gramma's voice rising peremptorily: *Don't coddle the boy, Ruth! Send him over here; I want to give him a hug.*

No. He's crying.

And as Gramma lowered her heavy arms from which the flesh hung in great, doughlike gobbets, a sly, senile smile had overspread her face and she had said: *Does he really look like Franklin, Ruth? I remember you saying he favoured Frank.*

Slowly, George stirred the macaroni and cheese and catsup. He hadn't remembered the incident so clearly before. Maybe it was the silence that made him remember. The silence, and being alone with Gramma.

So Gramma had her babies and taught school, and the doctors were properly dumbfounded, and Granpa carpentered and generally got more and more prosperous, finding work even in the depths of the Depression, and at last people began to talk, Mom said.

What did they say? George asked.

Nothing important, Mom said, but she suddenly swept her cards together. *They said your Gramma and Granpa were too lucky for ordinary folks, that's all.* And it was just after that the books had been found. Mom wouldn't say more than that, except that the school board had found some and that a hired man had found some more. There had been a big scandal. Granpa and Gramma had moved to Buxton and that was the end of it.

The children had grown up and had children of their own, making aunts and uncles of each other; Mom had gotten married and moved to New York with Dad (who George could not even remember). Buddy had been born, and then they had moved to Stratford and in 1969 George had been born, and in 1971 Dad had been hit and killed by a car driven by the Drunk Man Who Had to Go to Jail.

When Granpa had his heart attack there had been a great many letters back and forth among the aunts and uncles. They didn't want to put the old lady in a nursing home. And she didn't want to *go* to a home. If Gramma didn't want to do a thing like that, it might be better to accede to her wishes. The old lady wanted to go to one of them and live out the rest of her years with that child. But they were all married, and none of them had spouses who felt like sharing their home with a senile and often unpleasant old woman. All were married, that was, except Ruth.

The letters flew back and forth, and at last George's Mom had given in. She quit her job and came to Maine to take care of the old lady. The others had chipped together to buy a small house in outer Castle View, where property values were low. Each month they would send her a check, so she could 'do' for the old lady and for her boys.

What's happened is my brothers and sisters have turned me into a sharecropper, George could remember her saying once, and he didn't know for sure what that meant, but she had sounded bitter when she said it, like it was a joke that didn't come out smooth in a laugh but instead stuck in her throat like a bone. George knew (because Buddy had told him) that Mom had finally given in because everyone in the big, far-flung family had assured her that Gramma couldn't possibly last long. She had too many things wrong with her – high blood pressure, uremic poisoning, obesity, heart palpitations – to last long. It would be eight months, Aunt Flo and Aunt Stephanie and Uncle George (after whom George had been named) all said; a year at the most. But now it had been five years, and George called that lasting pretty long.

She had lasted pretty long, all right. Like a she-bear in hibernation, waiting for . . . what?

(you know how to deal with her best Ruth you know how to shut her up)

George, on his way to the fridge to check the directions on one of Gramma's special salt-free dinners, stopped. Stopped cold. Where had that come from? That voice speaking inside his head?

Suddenly his belly and chest broke out in gooseflesh. He reached inside his shirt and touched one of his nipples. It was like a little pebble, and he took his finger away in a hurry.

Uncle George. His 'namesake uncle', who worked for Sperry-Rand in New York. It had been his voice. He had said that when he and his family came up for Christmas two – no, three – years ago.

She's more dangerous now that she's senile.

[149]

George, be quiet. The boys are around somewhere.

George stood by the refrigerator, one hand on the cold chrome handle, thinking, remembering, looking out into the growing dark. Buddy *hadn't* been around that day. Buddy was already outside, because Buddy had wanted the good sled, that was why; they were going sliding on Joe Camber's hill and the other sled had a buckled runner. So Buddy was outside and here was George, hunting through the boot-and-sock box in the entryway, looking for a pair of heavy socks that matched, and was it *his* fault his mother and Uncle George were talking in the kitchen? George didn't think so. Was it George's fault that God hadn't struck him deaf, or, lacking the extremity of that measure, at least located the conversation elsewhere in the house? George didn't believe that, either. As his mother had pointed out on more than one occasion (usually after a glass of wine or two), God sometimes played dirty.

You know what I mean, Uncle George said.

His wife and his three girls had gone over to Gates Falls to do some last-minute Christmas shopping, and Uncle George was pretty much in the bag, just like the Drunk Man Who Had to Go to Jail. George could tell by the way his uncle slurred his words.

You remember what happened to Franklin when he crossed her.
George, be quiet, or I'll pour the rest of your beer right down the sink!
Well, she didn't really mean to do it. Her tongue just got away from her.
Peritonitis—
George, shut up!
Maybe, George remembered thinking vaguely, *God isn't the only one who plays dirty.*

Now he broke the hold of these old memories and looked in the freezer and took out one of Gramma's dinners. Veal. With peas on the side. You had to preheat the oven and then bake it for forty minutes at 300 degrees. Easy. He was all set. The tea was ready on the stove if Gramma wanted that. He could make tea, or he could make dinner in short order if Gramma woke up and yelled for it. Tea or dinner, he was a regular two-gun Sam. Dr Arlinder's number was on the board, in case of an emergency. Everything was cool. So what was he worried about?

He had never been left alone with Gramma, that was what he was worried about.

Send the boy to me, Ruth. Send him over here.
No. He's crying.

She's more dangerous now . . . you know what I mean.

We all lie to our children about Gramma.

Neither he nor Buddy. Neither of them had ever been left alone with Gramma. Until now.

Suddenly George's mouth went dry. He went to the sink and got a drink of water. He felt . . . funny. These thoughts. These memories. Why was his brain dragging them all up now?

He felt as if someone had dumped all the pieces to a puzzle in front of him and that he couldn't quite put them together. And maybe it was *good* he couldn't put them together, because the finished picture might be, well, sort of boogery. It might—

From the other room, where Gramma lived all her days and nights, a choking, rattling, gargling noise suddenly arose.

A whistling gasp was sucked into George as he pulled breath. He turned towards Gramma's room and discovered his shoes were tightly nailed to the linoleum floor. His heart was spike-iron in his chest. His eyes were wide and bulging. *Go now,* his brain told his feet, and his feet saluted and said *Not at all, sir!*

Gramma had never made a noise like that before.

Gramma had *never* made a noise like that before.

It arose again, a choking sound, low and then descending lower, becoming an insectile buzz before it died out altogether. George was able to move at last. He walked towards the entryway that separated the kitchen from Gramma's room. He crossed it and looked into her room, his heart slamming. Now his throat was *choked* with wool mittens; it would be impossible to swallow past them.

Gramma was still sleeping and it was all right, that was his first thought; it had only been some weird *sound,* after all; maybe she made it all the time when he and Buddy were in school. Just a snore. Gramma was fine. Sleeping.

That was his first thought. Then he noticed that the yellow hand that had been on the coverlet was now dangling limply over the side of the bed, the long nails almost but not quite touching the floor. And her mouth was open, as wrinkled and caved-in as an orifice dug into a rotten piece of fruit.

Timidly, hesitantly, George approached her.

He stood by her side for a long time, looking down at her, not daring to touch her. The imperceptible rise and fall of the coverlet appeared to have ceased.

Appeared.

That was a key word. *Appeared.*

But that's just because you are spooked, Georgie. You're just being Señor El-Stupido, like Buddy says – it's a game. Your brain's playing tricks on your eyes, she's breathing just fine, she's—.

'Gramma?' he said, and all that came out was a whisper. He cleared his throat and jumped back, frightened of the sound. But his voice was a little louder. 'Gramma? You want your tea now? Gramma?'

Nothing.

The eyes were closed.

The mouth was open.

The hand hung.

Outside, the setting sun shone golden-red through the trees.

He saw her in a positive fullness then; saw her with that childish and brilliantly unhoused eye of unformed immature reflection, not here, not now, not in bed, but sitting in the white vinyl chair, holding out her arms, her face at the same time stupid and triumphant. He found himself remembering one of the 'bad spells' when Gramma began to shout, as if in a foreign language – *Gyaagin! Gyaagin! Hastur degryon Yos-soth-oth!* – and Mom had sent them outside, had screamed *'Just GO!'* at Buddy when Buddy stopped at the box in the entry to hunt for his gloves, and Buddy had looked back over his shoulder, so scared he was walleyed with it because their mom *never* shouted, and they had both gone out and stood in the driveway, not talking, their hands stuffed in their pockets for warmth, wondering what was happening.

Later, Mom had called them in for supper as if nothing had happened.

(you know how to deal with her best Ruth you know how to shut her up)

George had not thought of that particular 'bad spell' from that day to this. Except now, looking at Gramma, who was sleeping so strangely in her crank-up hospital bed, it occurred to him with dawning horror that it was the next day they had learned that Mrs Harham, who lived up the road and sometimes visited Gramma, had died in her sleep that night.

Gramma's 'bad spells'.

Spells.

Witches were supposed to be able to cast spells. That's what made them witches, wasn't it? Poisoned apples. Princes into toads. Gingerbread houses. Abracadabra. Presto-chango. *Spells.*

Spilled-out pieces of an unknown puzzle flying together in George's mind, as if by magic.

Magic, George thought, and groaned.

What was the picture? It was Gramma, of course, Gramma and her *books*, Gramma who had been driven out of town, Gramma who hadn't been able to have babies and than had been able to. Gramma who had been driven out of the *church* as well as out of town. The picture was Gramma, yellow and fat and wrinkled and sluglike, her toothless mouth curved into a sunken grin, her faded, blind eyes somehow sly and cunning; and on her head was a black, conical hat sprinkled with silver stars and glittering Babylonian crescents; at her feet were slinking black cats with eyes as yellow as urine, and the smells were pork and blindness, pork and burning, ancient stars and candles as dark as the earth in which coffins lay; he heard words spoken from ancient books, and each word was like a stone and each sentence like a crypt reared in some stinking boneyard and every paragraph like a nightmare caravan of the plague-dead taken to a place of burning; his eye was the eye of a child and in that moment it opened wide in startled understanding on blackness.

Gramma had been a witch, just like the Wicked Witch in the *Wizard of Oz*. And now she was dead. That gargling sound, George thought with increasing horror. That gargling, snoring sound had been a . . . a . . . a *'death rattle'*.

'Gramma?' he whispered, and crazily he thought: *Ding-dong, the wicked witch is dead.*

No response. He held his cupped hand in front of Gramma's mouth. There was no breeze stirring around inside Gramma. It was dead calm and slack sails and no wake widening behind the keel. Some of his fright began to recede now, and George tried to think. He remembered Uncle Fred showing him how to wet a finger and test the wind, and now he licked his entire palm and held it in front of Gramma's mouth.

Still nothing.

He started for the phone to call Dr Arlinder, and then stopped. Suppose he called the doctor and she really wasn't dead at all? He'd be in dutch for sure.

Take her pulse.

He stopped in the doorway, looking doubtfully back at that dangling hand. The sleeve of Gramma's nightie had pulled up, exposing her wrist. But that was no good. Once, after a visit to the doctor when the nurse had pressed her finger to his wrist to take his pulse, George had tried it and hadn't been able to find anything. As far as his own unskilled fingers could tell, he was dead.

Besides, he didn't really want to . . . well . . . to *touch* Gramma. Even if she was dead. *Especially* if she was dead.

George stood in the entryway, looking from Gramma's still, bedridden form to the phone on the wall beside Dr Arlinder's number, and back to Gramma again. He would just have to call. He would—

—get a mirror!

Sure! When you breathed on a mirror, it got cloudy. He had seen a doctor check an unconscious person that way once in a movie. There was a bathroom connecting with Gramma's room and now George hurried in and got Gramma's vanity mirror. One side of it was regular, the other side magnified, so you could see to pluck out hairs and do stuff like that.

George took it back to Gramma's bed and held one side of the mirror until it was almost touching Gramma's open, gaping mouth. He held it there while he counted to sixty, watching Gramma the whole time. Nothing changed. He was sure she was dead even before he took the mirror away from her mouth and observed its surface, which was perfectly clear and unclouded.

Gramma was dead.

George realized with relief and some surprise that he could feel sorry for her now. Maybe she had been a witch. Maybe not. Maybe she had only *thought* she was a witch. However it had been, she was gone now. He realized with an adult's comprehension that questions of concrete reality became not unimportant but less *vital* when they were examined in the mute bland face of mortal remains. He realized this with an adult's comprehension and accepted with an adult's relief. This was a passing footprint, the shape of a shoe, in his mind. So are all the child's adult impressions; it is only in later years that the child realizes that he was being *made*; *formed*; shaped by random experiences; all that remains *in the instant* beyond the footprint is that bitter gunpowder smell which is the ignition of an idea beyond a child's given years.

He returned the mirror to the bathroom, then went back through her room, glancing at the body on his way by. The setting sun had painted the old dead face with barbaric, orange–red colours, and George looked away quickly.

He went through the entry and crossed the kitchen to the telephone, determined to do everything right. Already in his mind he saw a certain advantage over Buddy; whenever Buddy started to tease him, he would simply say: *I was all by myself in the house when Gramma died, and I did everything right.*

Call Dr Arlinder, that was first. Call him and say, 'My Gramma just died. Can you tell me what I should do? Cover her up or something?'

No.

'I *think* my Gramma just died.'

Yes. Yes, that was better. Nobody thought a little kid knew anything anyway, so that was better.

Or how about:

'*I'm pretty sure my Gramma just died*—'

Sure! That was best of all.

And tell about the mirror and the death rattle and all. And the doctor would come right away, and when he was done examining Gramma he would say, '*I pronounce you dead, Gramma,*' and then say to George, '*You laid extremely chilly in a tough situation, George. I want to congratulate you.*' And George would say something appropriately modest.

George looked at Dr Arlinder's number and took a couple of slow deep breaths before grabbing the phone. His heart was beating fast, but that painful spike-iron thud was gone now. Gramma had died. The worst had happened, and somehow it wasn't as bad as waiting for her to start bellowing for Mom to bring her tea.

The phone was dead.

He listened to the blankness, his mouth still formed around the words *I'm sorry, Missus Dodd, but this is George Bruckner and I have to call the doctor for my Gramma.* No voices. No dial tone. Just dead blankness. Like the dead blankness in the bed there.

Gramma is—

—is—

(oh she is)

Gramma is laying chilly.

Gooseflesh again, painful and marbling. His eyes fixed on the Pyrex teakettle on the stove, the cup on the counter with the herbal tea bag in it. No more tea for Gramma. Not ever.

(laying so chilly)

George shuddered.

He stuttered his finger up and down on the Princess phone's cutoff button, but the phone was dead. Just as dead as—

(just as chilly as)

He slammed the handset down hard and the bell tinged faintly inside and he picked it up in a hurry to see if that meant it had magically gone right again. But there was nothing, and this time he put it back slowly.

His heart was thudding harder again.

I'm alone in this house with her dead body.

He crossed the kitchen slowly, stood by the table for a minute, and then turned on the light. It was getting dark in the house. Soon the sun would be gone; night would be here.

Wait. That's all I got to do. Just wait until Mom gets back. This is better, really. If the phone went out, it's better that she just died instead of maybe having a fit or something, foaming at the mouth, maybe falling out of bed—

Ah, that was bad. He could have done very nicely without *that* horse-pucky.

Like being alone in the dark and thinking of dead things that were still lively – seeing shapes in the shadows on the walls and thinking of death, thinking of the dead, those things, the way they would stink and the way they would move toward you in the black: thinking this: thinking that: thinking of bugs turning in flesh: burrowing in flesh: eyes that moved in the dark. Yeah. That most of all. Thinking of eyes that moved in the dark and the creak of floorboards as something came across the room through the zebra-stripes of shadows from the light outside. Yeah.

In the dark your thoughts had a perfect circularity, and no matter what you tried to think of – flowers or Jesus or baseball or winning the gold in the 440 at the Olympics – it somehow led back to the form in the shadows with the claws and the unblinking eyes.

'Shittabrick!' he hissed, and suddenly slapped his own face. And hard. He was giving himself the whimwhams, it was time to stop it. He wasn't six anymore. She was dead, that was all, dead. There was no more thought inside her now than there was in a marble or a floorboard or a doorknob or a radio dial or—

And a strong alien unprepared-for voice, perhaps only the unforgiving unbidden voice of simple survival, inside him cried: *Shut up Georgie and get about your goddam business!*

Yeah, okay. Okay, but—

He went back to the door of her bedroom to make sure.

There lay Gramma, one hand out of bed and touching the floor, her mouth hinged agape. Gramma was part of the furniture now. You could put her hand back in bed or pull her hair or pop a water glass into her mouth or put earphones on her head and play Chuck Berry into them full-tilt boogie and it would be all the same to her. Gramma was, as Buddy sometimes said, out of it. Gramma had had the course.

A sudden low and rhythmic thudding noise began, not far to George's left, and he started, a little yipping cry escaping him. It was the storm door, which Buddy had put on just last week. Just the storm door, unlatched and thudding back and forth in the freshening breeze.

George opened the inside door, leaned out, and caught the storm door as it swung back. The wind – it wasn't a breeze but a wind – caught his hair and riffled it. He latched the door firmly and wondered where the wind had come from all of a sudden. When Mom left it had been almost dead calm. But when Mom left it had been bright daylight and now it was dusk.

George glanced in at Gramma again and then went back and tried the phone again. Still dead. He sat down, got up, and began to walk back and forth through the kitchen, pacing, trying to think.

An hour later it was full dark.

The phone was still out. George supposed the wind, which had now risen to a near-gale, had knocked down some of the lines, probably out by the Beaver Bog, where the trees grew everywhere in a helter-skelter of deadfalls and swampwater. The phone dinged occasionally, ghostly and far, but the line remained blank. Outside the wind moaned along the eaves of the small house and George reckoned he would have a story to tell at the next Boy Scout Camporee, all right . . . just sitting in the house alone with his dead Gramma and the phone out and the wind pushing rafts of clouds fast across the sky, clouds that were black on top and the colour of dead tallow, the colour of Gramma's claw-hands, underneath.

It was, as Buddy also sometimes said, a Classic.

He wished he was telling it now, with the actuality of the thing safely behind him. He sat on the kitchen table, his history book open in front of him, jumping at every sound . . . and now that the wind was up, there were a lot of sounds as the house creaked in all its unoiled secret forgotten joints.

She'll be home pretty quick. She'll be home and then everything will be okay. Everything
(you never covered her)
will be all r
(never covered her face)
George jerked as if someone had spoken aloud and stared wide-eyed across the kitchen at the useless telephone. You were supposed to pull the sheet up over the dead person's face. It was in all the movies.

Hell with that! I'm not going in there!

No! And no reason why he should! Mom could cover her face when she got home! Or *Dr Arlinder* when he came! Or the *undertaker*!

Someone, anyone, but him.

No reason why he should.

It was nothing to him, and nothing to Gramma.

Buddy's voice in his head:

If you weren't scared, how come you didn't dare to cover her face?

It was nothing to me.

Fraidycat!

Nothing to Gramma, either.

CHICKEN-GUTS fraidycat!

Sitting at the table in front of his unread history book, considering it, George began to see that if he *didn't* pull the counterpane up over Gramma's face, he couldn't claim to have done everything right, and thus Buddy would have a leg (no matter how shaky) to stand on.

Now he saw himself telling the spooky story of Gramma's death at the Camporee fire before taps, just getting to the comforting conclusion where Mom's headlights swept into the driveway – the reappearance of the grown-up, both reestablishing and reconfirming the concept of Order – and suddenly from the shadows, a dark figure arises, and a pine-knot in the fire explodes and George can see it's Buddy there in the shadows, saying: *If you was so brave, chicken-guts, how come you didn't dare to cover up HER FACE?*

George stood up, reminding himself that Gramma was *out of it*, that Gramma was *wasted*, that Gramma was *laying chilly*. He could put her hand back in bed, stuff a tea bag up her nose, put on earphones playing Chuck Berry full blast, etc., etc., and none of it would put a buzz under Gramma, because that was what being dead was *about*, nobody could put a buzz under a dead person, a dead person was the ultimate laid-back cool, and the rest of it was just dreams; ineluctable and apocalyptic and feverish dreams about closet doors swinging open in the dead mouth of midnight, just dreams about moonlight skating a delirious blue on the bones of disinterred skeletons, just—

He whispered, 'Stop it, can't you? Stop being so—'

(*gross*)

He steeled himself. He was going to go in there and pull the coverlet up over her face, and take away Buddy's last leg to stand on. He would administer the few simple rituals of Gramma's death perfectly. He would cover her face and then – his face lit at the symbolism of this – he would put away her unused tea bag and her unused cup. Yes.

He went in, each step a conscious act. Gramma's room was dark, her body a vague hump in the bed, and he fumbled madly for the light switch, not finding it for what seemed to be an eternity. At last it clicked up, flooding the room with low yellow light from the cut-glass fixture overhead.

Gramma lay there, hand dangling, mouth open. George regarded her, dimly aware that little pearls of sweat now clung to his forehead, and wondered if his responsibility in the matter could possibly extend to picking up that cooling hand and putting it back in bed with the rest of Gramma. He decided it did not. Her hand could have fallen out of bed any old time. That was too much. He couldn't touch her. Everything else, but not that.

Slowly, as if moving through some thick fluid instead of air, George approached Gramma. He stood over her, looking down. Gramma was yellow. Part of it was the light, filtered through the old fixture, but not all.

Breathing through his mouth, his breath rasping audibly, George grasped the coverlet and pulled it up over Gramma's face. He let go of it and it slipped just a little, revealing her hairline and the yellow creased parchment of her brow. Steeling himself, he grasped it again, keeping his hands far to one side and the other of her head so he wouldn't have to touch her, even through the cloth, and pulled it up again. This time it stayed. It was satisfactory. Some of the fear went out of George. He had *buried* her.

Yes, that was why you covered the dead person up, and why it was right: it was like *burying* them. It was a statement.

He looked at the hand dangling down, unburied, and discovered now that he could touch it, he could tuck it under and bury it with the rest of Gramma.

He bent, grasped the cool hand, and lifted it.

The hand twisted in his and clutched at his wrist.

George screamed. He staggered backward, screaming in the empty house, screaming against the sound of the wind reaving the eaves, screaming against the sound of the house's creaking joints. He backed away, pulling Gramma's body askew under the coverlet, and the hand thudded back down, twisting, turning, snatching at the air . . . and then relaxing to limpness again.

I'm all right, it was nothing, it was nothing but a reflex.

George nodded in perfect understanding, and then he remembered again how her hand had turned, clutching his, and he shrieked. His eyes bulged in their sockets. His hair stood out, perfectly on end, in a cone. His heart was a runaway stamping-press in his chest. The world tilted crazily, came back to the level, and then just went on moving until it was tilted the other way. Every time rational thought started to come back, panic goosed him again. He whirled, wanting only to get out of the room

[159]

to some other room – or even three or four miles down the road, if that was what it took – where he could get all of this under control. So he whirled and ran full tilt into the wall, missing the open doorway by a good two feet.

He rebounded and fell to the floor, his head singing with a sharp, cutting pain that sliced keenly through the panic. He touched his nose and his hand came back bloody. Fresh drops spotted his green shirt. He scrambled to his feet and looked around wildly.

The hand dangled against the floor as it had before, but Gramma's body was not askew; it also was as it had been.

He had imagined the whole thing. He had come into the room, and all the rest of it had been no more than a mind-movie.

No.

But the pain had cleared his head. Dead people didn't grab your wrist. Dead was dead. When you were dead they could use you for a hat rack or stuff you in a tractor tyre and roll you downhill or et cetera, et cetera, et cetera. When you were dead you might be acted *upon* (by, say, little boys trying to put dead dangling hands back into bed), but your days of *acting* upon – so to speak – were over.

Unless you're a witch. Unless you pick your time to die when no one's around but one little kid, because it's best that way, you can . . . can . . .

Can what?

Nothing. It was stupid. He had imagined the whole thing because he had been scared and that was all there was to it. He wiped his nose with his forearm and winced at the pain. There was a bloody smear on the skin of his inner forearm.

He wasn't going to go near her again, that was all. Reality or hallucination, he wasn't going to mess with Gramma. The bright flare of panic was gone, but he was still miserably scared, near tears, shaky at the sight of his own blood, only wanting his mother to come home and take charge.

George backed out of the room, through the entry, and into the kitchen. He drew a long, shuddery breath and let it out. He wanted a wet rag for his nose, and suddenly he felt like he was going to vomit. He went over to the sink and ran cold water. He bent and got a rag from the basin under the sink – a piece of one of Gramma's old diapers – and ran it under the cold tap, snuffling up blood as he did so. He soaked the old soft cotton diaper-square until his hand was numb, then turned off the tap and wrung it out.

He was putting it to his nose when her voice spoke from the other room.

'Come here, boy,' Gramma called in a dead buzzing voice. 'Come in here – *Gramma wants to hug you.*'

George tried to scream and no sound came out. No sound at all. But there were sounds in the other room. Sounds that he heard when Mom was in there, giving Gramma her bed-bath, lifting her bulk, dropping it, turning it, dropping it again.

Only those sounds now seemed to have a slightly different and yet utterly specific meaning – it sounded as though Gramma was trying to . . . to get out of bed.

'*Boy! Come in here, boy! Right NOW! Step to it.*'

With horror he saw that his feet were answering that command. He told them to stop and they just went on, left foot, right foot, hay foot, straw foot, over the linoleum; his brain was a terrified prisoner inside his body – a hostage in a tower.

She IS a witch, she's a witch and she's having one of her 'bad spells', oh yeah, it's a 'spell' all right, and it's bad, it's REALLY bad, oh God oh Jesus help me help me help me—

George walked across the kitchen and through the entryway and into Gramma's room and yes, she hadn't just *tried* to get out of bed, she *was* out, she was sitting in the white vinyl chair where she hadn't sat for four years, since she got too heavy to walk and too senile to know where she was, anyway.

But Gramma didn't look senile now.

Her face was sagging and doughy, but the senility was gone – if it had ever really been there at all, and not just a mask she wore to lull small boys and tired husbandless women. Now Gramma's face gleamed with full intelligence – it gleamed like an old, stinking wax candle. Her eyes drooped in her face, lacklustre and dead. Her chest was not moving. Her nightie had pulled up, exposing elephantine thighs. The coverlet of her deathbed was thrown back.

Gramma held her huge arms out to him.

'*I want to hug you, Georgie,*' that flat and buzzing deadvoice said. '*Don't be a scared old crybaby. Let your Gramma hug you.*'

George cringed back, trying to resist that almost insurmountable pull. Outside, the wind shrieked and roared. George's face was long and twisted with the extremity of his fright; the face of a woodcut caught and shut up in an ancient book.

George began to walk toward her. He couldn't help himself. Step by dragging step toward those outstretched arms. *He would show Buddy that he wasn't scared of Gramma, either. He would go to Gramma and be hugged because he wasn't a crybaby fraidycat. He would go to Gramma now.*

He was almost within the circle of her arms when a window to his left crashed inward and suddenly a wind-blown branch was in the room with them, autumn leaves still clinging to it. The river of wind flooded the room, blowing over Gramma's pictures, whipping her nightgown and her hair.

Now George could scream. He stumbled backward out of her grip and Gramma made a cheated hissing sound, her lips pulling back over smooth old gums; her thick, wrinkled hands clapped uselessly together on moving air.

George's feet tangled together and he fell down. Gramma began to rise from the white vinyl chair, a tottering pile of flesh; she began to stagger towards him. George found he couldn't get up; the strength had deserted his legs. He began to crawl backward, whimpering. Gramma came on, slowly but relentlessly, dead and yet alive, and suddenly George understood what the hug would mean; the puzzle was complete in his mind and somehow he found his feet just as Gramma's hand closed on his shirt. It ripped up the side, and for one moment he felt her cold flesh against his skin before fleeing into the kitchen again.

He would run into the night. Anything other than being hugged by the witch, his Gramma. Because when his mother came back she would find Gramma dead and George alive, oh yes ... but George would have developed a sudden taste for herbal tea.

He looked back over his shoulder and saw Gramma's grotesque, misshapen shadow rising on the wall as she came through the entryway.

And at that moment the telephone rang, shrilly and stridently.

George seized it without even thinking and screamed into it; screamed for someone to come, to please come. He screamed these things silently; not a sound escaped his locked throat.

Gramma tottered into the kitchen in her pink nightie. Her whitish-yellow hair blew wildly around her face, and one of her horn combs hung askew against her wrinkled neck.

Gramma was grinning.

'Ruth?' It was Aunt Flo's voice, almost lost in the whistling wind-tunnel of a bad long-distance connection. 'Ruth, are you there?' It was Aunt Flo in Minnesota, over two thousand miles away.

'*Help me!*' George screamed over the phone, and what came out was a tiny, hissing whistle, as if he had blown into a harmonica full of dead reeds.

Gramma tottered across the linoleum, holding her arms out for him. Her hands snapped shut and then open and then shut again. Gramma wanted her hug; she had been waiting for that hug for five years.

'Ruth, can you hear me? It's been storming here, it just started and I . . . I got scared. Ruth, I can't hear you—'

'Gramma,' George moaned into the telephone. Now she was almost upon him.

'George?' Aunt Flo's voice suddenly sharpened; became almost a shriek. 'George, is that *you*?'

He began to back away from Gramma, and suddenly realized that he had stupidly backed away from the door and into the corner formed by the kitchen cabinets and the sink. The horror was complete. As her shadow fell over him, the paralysis broke and he screamed into the phone, screamed it over and over again: '*Gramma! Gramma! Gramma!*'

Gramma's cold hands touched his throat. Her muddy, ancient eyes locked on his, draining his will.

Faintly, dimly, as if across many years as well as many miles, he heard Aunt Flo say: 'Tell her to lie down, George, tell her to lie down and be still. Tell her she must do it in your name and the name of her father. The name of her taken father is *Hastur*. His name is power in her ear, George – tell her *Lie down in the Name of Hastur* – tell her—'

The old, wrinkled hand tore the telephone from George's nerveless grip. There was a taut pop as the cord pulled out of the phone. George collapsed in the corner and Gramma bent down, a huge heap of flesh above him, blotting out the light.

George screamed: '*Lie down! Be still! Hastur's name! Hastur! Lie down! Be still!*'

Her hands closed around his neck—

'You gotta do it! Aunt Flo said you did! In *my* name! In your *Father's* name! Lie down! Be sti—'

—and squeezed.

When the lights finally splashed into the driveway an hour later, George was sitting at the table in front of his unread history book. He got up and walked to the back door and opened it. To the left, the Princess phone hung in its cradle, its useless cord looped around it.

His mother came in, a leaf clinging to the collar of her coat. 'Such a wind,' she said. 'Was everything all – George? *George, what happened?*'

The blood fell from Mom's face in a single, shocked rush, turning her a horrible clown-white.

'Gramma,' he said. 'Gramma died. Gramma died, Mommy.' And he began to cry.

She swept him into her arms and then staggered back against the wall, as if the act of hugging had robbed the last of her strength. 'Did . . . did anything happen?' she asked. '*George, did anything else happen?*'

'The wind knocked a tree branch through her window,' George said.

She pushed him away, looked at his shocked, slack face for a moment, and then stumbled into Gramma's room. She was in there for perhaps four minutes. When she came back, she was holding a red tatter of cloth. It was a bit of George's shirt.

'I took this out of her hand,' Mom whispered.

'I don't want to talk about it,' George said. 'Call Aunt Flo, if you want. I'm tired. I want to go to bed.'

She made as if to stop him, but didn't. He went up to the room he shared with Buddy and opened the hot-air register so he could hear what his mother did next. She wasn't going to talk to Aunt Flo, not tonight, because the telephone cord had pulled out; not tomorrow, because shortly before Mom had come home, George had spoken a short series of words, some of them bastardized Latin, some only pre-Druidic grunts, and over two thousand miles away Aunt Flo had dropped dead of a massive brain haemorrhage. It was amazing how those words came back. How *everything* came back.

George undressed and lay down naked on his bed. He put his hands behind his head and looked up into the darkness. Slowly, slowly, a sunken and rather horrible grin surfaced on his face.

Things were going to be different around here from now on.

Very different.

Buddy, for instance. George could hardly wait until Buddy came home from the hospital and started in the Spoon Torture of the Heathen Chinee or an Indian Rope Burn or something like that. George supposed he would have to let Buddy get away with it – at least in the daytime, when people could see – but when night came and they were alone in this room, in the dark, with the door closed . . .

George began to laugh soundlessly.

As Buddy always said, it was going to be a Classic.

THE HOLLOW OF
THE THREE HILLS

Nathaniel Hawthorne

Nathaniel Hawthorne (1804–64) was born in
Salem, Massachusetts, celebrated for its 1692
witchcraft trials, in which one of his ancestors
(Colonel John Hathorne) was closely involved.
Many of his stories in *Twice-Told Tales, Mosses
from an Old Manse*, and *The House of the Seven
Gables* reflect his keen interest in witchcraft.

In those strange old times, when fantastic dreams and madmen's
reveries were realized among the actual circumstances of life, two
persons met together at an appointed hour and place. One was a lady,
graceful in form and fair of feature, though pale and troubled, and
smitten with an untimely blight in what should have been the fullest
bloom of her years; the other was an ancient and meanly-dressed woman,
of ill-favoured aspect, and so withered, shrunken, and decrepit, that even
the space since she began to decay must have exceeded the ordinary term
of human existence. In the spot where they encountered, no mortal
could observe them. Three little hills stood near each other, and down in
the midst of them sunk a hollow basin, almost mathematically circular,
two or three hundred feet in breadth, and of such depth that a stately
cedar might but just be visible above the sides. Dwarf pines were
numerous upon the hills, and partly fringed the outer verge of the
intermediate hollow; within which there was nothing but the brown
grass of October, and here and there a tree trunk that had fallen long ago,

and lay mouldering with no green successor from its roots. One of these masses of decaying wood, formerly a majestic oak, rested close beside a pool of green and sluggish water at the bottom of the basin. Such scenes as this (so grey tradition tells) were once the resort of the Power of Evil and his plighted subjects; and here, at midnight or on the dim verge of evening, they were said to stand round the mantling pool, disturbing its putrid waters in the performance of an impious baptismal rite. The chill beauty of an autumnal sunset was now gilding the three hill tops, whence a paler tint stole down their sides into the hollow.

'Here is our pleasant meeting come to pass,' said the aged crone, 'according as thou hast desired. Say quickly what thou wouldst have of me, for there is but a short hour that we may tarry here.'

As the old withered woman spoke, a smile glimmered on her countenance, like lamplight on the wall of a sepulchre. The lady trembled, and cast her eyes upward to the verge of the basin, as if meditating to return with her purpose unaccomplished. But it was not so ordained.

'I am a stranger in this land, as you know,' said she at length. 'Whence I come it matters not; but I have left those behind me with whom my fate was intimately bound, and from whom I am cut off forever. There is a weight in my bosom that I cannot away with, and I have come hither to inquire of their welfare.'

'And who is there by this green pool, that can bring thee news from the ends of the earth?' cried the old woman, peering into the lady's face. 'Not from my lips mayst thou hear these tidings; yet, be thou bold, and the daylight shall not pass away from yonder hill top before thy wish be granted.'

'I will do your bidding though I die,' replied the lady desperately.

The old woman seated herself on the trunk of the fallen tree, threw aside the hood that shrouded her grey locks, and beckoned her companion to draw near.

'Kneel down,' she said, 'and lay your forehead on my knees.'

She hesitated a moment, but the anxiety that had long been kindling, burned fiercely up within her. As she knelt down, the border of her garment was dipped into the pool; she laid her forehead on the old woman's knees, and the latter drew a cloak about the lady's face, so that she was in darkness. Then she heard the muttered words of prayer, in the midst of which she started, and would have arisen.

'Let me flee, – let me flee and hide myself, that they may not look upon me!' she cried. But, with returning recollection, she hushed herself, and was still as death.

For it seemed as if other voices – familiar in infancy, and unforgotten through many wanderings, and in all the vicissitudes of her heart and fortune – were mingling with the accents of the prayer. At first the words were faint and indistinct, not rendered so by distance, but rather resembling the dim pages of a book which we strive to read by an imperfect and gradually brightening light. In such a manner, as the prayer proceeded, did those voices strengthen upon the ear; till at length the petition ended, and the conversation of an aged man, and of a woman broken and decayed like himself, became distinctly audible to the lady as she knelt. But those strangers appeared not to stand in the hollow depth between the three hills. Their voices were encompassed and re-echoed by the walls of a chamber, the windows of which were rattling in the breeze; the regular vibration of a clock, the crackling of a fire, and the tinkling of the embers as they fell among the ashes, rendered the scene almost as vivid as if painted to the eye. By a melancholy hearth sat these two old people, the man calmly despondent, the woman querulous and tearful, and their words were all of sorrow. They spoke of a daughter, a wanderer they knew not where, bearing dishonour along with her, and leaving shame and affliction to bring their grey heads to the grave. They alluded also to other and more recent woe, but in the midst of their talk, their voices seemed to melt into the sound of the wind sweeping mournfully among the autumn leaves; and when the lady lifted her eyes, there was she kneeling in the hollow between three hills.

'A weary and lonesome time yonder old couple have of it,' remarked the old woman, smiling in the lady's face.

'And did you also hear them?' exclaimed she, a sense of intolerable humiliation triumphing over her agony and fear.

'Yea; and we have yet more to hear,' replied the old woman. 'Wherefore cover thy face quickly.'

Again the withered hag poured forth the monotonous words of a prayer that was not meant to be acceptable in Heaven; and soon, in the pauses of her breath, strange murmurings began to thicken, gradually increasing so as to drown and overpower the charm by which they grew. Shrieks pierced through the obscurity of sound, and were succeeded by the singing of sweet female voices, which in their turn gave way to a wild roar of laughter, broken suddenly by groanings and sobs, forming altogether a ghastly confusion of terror and mourning and mirth. Chains were rattling, fierce and stern voices uttered threats, and the scourge resounded at their command. All these noises deepened and became substantial to the listener's ear, till she could distinguish every soft and dreamy accent of the love songs, that died causelessly into funeral hymns. She shuddered at the unprovoked wrath which blazed up like the spontaneous kindling of flame, and she grew faint at the fearful merriment raging miserably around her. In the midst of this wild scene, where unbound passions jostled each other in a drunken career, there was one solemn voice of a man, and a manly and melodious voice it might once have been. He went to and fro continually, and his feet sounded upon the floor. In each member of that frenzied company, whose own burning thoughts had become their exclusive world, he sought an auditor for the story of his individual wrong, and interpreted their laughter and tears as his reward of scorn or pity. He spoke of woman's perfidy, of a wife who had broken her holiest vows, of a home and heart made desolate. Even as he went on, the shout, the laugh, the shriek, the sob, rose up in unison, till they changed into the hollow, fitful, and uneven sound of the wind, as it fought among the pine trees on those three lonely hills. The lady looked up, and there was the withered woman smiling in her face.

'Couldst thou have thought there were such merry times in a madhouse?' inquired the latter.

'True, true,' said the lady to herself; 'there is mirth within its walls, but misery, misery without.'

'Wouldst thou hear more?' demanded the old woman.

'There is one other voice I would fain listen to again,' replied the lady, faintly.

'Then, lay down thy head speedily upon my knees, that thou mayst get thee hence before the hour be past.'

The golden skirts of day were yet lingering upon the hills, but deep shades obscured the hollow and the pool, as if sombre night were rising thence to overspread the world. Again that evil woman began to weave her spell. Long did it proceed unanswered, till the knolling of a bell stole in among the intervals of her words, like a clang that had travelled far over valley and rising ground, and was just ready to die in the air. The lady shook upon her companion's knees, as she heard that boding sound. Stronger it grew and sadder, and deepened into the tone of a death bell, knolling dolefully from some ivy-mantled tower, and bearing tidings of mortality and woe to the cottage, to the hall, and to the solitary wayfarer, that all might weep for the doom appointed in turn to them. Then came a measured tread, passing slowly, slowly on, as of mourners with a coffin, their garments trailing on the ground, so that the ear could measure the length of their melancholy array. Before them went the priest, reading the burial service, while the leaves of his book were rustling in the breeze. And though no voice but his was heard to speak aloud, still there were revilings and anathemas, whispered but distinct, from women and from men, breathed against the daughter who had wrung the aged hearts of her parents – the wife who had betrayed the trusting fondness of her husband – the mother who had sinned against natural affection, and left her child to die. The sweeping sound of the funeral train faded away like a thin vapour, and the wind, that just before had seemed to shake the coffin pall, moaned sadly round the verge of the Hollow between three Hills. But when the old woman stirred the kneeling lady, she lifted not her head.

'Here has been a sweet hour's sport!' said the withered crone, chuckling to herself.

THE TAKING

Roger Johnson

Roger Johnson (b. 1947) has lived most of his
life in Chelmsford, Essex – aside from five years
at university in London and at library college,
and six years living and working in Harlow New
Town. He now works as a librarian in
Chelmsford. His earliest published pieces were
three sonnets which appeared in August
Derleth's *Arkham Collector* (USA) in 1971.
Johnson did not return to the horror genre until
1983 when his fine ghost story 'The Wall
Painting' was published in *Saints and Relics*
(1983). This was selected for inclusion in that
year's *Best Horror* anthology. He has written
several more equally fine ghost and horror
stories, two of which have also been selected for
the prestigious *Year's Best Horror* anthologies:
'The Scarecrow' (1984), and 'The Soldier'
(*Mystery for Christmas*, 1990).
Among his other stories are 'The Dog', 'The
Searchlight', and 'The Watchman' (all 1985);
and seven more collected and published as *Deep
Things Out of Darkness* (1987), from which 'The
Taking' (in a revised form) has been selected here.
In his spare time Johnson edits an invaluable
newsletter, *The District Messenger*, for the
Sherlock Holmes Society.

R obert Lovewell looked at each of us in turn over his glass of John
Jameson. He glanced thoughtfully for a moment at the whiskey
itself, and then asked diffidently, 'Did you ever see Carl Dreyer's
film *Vampyr?*'

George Cobbett drew his heavy grey eyebrows down in a momentary scowl, but merely said, 'No.'

'I've seen it,' I said. 'It was at the Scala in Bloomsbury, on a double bill with the silent *Nosferatu*. The print was pretty bad, but for all that it was a wonderfully strange and powerful film. Why do you ask?'

'Well, because I'd like you to consider a remark that Dreyer made about the film. "Imagine," he said, "that we are sitting in an ordinary room. Suddenly we are told that there is a corpse behind the door. In an instant, the room we are sitting in is completely altered: everything in it has taken on another look: the light, the atmosphere have changed, and the objects are as we conceive them."'

'"As we conceive them,"' George repeated. 'Well, that's an interesting way of putting it. But look here, young Lovewell, I thought you were an artist, not an expert on the European cinema.'

Robert took a sip of his whiskey. 'I'm a professional painter,' he said, 'as you well know. Whether I'm as much of an artist as Dreyer is another matter, but my line of work does have some bearing on the story, as otherwise I shouldn't have gone to stay at Abbotts.' He glared briefly at the old man. 'Don't sidetrack me again, George, or you won't hear the story at all. Ha! Very well . . .

Abbotts Farm (he continued) was a smallish concern that had been bought up by a neighbouring farmer in the early fifties. Most of the farmyard buildings were pulled down, and the new owner was wondering what to do with the old house when Jack Iszatt, the RA, happened to spot it and made him an offer. As a result, Iszatt found himself the owner of a country retreat at a price that would seem ludicrously small today.

Iszatt is a good fellow, and not one to keep his fortune to himself. I suppose that by now nearly all his friends have been offered the use of the house for a couple of months or so. My turn came about six years ago, in early September, and I accepted it most gratefully. I was going through a bad period creatively – it was something like writer's block – and a change of situation seemed the best possible answer. North Essex landscape in the late summer – it sounded perfect.

Abbotts stands just outside a village or hamlet called Winstock. You'd need a pretty large-scale map to find it, but it's just off the road between Thaxted and Little Sampford. On the corner is the local pub, The Whalebone; then there are a couple of cottages and an evangelical chapel, and then no buildings at all for half a mile or so – just a high hedge on both sides of the road. At last the road takes a turn to the north, and just around the corner, on the left, is the house.

It's an attractive building, without being particularly distinguished. You can see similar houses all over the eastern counties. The shape is that of a flattened letter H, with the crosspiece as the main part. The upper storey on each of the two wings juts out a little at the gable end. I could bore you with a lot of technical terminology, but I'd rather not; you'll have the essentials in your minds. The roof is tiled, though it may have been thatched at one time, and the walls are of lath and plaster over strong wooden beams. I was pleased to see that successive inhabitants had resisted the urge to strip off the plaster and expose the beams. It's a practice that our ancestors would have thought about as logical as stripping away your own flesh to expose the bone.

I was able to draw the car up to the front door – which is over to the right in the central block, facing east – and while I carried my bags inside I found myself trying to estimate the age of the building. It appeared to have been built from the first with two storeys, which suggested that it was no older than the fifteenth century. Another possible clue might be in the name. Had the place been built or owned at some time by a man named Abbott, or had it perhaps originally belonged to a monastery? At some time, I thought, I would look at the parish records.

I found myself upon entering in a fairly narrow hallway, with the main staircase at the far end. On the right, as I knew, were the kitchen and pantry, while to the left were the sitting room, dining room and study. Behind the house was a small plot of land, where Iszatt had converted one of the original farm buildings into a rather nice studio, small but airy and light.

The sitting room somehow managed to combine spaciousness and cosiness. No doubt it had been larger originally, taking in the hallway, with the front door leading directly into it. As it was, it stretched from the front to the back of the house. In each outer wall were two windows, which had probably been enlarged in the seventeenth or eighteenth century. Between each pair of windows was a tall bookcase, one containing a nice selection on the pictorial arts and the other a surprising little library of rather tempting antiquarian books. Facing you as you entered the room was the big fireplace – early Victorian, I think – with the door to the dining room on its left. Over the mantel Iszatt had hung one of his own paintings, a very fine watercolour of the Abbey at Bury St Edmunds – you know, the west front of the church, with the houses built into it – and elsewhere in the room were other pictures. I remember a rare couple of Lafcadio's early figure studies and a good Welsh landscape by Boddington.

A rich green carpet covered the middle of the floor. Remember that carpet, by the way: it's important. And there's another feature of the room that's relevant: all the illumination came from wall lamps. Iszatt had told me that he disliked ceiling lights, so I wasn't surprised to see a cluster of lamps on each side of the fireplace and another on each side of the door opposite, the one into the hall.

I settled for a lazy evening on that first day, leaving work until the following morning. I didn't even bother to check out the studio right away. Well, I got my things stowed away in one of the guest bedrooms and then went to see that the kitchen was properly stocked up. Having satisfied myself on that point, I thought it'd be a nice idea to make myself known at the local pub, and as the time by now was coming up to eight o'clock I took a walk down to The Whalebone. There I had a sandwich and a couple of drinks, a chat with the barmaid and a game of darts. Then I walked back to Abbotts.

I suppose it was getting on for eleven when I arrived back, but I wasn't feeling particularly tired, just comfortably lazy, so I helped myself to a glass of whiskey from the sideboard, put a record on the gramophone, and settled down in an armchair with an early volume of *Punch* cartoons. Nothing deep, you see, I didn't want to bother with anything taxing. The music was Vaughan Williams' *Job* – the Adrian Boult recording – which suited both the place and my mood deliciously. In any case, it's a work that I'm particularly fond of, one that perfectly bears out Sidney Smith's dictum that music is the only cheap and unpunished rapture upon earth. I actually played the whole thing through twice, though I did refrain from refilling my glass, but at last it seemed that it really was time I turned in. I switched off the record-player, put the book back on the shelf, and went over to the door. Before turning out the lights, I just stood for a moment or two, looking at the room, drinking it in, as it were. Perhaps you've done the same thing. Then I opened the door, flicked the light switches off, and turned to go out.

I must be rather precise about this, because it's quite important, as you'll see. Now, there were two switches by each door, so that you could turn off both sets of lights whichever way you went out of the room. Being unfamiliar with the switches, I inadvertently turned off the nearer lights first, so that for a moment all the illumination was directed towards me, throwing shadows in my direction. The next moment the room was in darkness, and I was halfway out into the hall. Only then did

I realize that I had seen something on the floor, something rather curious. You know how you sometimes see a thing but don't immediately register the fact? Well, I went straight back into the room and pressed those switches again until the lights were on as before, on the far side of the room only. Then I crawled on my hands and knees the length and breadth of that nice green carpet, but there was nothing. Not a single blessed thing out of the way at all. At last, thinking that my imagination must be stronger than I'd given it credit for, I left the room again.

What was it I'd seen? Well, you'll remember that just for a moment all the illumination, shadows and all, was directed towards me. On the carpet I had clearly seen the impressions of a dozen or more pairs of feet, large and small, all sharply defined, as if they'd been made in damp sand. Now, I said that the carpet was important, didn't I? You see, it was made of pure wool, and wool has one very interesting property which the man-made fibres don't have: it doesn't retain impressions. After the pressure is lifted, the pile springs right back into place. Odd, eh? Besides, you know, if they were just footprints left in the ordinary way there ought to have been many more than just the dozen or so that I'd seen. It occurred to me that perhaps I'd been visited by a group of invisible people; and with that rather bizarre thought I gave the whole thing up as a mystery and went to bed.

I fell asleep pretty quickly, and at once found myself dreaming. Now, this dream is really the greater part of my story, so again I'll have to be rather specific. The effect was not one I'd experienced before – and nor have I since, though I understand that it's not actually unknown. I was myself, Robert Lovewell, and perfectly aware of it, but I wasn't in my own body. Not that this was a wish-fulfilment fantasy, where I suddenly found myself a Hercules or Adonis. I mean exactly what I say: the body belonged to someone else, and that someone was there as well. Whoever my – er – host was, he was unaware of the fact, that much was plain; but he was in full control of our shared flesh. I couldn't either influence or anticipate, but only observe. With his eyes and ears and nerves, I could see, hear and feel – but that's all.

No, not quite all, because I could smell things too, and it was this that suggested that I might be in a real situation, rather than your usual surrealist dreamland. The odour that reached me was mostly a mixture, I think, of dust, sweat and dung. That last was rather faint, but it struggled bravely against the scent of flowers that someone had thoughtfully provided to cover it all. The sense of smell was the first to clarify, so to speak, forcing upon my mind that it had encountered something physical. Admitting this, I had to admit the evidence of the other senses. It came to me that I could distinctly feel the rather coarse stuff of the leggings that my man was wearing, with a much finer shirt, and what I took to be soft leather boots. The temperature, for what it's worth, was comfortably mild, like a good day in late spring. For a little while my sight was fixed upon the floor immediately in front of me. It was made of stone flags, partly covered with, I think, dried rushes – quite clean, it was – and just at the edge of my vision there was someone standing. I could make out a long robe or gown that just avoided brushing the floor. A woman, probably. For a second my gaze flicked towards this figure, and then back again immediately. And I distinctly felt a frown on my forehead.

You've probably seen films which are shot in the first person, so to speak; Mamoulian used the technique for the opening sequence of *Dr Jekyll and Mr Hyde*, where everything is shown as through Jekyll's eyes. But it's a very strange sensation indeed to feel another person's frown! While my eyes were set on the floor before me, my mind turned to what I could hear. It was Babel. From a little way off came the squawking, clucking and grunting sounds of a well-stocked farmyard, and above this, within the room, a dozen voices were talking, subdued but desperate, and in a tongue that meant nothing to me. From the vowel sounds and the occasional guttural, I thought that it might be Dutch, or possibly Scandinavian, but even as my eyes were raised at last to view the figure in front of me I could not be sure.

Slowly, even with reluctance, my host's gaze took in the long dark grey robe or dress, moving upwards to rest for a moment on the hands. They were beautiful hands, slender and elegant, meekly folded, the left over the right, but tense with a disconcerting nervousness. The skin was of that exquisite glowing pink that sometimes goes with real pure blonde hair. When you've spent much of your life studying the human body from an aesthetic viewpoint, you come to realize that each part can have its own special beauty. I tell you, those hands were remarkably beautiful. They made me very curious to see the face of the woman who owned them.

I became aware of other people in the room. With something of a shock, I realized that there were two large men standing firmly, one on either side of the young woman. Oh, I was convinced by now that she was young, and as beautiful *in toto* as her hands. For some reason, my host seemed reluctant to look her in the face. He turned his gaze away abruptly to the left, to where a little knot of people stood nervously chattering by an open door, casting occasional uneasy glances in my direction. Now that I could see them and how they were dressed, a part of the puzzle fell into place, and it seemed the most natural thing in the world that I should find myself among country folk in the late sixteenth century. And the room – yes, that looked familiar now, as it should, for I'd spent much of the previous evening in it. There was no separate hallway then, of course, and the sturdy front door led directly into the room. The furniture, what I could see of it, was quite different, being much more chunky and solid, but with that curious dignity that perfect rightness achieves. The walls were covered with linenfold panelling to a height of about six feet, with plain lime-wash above. All this I had to notice when I could, being wholly at the mercy of my unwitting host, but there could be no doubt about it: I was in the main room of Abbotts Farmhouse.

That would explain the apparently foreign language. My guess at a Nordic tongue hadn't been a bad one. As you know, Elizabethan English really did sound rather like that, and in such a remote place there would be the local accent to confuse things further. Even now it's very strong in some areas, despite growing uniformity, but can you imagine how it was four hundred years ago? Realizing this, I discovered that I could now actually distinguish an occasional phrase from the subdued babble that came to my ears. At this point, my host turned his gaze away from that of an elderly, strong-faced woman who stood near the door, but a little apart from the group. He had at last resolved to look fully upon the young woman who was the centre of the drama.

Yes, she was young – no more than twenty-five – and she was beautiful, though not with a classical, superficial beauty. Above the plain grey gown and white lace collar, she wore a close-fitting cap of grey velvet that framed her face. It hid most of her hair, but a stray lock on her left cheek was of the perfect pure gold that I had expected. The mouth was neither large nor small, but well-shaped, and the eyes, though not exceptionally large, were of a very clear grey. It was a finely proportioned face, but what made it beautiful was the very evident spirit within. I never saw a smile on that face, but its smile, I think, would have been ravishing.

Her grey eyes returned my stare, and noticeably hardened, though she said nothing. Her mouth was calm and apparently without expression. That she was contemptuous of this man I was sure, for all that fear might be mingled with the scorn. But what were his own feelings? I thought I could sense in him a strong nervous tension, and something that was only too plain to read as lust.

The two men standing beside her were massive brutes, roughly dressed, who might perhaps have been labourers on this very farm. In their bovine faces I could see only a rather frightening blankness. They stood so close to her, as if guarding her, that they put me in mind of policemen effecting an arrest. And plainly the situation was something very like that. As this fact forced itself upon me, I found that I could distinguish more and more what the people around me were saying, though there was one word, muttered or whispered, that somehow eluded me. Then this puzzle too was solved, by a voice behind me, masculine and assured, which cut through the chatter and silenced it. Some official paper was read or quoted, and with this at last the whole tragedy became clear. The word that seemed to form most of the conversation in the room, the word that I could not quite make out, was 'witch'.

The tension in my body was painful, seeming about to erupt, as if the man had been waiting for this. Briefly his right hand clenched, and, horribly, I could feel sweat starting from his forehead. He looked sharply at the girl, but her grey eyes were like slivers of ice in the warmth of her pink skin, and he turned his gaze away to where the older woman stood, rather aloof from the crowd. He looked long at that still-handsome face, and the tension gradually came under control.

This woman, now – I called her elderly, but the word isn't quite right. People did grow old before their time in those days, of course, but for all her fifty or so years she was not old, but rather in vigorous middle age. She looked as if she could live for ever by the strength of her will. Her eyes gazed very steadily into mine – his – and I fancy that there was something like suppressed amusement there. Only once did she glance towards the younger woman, and even then not a flicker of expression crossed her handsome features. I think the man took strength from her. At last he looked back at the girl, meeting her own cold stare with growing confidence.

The voice behind us finished speaking, and the silence that followed was like something tangible. The girl's elegant little hands were clasped now, so tightly that the knuckles showed a vivid white. It was the only sign of fear that she showed, and her voice was quite calm as she spoke. The accent was still strange to me, but that voice was pure and clear. She said, 'Before God and His angels, I do swear my innocence.'

She was allowed no more, for with a terrifying suddenness the man's hand – my hand, God help me! – had drawn from its sheath a long-bladed knife, and he had leapt at her, bellowing like an animal. The abrupt release of rage appalled me. In my mind I was cursing with frustration that I could not stop him. I could only watch, through his own damned eyes, as the knife swept across her face – as she started back, but was firmly held by the two uncomprehending oafs beside her – as she threw up her right hand to save her eyes – and as the sharp blade sheared cleanly through flesh and bone, severing the slender forefinger.

Strong hands grasped my arms, pulling me back, that fearful rage still burning throughout my body – and I awoke. Awoke, with the girl's scream of bewildered pain sounding about me, and her horrified eyes clear in my sight, staring with appalled accusation directly at me.

I felt foul. My vision was blurred, my head had a dull ache, and I was thinking quite lunatic thoughts. Fortunately sleep came over me again, and the next I knew was that I was fully awake in bright daylight. I began to think again, but coherently this time. What should I make of it all? The few dreams I'd had before that I could recall in any detail had been thoroughly inconsequential affairs – 'as beautiful as the meeting of an umbrella and a sewing-machine upon an operating-table', which after all is the essence of surrealism. But there was nothing surreal about this. It was solid and logical. I couldn't doubt that I had been a party to some real event. Well, I decided to spend a while that day in the studio, where I could occupy my hands and make up my mind what course to take. Having reached that small decision, I washed, dressed and went downstairs.

In the sitting room I found something that set my mind racing again. It was a small enough thing, but – the significance of it! In the middle of that nice green carpet it lay, just where the girl had stood in my dream, and where I couldn't possibly have missed it the night before. You've guessed, of course. It was a severed finger. There was nothing of beauty left in it. It was quite clean, but withered and almost fleshless, though the nail was intact, and I could clearly see how the blade had cut through the bone. It looked, as it was, I suppose, some hundreds of years old.

I examined it very carefully, even minutely, and then wrapped it in cotton wool and locked it in a little box in the cabinet beside my bed. Then I took paper and chalks over to the studio, where I spent most of the day. It was already plain that I should have to make some research into the history of the house, but what was I to do with the – the object found? That was the question that kept nagging at me, and by the evening I was no nearer to an answer, though I had got down on paper quite a good portrait from memory of the two women I'd dreamed of, so the day hadn't been wholly wasted.

I dined on something from a tin and then went off to The Whalebone, as before, where I struck up a conversation with the landlord. He was an affable fellow enough, but unfortunately a foreigner – which is to say that he'd come from Cambridge and hadn't lived in Winstock above twenty years. Neither he nor the two old boys from the local farms, who spent the evening hunched over a game of crib, could tell me anything of the village during the period that I was interested in. One of them suggested that I ask the local vicar, but the landlord scorned the idea, pointing out that Winstock church no longer had its own incumbent. The vicar of Great Sampford would drive over every third Sunday to conduct a single service, and as he'd only been resident for a few months it was unlikely that he could help me. At least the landlord made the suggestion that should have occurred to me; that I should come into Chelmsford and consult the archives at the County Record Office.

Do I need to tell you that I dreamed again that night? But the dream was not the same. The hint, if that's the word, had been taken, and I need not take part in the drama again. What I saw that night – what I remember, at least – was the young woman herself, alone and standing by my bedside in the moonlight. Her face was calm, and there was none of the pain in her eyes that I had last seen there. I was relieved at that, for although I'd had no deliberate part in the events of her taking I hadn't been able to forget the bewildered accusation in those grey eyes. She stood quite still, until I had stopped gawping like an imbecile, and then she simply held out her hands to me, so that I could see clearly how sadly mutilated the right one was. The forefinger had been cleanly severed, and there were sharp cuts, dark with blood, across the lower joints of the middle and ring fingers. Anger rose in me, perhaps at the marring of such beauty, and I abruptly reached a decision. The thing was obvious, after all. 'Yes,' I said, just that; and although she made no reply, I knew that I had done right. She closed her eyes for a moment and expelled a gentle sigh. When she looked at me again, I could see relief in every feature. Then she was gone, and the morning was upon me. Perhaps it wasn't a dream this time. I'd like to believe that, but who can tell?

It took the best part of an hour for the people at the Record Office to find what I wanted, but they know their job, and in the end I had the whole sad tale. The information wasn't, as I'd expected, in the Winstock parish records, but in a copy of a report from the archives at Lambeth Palace. It was an account of the arrest, trial and execution for witchcraft of one Mistress Jennet or Janet Fisher of Winstock in the County of Essex in the year of Grace 1585, before Lord Brian Darcy.

Janet Fisher was the young widow of a farmer, whose house and land were 'late the property of the Prior of Tilty in the same County'. He inherited the place from his father, who had bought it at the Dissolution, but he, the son, survived only a few years, being killed in a riding accident at the age of twenty-seven. Having no other immediate family, he had willed the property to his wife. And this bequest, it seems, was the basis for the whole drama. It would have been unusual anyway for a woman to have sole charge of a farm, and this particular woman was both young and marriageable. In short, both the estate and its owner were desirable.

Desirable, eh? Well, she's described in the report as 'fair and slender, full-eyed, her feet and hands of singular beauty'. It's understandable that more than one young man should have had his eye on her. And one young man's mother, as well. She was another widow, one Dame Alice Rosemary, whose only surviving son, Thomas, was the master of a larger neighbouring farm. Having so much, they wanted more, and although young Mistress Fisher – she was just twenty-four, and a widow for eighteen months – showed no desire to marry again, it seems that Alice Rosemary had determined that she should. The happy bridegroom, of course, would be Thomas. Neither mother nor son comes out well from the affair, unless you count maternal ambition as a virtue. Alice Rosemary seems to have worshipped her late husband, and when he died she transferred that worship to their son, a taciturn lout of about twenty-five, strong and quick-tempered. From his own later account it appears that he considered himself happy only when in his mother's company, and he would do anything to ensure her approval. She must have been a remarkable woman, you know. In a less patriarchal age she might have made good use of her verve and intelligence. As it was . . .

Thomas Rosemary seems to have been pretty well indifferent to Janet Fisher until, as he said much later, his mother advised him to court the young widow. Even so, it appears that for the son as for the mother the main object was to gain possession of Abbotts Farm. To this end he did his clumsy best to woo the girl, and she, an intelligent creature, would have none of him. Every day Thomas would recount his lack of progress, and every day Alice would chide him for the fool that he was. So matters went for some months, and then Alice Rosemary chanced to consult a lawyer and learned something that put the whole affair in a new light.

Janet Fisher was an orphan with no surviving family. If she were to die unmarried then the estate would revert to her late husband's family. So far, all was straightforward. The shock was to learn that the late Walter Fisher's nearest living male relative was Thomas Rosemary himself. This gave a new urgency to the matter, for although the young widow might refuse to marry Thomas, there was no telling when she might meet a more attractive suitor. Alice found herself with two choices: she could reinforce the efforts of her miserable son to make love to the girl, or she could see to it that Janet Fisher simply did not live to marry again. Rejecting straightforward murder, she made up her mind to a simple and devastating plan. She would see that the respectable Mistress Fisher died as a witch.

Thomas Rosemary, some fifteen years later, confessed to his own part in the whole nasty business. He claimed that the idea was entirely his mother's, and I see no reason to doubt him. He was violent enough by nature, and ready to avenge what he saw as the slighting he'd received from this stubborn chit, but he lacked the intelligence that his mother had. And in those superstitious times, you know, the plan could hardly fail; an accusation of witchcraft was almost proof of guilt in itself. Oh, there were a few enlightened souls about, like George Gifford of Maldon; but even he didn't deny the reality of sorcery, and for the most part opinion went along with writers like William Perkins. Well, you can look him up if you like: he wrote A Discourse of the Damned Art of Witchcraft, and it's a very disturbing glimpse into the mind of a fanatic.

Dame Alice set to her filthy task – with some relish, if we may believe her son; certainly with effect. Rumours were spread. Simple folk began to believe that they had seen what they had only been told. Those who were sick or wounded became convinced that they were actually bewitched. Even Mistress Fisher's own servants came to be wary of her, while she, poor child, remained falsely secure in her real innocence. Then came the taking. On the morning of the fifteenth of May, the widow Rosemary and her son triumphantly conducted three officers of the County Sheriff, followed by a nervous group of village folk, to Abbotts Farm, where Janet Fisher was formally accused by that public-spirited citizen Master Thomas Rosemary, whose own bailiff, he said, had but recently been stricken lame through the sorcerous arts of the said woman. All this was recounted in some detail at the trial, so we know pretty well exactly what happened. At first the young woman was struck with horrified disbelief, but quickly controlled herself, and appeared to all to be quite calm. The fact was noted against her, but I suspect that she'd been overtaken by that comforting sense of unreality that's sometimes instilled in us by the utterly outrageous.

She spoke only once on that occasion, and I can quote the words exactly. After the Sheriff's man had read the formal deed of arrest, she said, 'Before God and His angels, I do swear my innocence.' You can imagine what a queer feeling it gave me to read that simple statement in the cramped print of the old pamphlet! All this was minutely recorded, because something quite unexpected followed. The brazen words of the witch aroused such an excess of wrath in the good Master Thomas that before he could be restrained he had drawn his long-bladed knife and attempted to slash at her face. She threw up her right hand, saving her eyes, but receiving a savage wound none the less. In short, one of her fingers was wholly severed, and the hand badly cut. At this, she cried aloud and swooned. The constables had to carry her from the house.

The trial was held at Chelmsford on the twenty-seventh of June, and Janet Fisher found herself only one of three women arraigned before Lord Brian Darcy. The others were simple, ignorant souls, and their cases were speedily despatched. It isn't surprising that more attention was paid to the young, intelligent and attractive mistress of Abbotts Farm. I wonder now if she was at all aware of Darcy's reputation. If so, she must have known already that she was lost. He'd been the presiding judge in at least two previous witchcraft trials and had proved himself to be quite without mercy.

I read the whole report very thoroughly, though it told me nothing that I hadn't anticipated. The several villagers who gave evidence were plainly overawed by the situation, and in one or two cases words were actually put into their mouths by the prosecution in a way that quite sickened me. Nearly all mentioned the part played by Master Rosemary in building up suspicion against the accused, and yet none of them was questioned upon this point. Every insinuation appeared to be accepted as fact. Dame Alice didn't testify, and her son's evidence was kept to a minimum. No mention at all was made of the fact that he was the sole heir to the estate of Abbotts.

The verdict was inevitable – guilty. The sentence was death by hanging. It was carried out the following day in the open space in front of the Sessions House, where Tindal Square is now. The old courthouse was replaced, as you know, in 1789 by John Johnson's Shire Hall, and the whole place is so changed that when I walked around there after leaving the Record Office I could gain no impressions from it at all.

That was the end of Janet Fisher: branded as a witch and hanged without compassion. But it wasn't the end of the affair, because about fifteen years later Alice Rosemary died of a fall. Her son Thomas must have had a spark of independent humanity in him after all, because the day after her funeral he went to the Sheriff's office and confessed to the whole sordid plot. He said that he was troubled by the thought of eternal ignominy attaching to the memory of an innocent woman. Maybe he really did love her a little, or had at least managed to persuade himself that he did. His confession was duly noted, and a copy of it survives in the County Archives, but no action was taken. Can you beat it? Nothing was done, and Thomas Rosemary went back to Winstock and his family. He died, according to the parish register, in March of 1611, much mourned by his wife and three sons.

Well, that's the story of the reality behind my vision, but of course I already knew that it was so, and the details of the story had combined to explain my own part in it. I knew what I was to do with the severed finger, and now I knew why.

Oh, I must tell you what the account said on that point, because it clarified matters wonderfully. There was just a brief, casual statement in the report of Janet Fisher's arrest. Thomas Rosemary, in his savage attack on her, had managed to cut off one of the fingers of her right hand – and as I knew, because I had seen, it was the forefinger. Now, in the confusion following all this, when the poor child had collapsed, nobody had given any thought to the severed finger, and when one of the constables had looked for it later it was not to be found. The assumption was that some servant, still faithful, or some ghoul among the bystanders had pocketed it as a gruesome memento. It was a reasonable notion, but quite wrong, as you can see. Quite wrong.

I am certain, positive, that it had been waiting for me. Somewhere – or nowhere – it had been waiting for me.

George was busily filling his pipe. Without looking up, he asked – although we both knew the answer – 'What did you do with it?'

Robert spread out his strong hands. 'Just what I'd promised I'd do. I sealed the box that I'd put it in, and that night I took it along to Winstock churchyard. I found a quiet corner where it wouldn't be disturbed, and I buried it.' He looked sharply at us, as if daring us to dispute the rightness of the action. 'I took along a copy of *The Book of Common Prayer* that I'd bought at Clarke's in Chelmsford, and I read over the burial service. She wouldn't have had a Christian burial, you see.'

I toyed with my glass for a moment, and as George didn't seem inclined to speak I asked the obvious question: 'Why? I mean, it was a nice gesture, and a good one – perhaps I'd have done the same. But why this insistence on it? You speak as though you were paying off a debt.'

'I'm sorry, but I thought you knew. "Paying off a debt" is about right.

Ah, well . . . I've not been able to trace the family all the way back, but it's a pretty distinctive name, and there's no doubt at all in my own mind. You see, my mother's maiden name was Rosemary.'

THE DAY OF
THE UNDERDOG

Ronald Chetwynd-Hayes

Ronald Chetwynd-Hayes (b. 1919) has been
dubbed 'Britain's Prince of Chill', and is the
doyen of this country's fantasy and horror
writers. 'The Day of the Underdog' originally
appeared in his paperback collection *Tales of
Fear and Fantasy* (1977).

Arthur Collins had always been oppressed.

But, he had never been a happy underdog, or even a resigned underdog, and forever dreamed of the day – a glorious tomorrow that kept receding into the future – when he would miraculously grow fangs and bite his oppressors.

For, to your true underdog, the world is populated by oppressors. During childhood they take the form of schoolteachers, playground bullies and parents. On the battlefield of adolescence their number is reinforced by the majority of all adults over thirty. But it is not until middle age has wiped its clammy fingers across forehead and silvering temples, that the true oppressors stand out like snarling wolves on a treeless plain.

Arthur knew who his were – and they knew him. They were – in order of seniority – his managing director, his sales manager, and last, but by no stretch of imagination, least, his wife. Every one of these people, each in his or her individual way, contrived to and mostly succeeded in oppressing Arthur Collins.

Mr Rowe, the sales manager, conducted his oppressive campaign without the slightest pretence of respect, but the maximum of sarcasm.

'Made a muck-up again, Collins? Dropped the proverbial clanger, have we? Have to pull our socks up, won't we?' Then with a nasty, gloating leer, 'The old man wants to see you.'

Mr Carrington-Jones, for such was the managing director's name, had, over the years, developed a very nice line in veiled threats, interposed with caustic humour, delivered in a low, husky voice.

'Been with us twenty-two years, aye, Collins? Can't see you making twenty-three. No place for slackers. Find yourself with a slack sack. Eh!' Then after taking a deep breath, rather like a rhinoceros that has made up its mind to charge, Mr Carrington-Jones raised his voice to a full-throated roar. 'Wake up, man. Get stuck-in – pull the stops out. Improve or remove.'

Ethel – the wife who had taken him to her bed and board some twenty years earlier – conducted her battle of domestic aggression with the time-honoured weapons of ridicule and rhetoric.

'Call yourself a man? Do you! The cat has more go in him than you have. I must have been mad when I married you. Stark, raving mad. When I think that Mark Manby was mine for the taking, and now he's top man in Gresham Supermarket. When are you going to have a rise? I suppose that Mr Carrington-Jones doesn't think you're worth any more, and I can't say I blame him, but it's a bit hard on me. I said, it's a bit hard on me . . .'

So, it can be quite clearly understood, that Arthur Collins was indeed sorely oppressed, and was prepared to accept help from any source, and use any weapons against his enemies that came to hand. It was perhaps providential that on the day when he had been subjected to a three-pronged attack – to wit: sales manager, managing director, and wife – he stumbled over an old woman who was quietly dying on the pavement.

She was nothing more than a bundle of skin and bones, wrapped in a cocoon of old rags. She was furthermore wrinkled, dirty, smelly, had no teeth worth mentioning, and insisted on clutching Arthur's ankle when he attempted to run for assistance. When he bent down an awful-looking claw of a hand came up to grab his shoulder. Her voice sounded like a worn-out foghorn on a windy night.

'Don't want nobody . . . get me upstairs . . . die in me own bed . . .'

Another claw crept out from beneath the rags and pointed to an open doorway, and Arthur, who had been trained from childhood to do what he was told, promptly slid an arm under her shoulders and raised the barely living scarecrow to its feet. Together, two of the world's underdogs ascended three flights of dimly lit stairs, and presently came up on to a really evil-looking landing, that had damp, crumbling walls on three sides and a cracked, dirt-grimed door on the fourth. Arthur's companion, who by now was groaning in a most blood-curdling fashion, somehow found strength to push a key into a tarnished Yale-lock, before collapsing over his supporting left arm. Arthur unlocked the door, pushed it open, then entered the room beyond. He had expected the worst and was not disappointed.

An unwholesome couch that apparently served as a bed lay under a dirt-fogged window. A sideboard on which was piled a collection of white bones, two skulls, a large leather-bound book and numerous bottles that contained blue or red powder appeared to prop up one wall. On a plastic clothes-line, which was slung from one wall to another, hung a gruesome array of mummified frogs, bats, rats, and to Arthur's disgust, snakes. A huge rusty cauldron sat on top of an ancient gas-stove, while bunches of dried herbs were piled on the plate-rack. For the rest, there was a sagging not-to-be-trusted armchair, a small wooden table, and a three-legged milking stool.

Arthur deposited his burden on to the bed, then tried to make up his mind as to what he should do next. His mind was wandering towards 999, police, ambulance and doctors, when the old woman opened her eyes and announced her return to consciousness by a loud groan. He approached the bed and stood looking down at the hideously wrinkled face, with the repugnance of the healthy in close proximity with the unsavoury sick. He made sympathetic noises.

'How do you feel? Would you like me to fetch a doctor?'

The lips twisted, the tongue flickered and the voice croaked: 'Don't want no doctor. Put me in 'ospital. You look after me.'

Arthur started like a rabbit that has stumbled in on a stoat's convention.

'Really, I'm afraid that would not be at all possible.'

'Only two days,' the old woman pleaded. 'Make it worth yer while. When I'm gone . . . treasure beyond price. No one to leave it to . . .'

Now, it is a well-known fact that there is no such animal as a rich underdog. Arthur could remember hearing stories of dirty, presumably poverty-stricken old women who had a fortune concealed under the floorboards or mattress. As any well-informed person is aware, every large city simply teems with these rag-clad misers, who are waiting to

[187]

enrich the kindly Samaritan. When the old woman moved, Arthur would have sworn that he heard the sound of rustling bank-notes.

'Anything I can do . . .'

'A drop of the 'ard stuff to wet me lips, and make sure me bones are burned. I wouldn't like to be up and about after the earth has been shovelled in. Me grandmother started wandering, and they 'ad to stake 'er down before she'd rest. You'll find a bottle in the oven.'

Arthur opened the gas-oven door and peered hopefully into the grease-coated interior. There was no pile of hoarded bank-notes, only a half-filled bottle of whisky and a chipped teacup. The croaking voice was tinted by an impatient undertone.

'Don't 'ang about. I wants me nourishment. Won't do for me to go down into the dark lands, before I've made me will.'

Arthur hastily grabbed the bottle and teacup and all but ran back to the bed. He half filled the cup with whisky, then looked enquiringly at the patient, who shook her head.

'Never allowed water to touch me lips or skin. Against nature, that's what it is. Let's get at it.'

The whisky did seem to do her a lot of good. She licked her one remaining tooth, smacked her black lips, then cackled her enjoyment.

'That's the stuff to warm the stummick. So long as I gets me ration regular like, I'll last for days.'

Arthur was struck by a sudden thought, but found it somewhat embarrassing to put into words.

'I really think you should see a doctor . . .'

'Don't want no doctor.'

'But . . . there is a little matter of a certificate . . . the death certificate.'

The old woman examined the whisky bottle with some anxiety, then turned her glittering little eyes in Arthur's direction.

'Better bring another bottle tomorrow. Death certificate, aye? Hadn't thought of that.'

'I fear there will be an inquest, unless a doctor has been in attendance . . .'

The old woman gave a squeal of terror and shook her head violently. 'Mustn't cut me open. Never know what they might find. Must be burned in one piece. Get a doctor. There's one round the corner in Angel Street.'

The doctor proved to be young, somewhat cynical, and the possessor of a black sense of humour. He felt the old woman's pulse, listened to her heartbeat, then pushed Arthur out on to the landing.

'You a relative?'

'No. A sort of . . . friend.'

'Go on! Well, your friend is on her way out. In fact I can't imagine how she manages to hang on. Good grief, how old is she?'

'I don't know. Eighty?'

'I'd say more like a hundred and eighty. She has a pulse beat of a hundred and thirty, and her liver and kidneys must have packed it in ages ago. I can get her into hospital if you like, although I doubt if it is worth the bother.'

'She doesn't want to go to hospital.'

The doctor looked round the landing with every indication of marked disgust before picking up his bag.

'Give me a call when she stops breathing and I'll come round and sign the certificate. By the way, what does she do with all that stuff in there? All those bones and skulls?'

'I don't know. Perhaps she collects them. You know, like stamps or bus tickets.'

The doctor ran down the first flight of stairs, then paused and stood looking up at Arthur.

'Mind she doesn't put a dying curse on you. She looks as if she was quite capable.'

Arthur brought a form from a stationer's, and uncomfortably aware of her sardonic smirk, sat down by the old woman's bedside, to make out her last will and testament. With surprising clarity, she dictated her wishes and kept snatching the document from Arthur's hand, so as to make sure he had written every word correctly. He read the completed will aloud.

'I, Tabitha Holbrook, being of sound mind, do hereby revoke all Wills heretofore made by me at any time and declare this to be my last Will and Testament.

'I give all my estate and effects and everything that I can give or dispose to Arthur George Collins of 24 Rampling Road, London, EC4.

'I hope and trust that he will live to enjoy all that I leave him, in particular the Great Treasure.

Signed. Tabitha Holbrook.'

Next day the young doctor witnessed the boldly written signature, and irritated Arthur by unnecessarily raised eyebrows and knowing smile. But finally the document that was to transform the underdog into the well-fleshed wolf was deposited in Arthur's bank, and he took a week off from work, so as to be on hand when his bread was returned unto him – hopefully – a hundredfold.

The old woman died three days later.

Needless to say, Arthur Collins did not wait for the will to be proved; for letters of administration, or any nonsense of that kind. Barely had the corpse been sent on its way to the local mortuary, than he was ripping the noisome mattress to pieces with a carving-knife, determined to lose no time in getting his hands on the 'great treasure'. His harvest consisted of a collection of rusty springs, a pile of flock and an army of blood-seeking insects that invaded his person with promptitude and tenacity. But no treasure.

He flung bones on to the floor, peered into skulls, wrecked the sideboard, prised up floorboards, tore what paper remained from the walls, opened the leather-bound book and shook it violently – but not so much as a bent sixpence to reward his efforts. The dream of saluting Mr Carrington-Jones with two raised fingers melted like snow in sunlight. The underdog collapsed under a burden of bitter disappointment and became a doormat.

Arthur went out and for the first time in his life, got drunk.

Mrs Collins – a lady with a long neck and a short temper – greeted Arthur on his return home from the office with a scowl and a statement.

'A vanman delivered a load of bones and rubbish this afternoon.'

Arthur hung his hat on the hall-stand and looked upon that which he liked to describe in his more jocular moments, as his worse-half, with some astonishment. Three months had passed since the remains of Tabitha Holbrook had been surrendered to the flames, and he had almost forgotten the entire unfortunate proceedings.

'Old bones . . . rubbish!'

'Yes.' His lady sniffed and watched her husband with grave suspicion. 'Bones, skulls and lots of other things that don't bear talking about. The vanman was most insolent and wouldn't take them away. So I told him to pile the lot in the garage. Good job we can't afford a car. Never get it in there.'

Arthur hurried to the garage, and there, sure enough, was a degutted mattress, a smashed sideboard, a chair, a milk-stool, an untidy pile of bones, two skulls, assorted dried toads, bats, rats, snakes, to say nothing of glass jars of coloured powder. And of course, there was the leather-bound book. It lay half buried in the gaping entrails of the mattress.

Arthur said, 'Oh, my God,' and wondered how his inheritance was going to be explained to a wife who never believed what she was told.

He prodded a skull and it rolled off the ruined sideboard and went clattering across the floor. He fingered a thigh-bone, then dropped it with a cry of disgust. Finally he picked up the leather-bound book, and turned back the front cover. The title page stared up at him and sent little thought-storms thundering across his brain.

YE GRATE TREASURE BOOK OF SPELLES
Both Big and Smalle.

So this was the old woman's great treasure. A book of spells. Arthur flicked the pages over and despite his scepticism began to experience a growing sense of excitement. Spell one was headed TO SOUR MILK ON A COLDE DAY AND DRIE UP A COWE SO SHE GIVETH NO MOOR. This act of unkindness was apparently accomplished by mixing: *One measure of drie batt with two measures of extrac of drie sirpent, stirr wel til ye powder is greene and mix with ye blud of ratt . . .*

Arthur shuddered and turned the page over, only to find himself reading YE WAYES AND MEENS OF CAUSING THY NAYBOUR TO BREAKE OUT IN SPOTS. But it was not until he reached spell twenty-two, that his interest was really aroused. He read it from beginning to end.

YE SHORE WAYE OF QUIETING A SCOLDING WIFE
Take one finger-length of her hare; ye clippings of her nails. Plaice in a vessel, then add sirpent powder, toad-eye and stirr with finger-bone. Take ye micture out into ye churchyard and burie in old grave when moon is behind steepel and chant ye spelle.

> *Curst wife who can but scold,*
> *Who du not wat she been told.*
> *Now I give you unpaid bill,*
> *May thy tunge bee er still.*

Arthur closed the book and returned – thoughtfully – to the house.

There could be no doubt, Ethel Collins was the prime candidate for the year's most scolding wife. Even while she dished up the baked beans and charred sausages, she poured out a torrent of abuse, that ably expressed her opinion of Arthur's past crimes, his present misdemeanours and his future prospects.

'Me mother always warned me. He's useless, she said. Dead useless and bone idle . . . no go . . . them were her very words . . . and how true

... as I stand here ... how true. You're worse now ... mad ... that's what you are ... filling the garage with bones and skulls and goodness knows what ... other men don't fill their garages with bones ... finish up in a mad-house, that's what you'll do ... did you hear what I said? Finish up in a mad-house ... but don't think I'm coming with you ...'

Arthur came to a decision.

Obtaining a finger-length of Ethel's hair presented no great problem. He cut it off with a pair of kitchen-scissors while she was asleep. Finger-nail clippings were another matter.

'What do you mean, isn't it about time I cut me nails?'

Arthur tore his eyes away from the large, blunt-fingered hand and looked longingly at the nail-scissors that he had thoughtfully laid on the table.

'You have such pretty hands and it would be a pity if they were spoilt by long nails.'

'You trying to be funny? Eh! Taking the mickey, are you?'

'Oh, no. But I thought ...'

'Don't. Thinking is not your strong point. You aren't equipped for it.'

But that night when Arthur went into the bathroom, he found nail-clippings all over the wash-basin, and he was able to wrap them carefully in the face-flannel. The other ingredients he – after many stomach-turning experiments – obtained from his inheritance, and the end result was stirred together by what he hoped was a finger-bone in one of Ethel's pudding-basins.

At two o'clock the following morning, he carried his basin of spell-binding mixture to St James's churchyard, and there solemnly buried it in a small hole which he carved out with a trowel on a suitably old grave. Then after looking round to ensure that he was not being watched, he chanted the memorized verse to the moon that was obligingly peering at him from behind the church steeple.

Later, as he crept upstairs to the matrimonial bedroom, he told himself what a fool he was to believe for one moment that a spell in an old book could possibly stop his wife from talking. Once back in the double bed, Ethel seemed to reinforce these doubts, for she muttered unendingly in her sleep, and once shouted: 'I should have married Harry Potter,' a regret that Arthur unreservedly shared.

The spell had not worked by breakfast time. Arthur was given a running commentary on his inability to do a simple domestic repair, paint the house front, cut the lawn ('it's a disgrace, I don't know what the neighbours think'), save enough money to buy a car ('not that you'd have the gumption to drive it'), and fit a new washer to the leaking tap. If he remained silent and allowed the storm to pass over him, he was told to stop sulking; when he said, 'Yes, dear' or, 'No, dear,' he was instructed not to answer back.

Without interrupting her tirade, Ethel collected the used plates and retired to the kitchen, where she raised her voice so that Arthur should not miss a single word. She had just reached the part he knew so well; the evergreen statement, which ran: 'The worst day's work that I ever did, was when I . . .', when she suddenly stopped. Arthur waited for the word 'married', but it never came. Instead, after a hopeful, but very anxious pause, a strange sound emerged from beyond the kitchen door. It was reminiscent of a pig that has found a brick in its feeding trough. This was explained when Ethel staggered out of the kitchen, clutching her throat with one hand, while she pointed to her mouth with the other. She repeated the sound: 'Ugh . . . ugh . . .'

Realization dawned and dispelled the dark clouds of doubt. Assisted by a few basic ingredients, Arthur Collins had performed one of the great miracles of modern times. Even now he could scarcely believe.

'Do you mean . . . you can't talk!'

Ethel again pointed to her mouth and repeated the 'Ugh . . . ugh' sound several times. Arthur did a little dance and expressed his proper gratitude by raising his eyes ceilingward, then remembering that such favours do not usually come from that direction, stared earnestly at the floor instead. 'Thank you . . . thank you. She can't talk. Please may it be permanent.'

Ethel's distress did not appear to be alleviated by this demonstration of thanksgiving, for she raised her guttural cries to a higher level and pounded the breakfast table with her clenched fists. It was then that Arthur realized that he had – to say the least – been guilty of committing an act of discourtesy, and did his very best to apologize. It was unfortunate that his best was not very convincing, for his face would persist in grinning, and the consoling words were interposed by an occasional gurgling chuckle.

'I say – I am sorry. It must be awful for you . . . Ye gods, you can't talk – What on earth will you do now?'

Ethel could not talk, but she could still communicate, for after running to a small bureau, she grabbed a sheet of paper and a ball-point pen, and scribbled furiously. Arthur read the message.

'Get doctor, you heartless, ungrateful, unnatural bastard.'

He shook his head in pretended sadness over the example of rhetoric prose, but decided to ignore the uncalled-for abuse.

'I do think it would be better if I took you straight to hospital. I mean to say, your case must be rather unique, and I should imagine – Oh, boy – they'll want to keep you in for observation.'

Despite his wife's protesting grunts, he rang for a taxi, then thoughtfully packed an overnight bag, to which he added – with cheerful optimism – a copy of *War and Peace*.

Ethel's predicament caused a great deal of interest at the local hospital. Several doctors took turns in peering down her throat; others felt it with exploring fingers, and one middle-aged surgeon took the apparently sorrowing husband to one side.

'You say she was *suddenly* struck dumb?'

Arthur nodded. 'In mid-sentence.'

The surgeon looked from left to right, then asked in a low but anxious whisper: 'If I got *my* wife to pay your good lady a visit – you don't suppose it might be catching?'

'You're the doctor,' Arthur pointed out.

The surgeon looked very thoughtful indeed, then asked softly: 'Do you wish your wife admitted as a private patient or . . .'

'National Health. Absolutely.'

The surgeon permitted himself a pale smile.

'We have a little industrial trouble. Nothing serious, but the cooking . . .'

Arthur could see in which direction the ball was travelling and quickly returned it to the surgeon's court.

'My wife is a small eater. I leave her in your capable hands.'

They gravely shook hands.

Mr Rowe was particularly offensive the following morning, and the soul of Arthur Collins positively trembled for joy. A reformed, courteous Mr Rowe would have been a great disappointment. The sales manager stalked up to Arthur's desk with the soft-footed approach of a man-eating tiger.

'We haven't seen much of you lately, Mr Collins. Wondered if you had decided to make an early retirement.'

'Sickness,' Arthur replied with calm simplicity.

The sales manager assumed an expression of grave concern.

'Sickness! Nothing serious I hope. Nothing to blunt that knife-sharp brain, and disrupt your well-known efficiency. Because if that happened,' Mr Rowe thumbed through a pile of papers he was carrying, 'you might make another balls-up. And we wouldn't want that, would we?'

'Anything wrong?' Arthur enquired, with breathtaking unconcern.

Mr Rowe smiled bitterly. 'Good heavens no. Of course, this contract for Danby and McCloud – there are one or two little errors – wrong date, wrong price – rather misleading wording – which does rather give the impression that we have to pay them, instead of the other way round. But I wouldn't say there was actually anything wrong. Just the usual muck-up we have come to expect from our senior clerk.'

Arthur inclined his head. 'Thank you.'

'Senior in age – not rank.'

'If,' Arthur said slowly, as though explaining a not very difficult problem to a backward child, 'there was not a loud-mouthed ignoramus constantly shouting down the back of my neck, I would be less inclined to make mistakes. Kindly leave the contract with me and I will correct it in due course.'

One might have supposed that Mr Rowe was a film mogul whose 'yes' man had suddenly said 'no'. His florid face assumed an even deeper shade of red, and his voice rose to a minor shout.

'Saucy, are we? Got a bit above ourselves – what? Well, let me tell you something. Something you won't like. Are you listening? When Mr Carrington-Jones comes back tomorrow, I'm going to have a few words with him. And when I have – we won't see your arse for dust.'

'We will see,' Arthur commented.

Mr Rowe nodded violently. 'Indeed we will. Oh, yes, when I've said what I'm going to say, we'll see all right. Make no mistake about that.'

Arthur grinned in a most irritating fashion and had the cool effrontery to light a cigarette and blow smoke into his superior's face.

During the course of the day he had occasion to see Mr Rowe's eyes watching him from behind the partly open office door. Once he waved and the resulting slam was like a clap of thunder on a clear night.

Spell thirty-one was more than enough to take care of Mr Rowe. Arthur, free now from any wifely interference, read the instructions carefully.

CAUSING PAINE IN YE GUTTS FOR ANY THAT DU SPEAKE
ILLE AGAINST YEW

Take ye likeness of him who is to bee afflicted and boor hol in that that du depict his stumach and fill same with blud from forefinger of left hand. Then burn likeness in fire and chant ye spelle.

[195]

Wen yew speake ille of me,
Belly full of paine bee,
Screem, yell, clutch gutt,
From now on keep mouth shut.

Mr Rowe's likeness was close to hand. A group photograph, taken at the last office Christmas party, had the sales manager standing well to the foreground, with a glass in one hand and a toy trumpet in the other. Arthur derived great satisfaction from driving one of Ethel's knitting needles into the likeness of Mr Rowe's protruding stomach, which more than compensated for the minor discomfort of cutting his forefinger with a dessert knife and filling the small hole with a modicum of blood. He then burned the photograph in the kitchen boiler, while loudly chanting the required spell, and was not in the least alarmed when a blue ball of fire shot up to the ceiling, where it exploded with a loud bang. Instead, he went early to bed and dreamed that Ethel was chasing Mr Rowe with a large knitting-needle.

Arthur sat at his desk and waited for retribution to strike down his second oppressor. Mr Rowe entered his small office at nine-thirty. Mr Carrington-Jones, in keeping with his august status, drifted into his large one at eleven o'clock. Ten minutes later Mr Rowe came out into the main office, gave Arthur one ominous glare, then tapped on the great man's door. A loud grunt was correctly translated as permission to enter and the sales manager went in unto the presence, with a smile on his face and a gleam in his eye. Arthur looked at his wrist-watch and counted fifteen seconds before he received confirmation that spell thirty-one was living up to its promise and a little to spare.

The loud groan became a scream, which in turn rose to an ear-piercing shriek. Mr Rowe's 'paine in ye gutt' must have been one of extreme severity, for not only was the sales manager vocally expressing his agony, but, judging by the accompanying sounds, jumping up and down as well. Presently Mr Carrington-Jones opened the door and called for assistance.

'Will someone . . .' he turned his head as a fresh outburst from the invisible Mr Rowe made it impossible for his voice to be heard. 'For heaven's sake, shut up, man. It can't be as bad as all that.' He again addressed the office staff. 'Will someone fetch a doctor – Mr Rowe appears to be having a nasty turn.'

For a little while Arthur was power drunk. He watched Mr Rowe, his eyes bulging, his mouth gaping, brought forth from the managerial office; saw him laid out on the floor, while Miss Hammond from accounts, who was the proud possessor of a first-aid certificate, applied a cold compress to his forehead, and poured hot, sweet tea down his throat. A doctor never did arrive – no one knew where to find one – but after a while the patient was sufficiently recovered to go home in a taxi. The general consensus of opinion was that Mr Rowe had been drinking cold beer on a hot stomach, a failing to which, apparently, the sales manager was much addicted.

Next morning he was back, none the worse for his mysterious attack, which he explained to an interested audience was the result of wind round the kidneys. But his doctor had given him some blue tablets, which had cleared up the matter in no time, and would without doubt prevent any reoccurrence. To Arthur's great annoyance he was ignored for the entire morning, and was forced to make a face at his immediate superior before he could obtain a resumption of his retributive action. Mr Rowe smiled – a nasty little sadistic smirk – and said: 'Oh, I had almost forgotten,' before hurrying to the font of managerial justice.

Twenty minutes later Arthur had the intense satisfaction of seeing his writhing, screaming oppressor carried away on a stretcher. Mr Rowe was about to join Ethel in the hospital for observation.

The crushing of Mr Carrington-Jones needed much thought.

As managing director and chairman of several large companies, he clearly could not be dismissed with a mere '*paine in ye gutt*' or as for that a '*ye shore waye of quieting a scolding employer*', beneficial as these treatments might be. Arthur pored over *Ye Grate Book of Spelles*, and at last decided the great man was worthy of spell fifty-four.

He had to admit that it was an unsettling spell – from everyone's point of view. Several times he was on the verge of discarding it for something more simple, as for example FOR MAKING UNSEEMLY GROUTHS ON YE FACE, which sounded rather jolly. There again MAKING THE MARSTER PASS CONSTANT AND VIOLENT WIND WEN IN POLITE COMPANEE had much to commend it. But these were but schoolboy japes when compared with the awesome spell fifty-four. The heading was very impressive.

FOR YE RAISING OF BLACK AND MOST MALICSUS DAMON WICH WILL GO IN
UNTO HIM HOO YU HATETH AND WILL TAKE HIS SOLE INTO HELL

The prospect of Mr Carrington-Jones being carried off to hell by a black and malicious demon was most pleasing. Arthur wasted no time in gathering together the list of ingredients which, due possibly to the necessary potency of the spell, was both lengthy and rather messy.

There was little trouble in obtaining *intrals of ye chicen* but *iye-balls of ye catt* presented untold difficulties. Fortunately for Arthur a black tom from down the road came out second best after an encounter with a passing lorry and he was able to secure the corpse before the bereft owner was aware of his loss. *Blud from a goodlie man*, was provided by the vicar, who, when he called to console the parishioner with a speechless wife, was prevailed upon to open a tin of baked beans. *Hair from ye chest of a fresh corpse*, had Arthur gnawing his nails for three days, and would never have been obtained had not old Mr Kempton from Number 24 suddenly decided that this was a convenient time to be gathered to his forefathers. When Arthur was invited to pay his respects, he went armed with a pair of scissors and a paper bag.

The remainder of the ingredients came from stock. Arthur – assisted by a hammer and mallet – ground a thigh-bone to powder, atomized rat-legs with a cheese-grater, minced bats, chopped snakes, then dumped the lot into the iron cauldron, added water, and simmered the evil-smelling stew for three hours on a low gas. Then he sat on the floor, crossed his legs and chanted the incantation.

> *Cum up from helle, oh damon black,*
> *And du my bidding without alack.*
> *Carry him that I du name,*
> *Down to torment and to flame.*
> *Burne his vitals, eat his heart,*
> *And rip his very sole apart.*

The stew seethed, bubbled and finally gave forth a plume of black smoke that drifted across the kitchen and made Arthur cough. Suddenly a strange cold wind sprang up in the vicinity of the sink – came up from the plug-hole, so far as a startled Arthur could ascertain – and went howling across the room. Then there was a loud bang, a flash of light – and something very nasty was standing by the gas-stove.

Black, pulsating, roughly human-shaped, with a horrible little white face that was unpleasantly familiar. The voice that sounded as if it were coming from a far distant and empty hall, had a cackling quality that once heard, could never be forgotten. It said: 'We meet again, ducky.'

Arthur gasped and exclaimed: 'No, it can't be!' but without much conviction, for when he came to think about it, this was the natural conclusion. The voice, not to mention the face, which was twisted up into a mocking grin, soon erased any lingering doubt.

'Oh, yes. Old Tabby is back. Very kind of you to call me up – but I thought you would. Never be able to resist me old Treasure Book.'

It was then that he realized that all the sense of power had gone. He was like a man who has been allowed to purchase a number of goods at bargain price, and must now give his all for the special item. He would have cancelled his contract if that had been at all possible, but the shade of Tabitha Holbrook was waiting.

'What little job would you like me to do, deary? Who's to be done dirt?'

'I don't want to trouble you,' Arthur protested. 'Perhaps it wasn't such a good idea. After all, Mr Carrington-Jones can't help being an old misery . . .'

The voice took on a threatening tone and the white face gleamed like a new tombstone in moonlight.

'Come off it, ducky. Once we're called up, we wants our meat, and if one joint isn't to hand – well, there's usually another one nearby. Get the message? So let's have no more argy-bargy – take me to 'im. NOW.'

'But it's late and the office will be empty . . .'

'But *he* is bound to be there,' the voice insisted. 'The top brass always work overtime. Don't they?'

Mr Carrington-Jones certainly did, and had loudly proclaimed the fact to the staff on numerous occasions. He made a fetish of working late, and had often expressed an ill-founded hope that his employees would follow his example.

The black shape glided forward and Arthur retreated.

'Let's be on our way, deary,' the voice said. 'I rather fancy a nice fat managing director. Set me up with the Black One. Don't worry – no one will see me – except you and 'im – when the time comes.'

Arthur Collins went forth and his demon went with him.

He boarded a bus and the shape became a black ball that nestled down on the seat beside him. On the tube train it was a dark shadow that wrapped itself round homeward-bound passengers, and seemed to grow denser when shoulders twitched and faces looked anxiously from left to right.

When Arthur entered the office building, he was followed by a black shadow-snake that writhed and coiled its long length over the tiled floor and up stone stairs – for the lifts were no longer working – and went undulating along the carpeted corridors. Night cleaners looked up as the little man with the frightened face went by, but not one glanced down and saw the twisting black streak.

The main office was still lit, but deserted. Cover-shrouded typewriters lurked on neat desks; files, ledgers, stacks of papers, all made Arthur think of an abandoned world. The door leading to the managing director's office was a white square of frosted light, on which was inscribed in thick black letters H. CARRINGTON-JONES. A name to be respected, hated, even feared. It looked well on cheques and letter-headings, and when written with a felt-pen made an awesome signature. Now, Arthur Collins, a miserable little middle-aged clerk whom no one respected, hated or feared, was going to destroy the bearer of that distinguished name. Burn the sanity from his mind, tear the soul from his body, and transform a big flesh and blood machine into an atom of quivering consciousness. He would have given much for the gift of free will, but terror stood in front of his desk and pointed a shadow arm towards the lighted door.

'I'm going in now, deary. When you hear 'im shriek, you'll know we're on our way. I hope you've got a strong stomach, for what will be left, won't be pretty. Not pretty at all.'

She – It – glided between desks and approached the lighted door. It shimmered – became thicker – blacker – sprouted long thin arms that appeared to terminate in gleaming knobs – then It merged into and through the door, like a cloud of smoke drawn into a funnel. Arthur waited while long-seconds crept out over a vast sea of time, before erupting into an explosive minute. From beyond the office door there came a scream, a flash of light and a loud bang. Then, for a long while – nothing. Arthur could only sit at his familiar desk and wait for the strength to return to his legs before departing and hiding himself in a darkened room.

But just as he was about to rise, the impossible happened.

From within the office came the sound of a chair being pushed back, and slow footsteps crossing the floor. The door opened and Mr Carrington-Jones came out and looked enquiringly along the row of desks. He smiled when his glance alighted on Arthur; an amused smile that made him look benign – rather like an indulgent father whose small son has contrived an unsuccessful booby-trap. He walked between the avenue of desks and seated himself opposite his senior clerk.

'There you are, Collins. Thought you must be nearby. How are you?'

Arthur said: 'Fine, thank you, sir,' before he realized what he was saying.

Mr Carrington-Jones sighed. 'I wish I could say the same. Frankly, getting shot of a top-grade, soul-snatching enmity, takes it out of me these days. Never thought you would bring one of those up, Collins. Of course I knew you had stumbled across some sort of power, when your wife was struck dumb and poor old Rowe had those awful pains in his tummy. But raising a Black – I do congratulate you.'

Arthur's mind was clouded by the mists of confusion, but he still retained a spark of understanding.

'You mean, sir – that you can . . . ?

Mr Carrington-Jones chuckled. 'I've been a master of the seventh circle for years. How do you suppose I've got where I am? Hard work and long hours? All my opposition is either in the hot place or stark, raving mad.'

Arthur did not comment on this statement. There did not seem much point. Mr Carrington-Jones sighed again.

'Pity about you. But still, it can't be helped. You've guessed what happens next, I suppose?'

Arthur shook his head, although he had a faint suspicion.

'Well, it's like this. You called up a soul-snatching Black and promised it a nice juicy tit-bit. Me. I turned out to be a member of the top management – if I might so describe myself – and knocked it for six with a defensive spell. Now – it can't go back empty handed. See what I mean?'

Arthur did, but was not at all keen to say so. Mr Carrington-Jones frowned and tapped his fingers impatiently on the desk.

'Oh, come now. Do I have to *spell* it out? If Blackie can't have the meat, it must eat the butcher. I would say you've got about twenty-four hours.'

Arthur's face turned white, then assumed a shade of pale-green. Mr Carrington-Jones rose and looked down upon his unfortunate employee with cold, stern eyes.

'Of course, I cannot continue to employ a man who keeps such low company. You will receive one month's pay in lieu of notice, plus whatever sums of money to which you are entitled. Kindly vacate the premises at once.'

Arthur – once again the underdog – crept out of the office, with his allegorical tail between his trembling legs, and ran through long corridors that smelled of detergent and disinfectant. Once out into the street, every shadow was a menace and every face a mocking mask.

The Treasure Book of Spelles contained not one word of comfort or the smallest shred of hope. Arthur could find no spell for putting down a black demon. But he did his poor best.

He drew a chalk circle on the dining-room floor; stole holy water from the Roman Catholic church; purchased crucifixes and Bibles by the dozen and added a score of prayer books for good measure.

The holy books made a wall round his circle, and he placed the crucifixes and cups of holy water on top, then knelt in his little fortress and tried to pray. But his thoughts kept straying to the room that lay beyond the frail wall, and his fear-sharp eyes darted from wall to wall, to rolled-up carpet, to chairs, table, curtained window, closed door – waiting for black terror to take on shape and assail his untested ramparts – blow upon his paper castle. But the room remained as snug and as innocent as a church hall at Christmas time.

Then – just as he was beginning to relax, to unclench his teeth, to breathe a little deeper – there came from behind him a tiny, cackling giggle. He could not move, let alone look around, and there was really no need – he knew who was there. The giggle died and a harsh, terrible voice whispered in his left ear.

'How cosy, deary. Just the two of us – inside.'

THE EXECUTOR

David G. Rowlands

David G. Rowlands (b. 1941), a biochemist by
profession, has had many excellent horror and
ghost stories published over the past twenty
years, and is a regular contributor to Haunted
Library publications and the *Holly Bough*,
a Christmas magazine published by the
Cork Examiner.
Father O'Connor, a Catholic priest with a keen
interest in the supernatural, is featured in many
of his best stories including the one reprinted
here (from *Ghosts & Scholars* 4, 1982).

Fr O'Connor made it a regular custom to invite other clergy to dinner from time to time, a pleasant little ecumenical exercise resisted only by a somewhat dour Presbyterian. On such occasions the table talk might centre on 'shop', local gossip, antiquities or anecdotes.

One particular evening, the Baptist and Anglican ministers only were present – a Mr Cummings and a Revd Timothy, respectively. A remark from the Revd Timothy about the grievous matter of one of his church bells needing to be recast had launched Fr O'Connor into anecdotes of early itinerant bellfounders. Beginning with Robert Catlin who had cast the local tenor bell in the churchyard, he came by devious routes to a sixteenth-century monk of St Milburg's – the Cluniac Abbey at Much Wenlock in Shropshire – one William of Corvehill: noted for many mechanical and artistic talents, but especially for bell casting and bell hanging . . . but – by your leave – I will keep that for another occasion.

Mention of Wenlock sufficed to enthuse the Revd Timothy, who was a keen student of architecture, and we had a long exposition of the beauties of the Guildhall in that quiet little Shropshire town. His panegyric on the panelling was interrupted by Mr Cummings, who inquired whether the wheeled stocks were still there.

'I believe so, my dear fellow,' replied the Anglican, 'but why do you mention them? There is a much better set in the Cardiff Folk Museum, you know.'

Mr Cummings laughed. 'No reason, really. It just reminded me that my great aunt Lucy was threatened once by the vicar of Wenlock (or is it rector? I forget) with being put in the stocks and wheeled through the town and surrounding villages.'

'She must have been a character,' I commented.

'Yes,' he said musingly. 'She was widely believed to be a Wise Woman or witch; certainly people came from miles around for her cures.' He laughed. 'It's a pity I haven't inherited her talents, maybe,' (the Baptist congregation being very small in our village). He grew suddenly serious: 'Though I'm glad I haven't.'

Fr O'Connor caught my eye and winked so that Mr Cummings could see.

'Ha,' he said. 'That sounds like the basis of a good story, Cummings. What about it?'

Mr Cummings thought for a moment. 'I don't see why not,' he said. 'It reflects badly on my relatives, but as they're all dead and buried long ago, I don't suppose any harm can come of telling the story now.'

'Well then, gentlemen, I propose we adjourn to the study, where we can talk in comfort over a pipe or two,' said the good Father, rising to say Grace.

When we were all comfortably ensconced, Mr Cummings began his story. 'My grandfather was the son of a Shropshire yeoman farmer,' he began. 'He blotted his copybook by marrying a Romany girl (of all people!) and his father threw him out in consequence. The couple went to Hereford, where my father was born, and they both worked in the cattle market. However, the girl tired of the restricted life, upped and went off with a drover, leaving him to raise my father alone. He moved to Gloucester as stockman for an auctioneer and lost touch with his family, apart from his sister, this eccentric old dame who lived on Wenlock Edge. (The family farm went to my grandfather's younger brother.) My father entered the auctioneer's as a trainee clerk, married the boss's daughter and ultimately managed the business for her family. All this is by the way however. What concerns my story is that at the age of ten, or thereabouts, I succumbed badly to bronchitis and the doctor recommended a holiday away from the lower reaches of Gloucester. My poor dad was at his wit's end what to do about it, since he was too proud to ask help from my mother's family, despite her urgings. Then he remembered his old aunt. Somehow, it was settled that I should go and stay there for six weeks or so.

'Longbury, where she lived, was a tiny community on the Wenlock Edge, immortalized by Housman's verses. Even such a communal backwater was a microcosm of a divided Christendom, however, for there were Anglicans (of high leaning), Methodists, Congregationalists, Baptists, Roman Catholics and even a few Friends of austere persuasion, who met over the village shop.

'My great aunt's residence, Rose Cottage, was a rambling place that had belonged to her husband's parents, who used to run the village school; and it was situated at the end of a little lane that led off the main street through the village. A single-storey wing had been added about a hundred years earlier and this was fitted out and used as the Baptist chapel. There was some mystique surrounding my great uncle, who had been custodian of the chapel and lay preacher as well, and I was told he had gone abroad in the "Lord's Service". It was only later that I learned he had actually disappeared – at the same time as, and presumably in the company of, a buxom young farm girl who had attended the chapel and in whose spiritual welfare he had shown great interest. Needless to say it had been the scandal of the district for years, though I daresay any eloping couple need have gone no further than had my grandfather to escape local opinion. So far as Shropshire villagers of that period were concerned Hereford and the North Pole were equidistant!

'My aunt had assumed the caretaker's role and a minister used to bicycle over from Stokesay, there being no Sunday train service.

'From the start of my visit I was afraid of the old lady, though she was kind enough to me in a gruff sort of way. She must have been in her sixties then, I suppose, dressed always in black material that had gone greenish with age, and which had been polished to a sheen from long use. She had rounded, vaguely benevolent features, belied both by a sharp pair of hazel eyes and a curiously sibilant voice that instilled respect far more than any stridency could have achieved. Her greeting was typical.

'"Well, Harold," she said, peering at me from top to toe, "I don't suppose you want to be here any more than I want you, but I suppose we must make the best of it; blood is blood, after all. Mind your manners and keep out of my way, and we shall get along, I daresay."

'How well I remember that cottage! There were two downstairs rooms. The one termed the scullery was dining and kitchen combined, dominated by a huge kitchen range which I had to blacklead every day as one of my tasks, and with red enamelled doors that had to be polished until I could see my face in them. The other downstairs room was next to the chapel, sharing a wall (though there was no door connection); cool and dark with chintzy furniture and pervaded by that unmistakable smell of the long-unlit coal fire. Occasionally if I entered on a Sunday, I could hear the chapel piano through the wall – played with more vigour than skill – and the discordant mumble of singing. There was a little alcove, curtained off, with scrubbed table, pair of scales, huge stoneware pestle and mortar and other impedimenta of the herbalist. The old lady was much in demand locally as a healer or Wise Woman and was clearly a thorn in the flesh of the local doctor. Indeed, she had a daily stream of visitors – some furtive, some defiant, some afraid, a few resigned; but all clearly in awe of the old curmudgeon. Since she was both astute and imperious, I imagine she must have accumulated more knowledge about local people and their affairs than was good for them.

The path outside divided in two – one main sweep going from the front door (there was no back!) to the gate into the lane; the other went past the new wing, crossing the chapel path (worshippers came in by a different gate) and on to a long dark shed, called the Wash House, with sagging rainwater barrel outside and mangles, stones, flatirons and sinks inside. A substantial hook and pulley system ran on a rusty wire the length of the shed, for easy handling of laundry baskets.

'My aunt lived alone since her husband's defection, and a daily woman came in: a Mrs Bardette, who was as taciturn as my aunt and a hard task-mistress. The reading matter available was unquestionably moral and wholesome for a young lad (Mary Webb herself could have grown up with my aunt), but the rewards of the excessively virtuous have never appealed to me as a theme. Missing the company of my Gloucester street chums, as I rubbed the graphite paste on to the range one day, I ventured to ask Mrs Bardette who there was of my age for me to play with.

'She gave a short bark of a laugh. "Playmates?" she cried. "You won't get local lads coming here, my boy, and that's a fact." When I asked the obvious, she retorted, "Because Mistress won't have them, that's why. She'd take her stick to them ... or something," (this last being something of an afterthought). She looked sideways at me, a slightly malicious nuance coming into her voice. "Not to say you mightn't get company sometimes; this was once a school you know," and she cackled to herself as she deposited the washing she was doing on to the big rubbing board and ladled more hot water from the iron pot on the range into the sink. She jumped rather guiltily as my aunt spoke from the doorway; neither of us knew how long she had been standing there.

'"Mrs Bardette, why are you washing in here? The Wash House is the place for that as you know very well. There's the copper ready for lighting and plenty of firewood."

'Mrs Bardette shook the suds of Sunlight soap from her arms before folding them akimbo.

'"You know why," she almost shouted. At this juncture my aunt seemed to notice my ears flapping and sent me off to the shop on a pretext. She watched me go, and since the scullery window overlooked the entire path, I could not creep back to overhear more. As I left she was hissing, "Now, Mrs Bardette, you know perfectly well . . ." and I heard the louder voice reply, "Oh yes, I *know* all right . . ."

'Now, whatever Mrs B might feel about the Wash House, I soon discovered what she had meant about the school and company (I only mention this, gentlemen, to give some idea of the atmosphere of the place; so far as I know it has absolutely nothing to do with the rest of the story). There was a wide staircase leading up to the bedroom and a bend in the stairs where a window looked across the slopes to Long Mynd. One afternoon, while all was quiet in the house I was running upstairs to my room, and I paused to look out of this window. To my amazement, children's voices – like the far-off clamour of a school playground – were all around me in the air, confused and incoherent, coming from nowhere. I shook my head, but the sound continued, without rhyme or reason. Then it ceased as suddenly as it had begun. I was strangely frightened and ran back downstairs and into the garden where my aunt was gathering herbs. She was muttering to herself as usual, a wooden lath basket over her arm. It was a measure of my fright that I poured it all out to her. She rose to her feet and put out a hand as if to touch me, then withdrew it.

'"Ah," she said. "You have the gift of hearing . . . Don't worry, it runs in the family. Sometimes you hear things; sometimes you don't; sometimes you *see* things . . .", and here she put her hand on my shoulder. I felt a strange sensation, that odd sweetness when a voice or timbre fascinates one; it vanished as she removed her hand . . .

[207]

"Sometimes you don't. It's nothing to worry about. You'll hear – yes, and see too – more than that in your life, Harold."

'Not a word more did I get from her on the subject; though I was conscious of her speculative glance on occasion and certainly her manner was less severe from that moment on.

'There was nothing to be got from Mrs Bardette either. "Pooh; that's nothing," she scoffed with a toss of her head to the window – which I took to indicate the Wash House.

'With the temerity of youth, and the curiosity of a kitten, I hung about the shed in the daytime. (I was not allowed out after 6 p.m. at night.) It was a gloomy, dank place frequented by the occasional frog and lit only by a much-dirtied skylight. It could be brilliant sunshine outside, but the minute I entered (there was no door), darkness closed in on me and had the physical effect of making me breathless. Overall hung an indescribable mustiness. I could see the old wrought-iron mangles, and the two coppers for heating water. In the dimness my eyes could just discern a brace of heavy flatirons on the stove top, and between the intangible outlines of the coppers gleamed the dull white of a sink. Close by this, further into the shadows, hung an inverted face. It was so grotesquely unrecognizable that I stared at it for several moments without realizing what it was. It was bloated and puffy and it began to drip water from the dangling hair to the floor. I had unconsciously advanced into the shed and I turned to run, only to be confronted by another, between me and the doorway. The hair from its sodden features trailed on to the floor. I shut my eyes and hurled myself at where I judged the opening to be, and so ran out into the sunlight, straight into the apron of Mrs B who was on the chapel path.

'"Hmm, I know where you've been," said she, dryly, and frog-marched me off to the chapel, where I sat on one of the chairs, trembling now, while she collected up the coconut mats. We hung them over the privet hedge and I helped her to beat them with the spider. She made no further allusion to the cause of my fright, except to growl "I'd keep out of there, my lad – and, whatever you do, say nothing to the mistress"; but she kept me beside her, and we went indoors and had a cup of tea together.

That was the eve of my departure, and nothing else untoward happened. I had expected fearsome dreams but in fact passed a quiet night. In the morning, my aunt walked with me to the station – getting much salutation from local people – and put me on the train home. To my utter amazement, she kissed my cheek and pressed half a crown into my hand. I was moved to wave from the carriage, but she had gone, and the interest of the journey dispelled all other thoughts.

'Doubtless you have already anticipated the outcome of my little experience, gentlemen?' remarked Mr Cummings, stirring in his chair and lighting a vile little cheroot that smelled like burning compost. (I had visions of poor Mrs Bailey trying to get the smell out of the curtains.) He waved the thing about like a joss-stick, describing smoky trails in the air, and at our lack of response, settled down again and continued.

'I heard nothing of my aunt for years, save that thereafter she sent me a pound on each successive birthday. My father's long illness intervened, and he died. She did not attend the funeral, nor did any others from the family in Shropshire; though I wrote to them all.

'I was at theological college when I got a letter forwarded from home. It was written in large, badly formed letters, and was from a second cousin I had never met, telling me of the old lady's sudden death. Due to the delay in forwarding, the funeral was imminent and it seemed that she had named me to the family lawyer, and they were inviting me to attend and – later – to execute the will. I got compassionate leave and caught a train within a couple of hours.

'The vagaries of railway timetables meant that I had to break my journey at Hereford. I could not resist revisiting the magnificent cathedral. Then, after a bun and an unpleasantly warm glass of milk in a teashop, I caught the Shrewsbury train and headed for Craven Arms.

'There I crossed to the platform for the Wellington branch, where a diminutive tank engine – running backwards – and two coaches were hopefully awaiting passengers. At 5 p.m. by the station clock we puffed out. Nostalgia awoke in me, for it had been this same train I had caught as a child of ten, a large and embarrassing label with my name and destination affixed to my best (and only) coat. The guard of the Shrewsbury train had handed me over to his counterpart of the branch line to ensure my alighting at Longbury. This time I would have to fend for myself! Even the engine was the same, for I remembered the number well – 4401. Surely the carriage too? Had I not seen the sepia picture of Dawlish sea wall before? (But then it is in so many carriages!)

'The little train left the main line at Marsh Farm Junction and headed out across Wenlock Edge, that lovely country of Housman's verses. (I will refrain from comment on Mary Webb, that other Salopian writer of note – since I know her bilge is popular with Mr Timothy!) The sun was behind Long Mynd and one could not have guessed from the wild beauty of the scene that a little further along this rural railway lay Shropshire's "black country" – the iron foundries of Coalbrookdale and Horsehay & Dawley (what a deceptively lovely name!), dating back to 1709 and the Dudley family; though I believe charcoal forges had heated iron in those hills since Tudor times.

'I was the only passenger to alight in the soft warm air at Longbury. The porter took my ticket, and replied to my compliment on the well-kept flower beds on the platform. "A welcome to you, Mr Cunningham," he said, with a rather odd look at me, and signalled to a waiting car outside before marching off to the little cabin at the end of the platform to receive the tablet back from the engine driver. Clearly my coming was known in the village.

'As I stepped forward to meet my cousin I could hear the explosive staccato bark of the train pulling away from the station and off towards Much Wenlock.

'My cousin Sefton was a likable enough chap, who was obviously intending me to stay at his farm. However, in course of conversation on details of the morrow's funeral, it transpired that my great aunt's body was lying alone at her cottage. "Harry Jones, the undertaker, wouldn't take her to his parlour of course," was the bald statement in Sefton's Shropshire accents. When I asked the reason, and why "of course", I was met with a shrug of the shoulders. In my stubborn way, I therefore determined to spend the night at the cottage, if only for the remembrance of her kiss, half-crown and annual pound! Seeing I meant what I said, Sefton made no argument – though he was clearly surprised – gave me the key and said there would doubtless be provisions in the larder. He gave me his telephone number "in case" (there were phones at the pub, village store and vicarage). As he dropped me with my suitcase at the gate to the cottage, I said brightly, "Well, if I'm lonely, I'll drop into the pub."

'"Mebbee you'd better not," he said with an odd look. "In any case, you won't lack for company." And with that he drove off.

'I walked up the well-remembered path through the tidy garden, full of the scent of thyme and other herbs, and with roses and honeysuckle over the porch and walls, opened the door and put on the light. Great Aunt Lucy was lying in her open coffin in the old parlour. Even the tang of medication could not mask the all-pervading smell of unlit fire. What memories that smell evoked! I looked at my aunt's waxen features. She was smaller than I remembered and her face had got thinner and more lined. As I bent and kissed her cold forehead, I became conscious of a murmur of voices from beyond the chapel wall. There must be a

Covenanters' meeting or something in progress – though six o'clock of an evening was an odd time to have it. I put my ear to the wall. The murmur resolved into the voices of a man and woman, but I could catch nothing of what they had said. I went outside to look at the chapel wing, but it was immediately obvious in the gloaming that there were no lights within. Indeed, the door was locked. How peculiar! However, remembering my childhood terror on the stairs, I just had to accept that this was a house of inexplicable sounds. This put me in mind of my other fright and I looked apprehensively toward the louring bulk of the Wash House, thought better of it and went back into the cottage. The muffled voices had, I thought, sunk to whispers, but might have ceased altogether. I gave it up and went into the scullery to forage.

'My accomplishments of yesteryear returned, and I soon had a fire going in the range and a kettle on the hob before the open enamel door. I managed very well with some eggs that proved to be quite fresh and some slices of cured ham. There was a big valve radio and I switched it on to have some noise about me: the place was deathly quiet, which I found uncanny – there were not even the usual mice or cockroaches of the country cottage. Maybe my aunt's herbal knowledge had kept them at bay. Thinking of this, I returned to the front room where she lay, and looked into the curtained alcove. Her equipment was still there. I swung the pans of the scale idly and my eye caught a protruding knothole in the wall panelling. It came out easily into my hand leaving a small black hole. Selecting a dried grass stem from a small bundle on the table top, I poked it into the hole – it went through. So, the old lady had a peephole into the chapel from her seat at the table. I leaned forward to apply my eye to the hole, but of course all was dark within; though, I must say, I felt there was a cautious shifting movement beyond me in the murk. After all, it was now quite dark outside. However, in leaning forward I had put all my weight on the edge of the table, which must have loosed some spring or catch, for an unsuspected drawer appeared – stealthily as it were – without a sound from underneath. It gave me quite a start. The drawer was large and shallow, cleverly concealed to fit flush to the side of the table and remain undetected. In it were several books of the ledger type. Pushing the drawer back I took them to read beside the scullery range, for the room was becoming decidedly chilly. At any rate they might make better reading than *Virtue's Reward* or *Little Jeremy's Prayers*, offered by the bookcase.

'As I crossed to the door I got a severe shock and dropped the books. Aunt Lucy's head had turned in the coffin and had tensed or contracted

[211]

into a distinctly malevolent leer, as if she were sharing a secret – and that none too pleasant a one – with me. Startled, but reassuring myself, from my ignorance, that such muscular contractions might be quite normal in corpses, I bent and put my ear to her chest (I must admit to a fear that her arms would rise from her sides and clasp me!), but there was no heartbeat of course. I took a small glass dish from the herb table and held its cold surface to her lips and nostrils, but there was no dimming at all: that was enough for me . . . I left the range fire to die out, put out the lights and radio, and scuttled off down the drive to the pub. I had fully intended to visit the Wash House with an electric torch to dispel my childish dread of its gloomy shadows, but now – admitting my unreasoning cowardice to myself – I no longer had any such notion.

'Clearly both publican and villagers knew who I was. They weren't hostile – simply wary and offhand. There was no room to let, it seemed. (I almost expected the landlord to add "Leastways not to *you*".) A fine situation: either I could go back to the cottage, or phone Sefton and admit that I couldn't stay with one dead old lady for whom I had previously and arrogantly asserted pity and dutiful affection. Clearly I should get nowhere asking any villager for a bed . . .

'So I went back to the cottage, poked and fuelled the fire back to life and put the radio on loud for company. Jeff and Luke, and the other "Riders of the Range", investigating a ghost town in the West did not help my mood much, what with the creaking doors and mysterious footsteps: I found some music instead. Then I settled myself in the chimney corner, back to the two walls, to browse through the books. All were painstakingly compiled in longhand, making use of extensive but simple abbreviations. Although not copperplate, the hand was bold and clear and the first tome proved to be the old girl's herbal, clearly a valuable compilation. (I subsequently presented it to the library at Kew.) Aunt Lucy had obviously been an amateur botanist of very practical bent: there were notes of where plants could be found in the locality, sketches of their anatomy and counsel on how to propagate them. There was an extensive cross-indexing of entries and a long list of ailments and cures, some of the latter distinctly odd. The second book was heavier and thicker, and had an alphabetical thumb-index. It was rather like a doctor's case book, for under family names it contained details of treatments and transactions she had carried out. To my surprise and dismay however, on closer reading it also contained a great deal of intimate, scandalous and often sordid detail about persons in the parish. Clearly her view had been "knowledge is power" and there could be no doubt she had shamelessly and callously exploited the confidences (willing or unwilling) of her clients. Thus I could read of Maisie Bassett's indiscretions, unwanted pregnancy and the conclusion of that little affair, and the subsequent use my aunt had made of her knowledge; or the "threats" of local doctor and clergy – to whom one hapless victim had obviously confessed; and so on. I'm ashamed to say that the horrible fascination of the pathetic (and very human) errors catalogued in detail kept me reading. By the time I'd read for several hours, I was feeling extremely tired. In a fit of disgust I threw the book on to the range fire and poked and stoked at it, until the ghastly catalogue of human frailties was consumed.

'To be quite frank, I did not fancy going upstairs, and arranged chairs before the fire so that I could stretch out; made some more milkless tea and settled down with the final volume.

'This appeared to be an attempt at a narrative or journal based on her daily round, but the writing – which started out legible and clear – became much less so, showing clear signs of hasty setting down and lack of care, in contrast to the other books. It deteriorated so that letters were often unformed or words missed out – so fast, I judged, had the writer's thoughts flowed ahead of the pen. With the heat from the range and the sighing of the fire within (the radio broadcasts having ceased), I drowsed over the lines of barbed-wire script, which blurred my eyes as if water had poured across the page.

'I found myself rethinking some details of my visit of ten years earlier. I had slept in the little front room upstairs where the ceiling sloped down to a tiny window that overlooked the pathways and village lane. In my mind's eye, I could see that fresh, whitewashed room with rush mats on the floor and rough but comfortable bedding scented with dried lavender heads. There was a biblical picture, "The Light of the World", over the bed. I knew I had suddenly woken, for the harvest moon shone direct on my face through the open window. I heard a sound outside and climbed up, with some difficulty for my legs were short, into the tiny window recess up in the wall, to look out. The gardens and paths were bathed in ethereal brilliance and there was a slight ground mist. To my surprise, two figures were standing by the chapel, locked in each other's arms. A stealthy sound came from the house below me and someone – it could only be my aunt – came out of the front room and into the garden. She came from under the porch into my range of vision, down the chapel path to the herb garden, and towards the couple, making shooing gestures with her hands. They had turned to face her, the man's arm

[213]

protectingly round the woman. Then I must have blinked or something, for all of an instant they were gone, and my aunt was pacing sedately back to the house. As luck would have it, she looked up and saw me leaning from the window, and that strange grimace I had seen earlier crossed her face. I shot back into bed, overturning the chair with a clatter, and lay quiet, frozen with fear between the sheets. I heard her come upstairs and pause on the landing outside my door, with creaking of floorboards. "Please don't let her come in," my child's mind was praying. Came a further creaking of the boards and a low laugh . . . and I awoke, with that laugh still held in my ears, to find myself back in the present, a grown man, but upstairs in the dark, crouched on the small bed and clutching a handful of counterpane!

'As a grown man, I could stand on the chair (which I righted!) and look out of the window without getting on to the ledge. It was nearly morning. The moon had waned and there was nothing to be seen. It was, indeed, that 'darkest hour'. I pulled myself together, put on the landing light and went downstairs, nerving myself to enter the front room. There lay Aunt Lucy in her coffin, head turned to face the ceiling. The *risus sardonicus*, or whatever it might be, had gone and her features were composed.

'There was plenty of life in the range fire, and I drew it up to boil water for tea and to fry some eggs. I picked up the books where they had fallen to the floor and put them on the table. After eating I washed myself at the sink and went up the lane for a walk, to see the welcome dawn break over the hills and to enjoy the birds' chorus.

'I was listening to the nine o'clock news on the radio when the undertaker's men arrived to close the coffin. Not long after, Sefton and some others of the family arrived, and after introductions we preceded the pall bearers into the chapel, where the itinerant preacher was removing his bicycle clips. After a brief service and tribute to Aunt Lucy's long years of caretaker duty, we marched ahead of the hearse up the village street to the new burial ground beyond the churchyard. Few if any of the villagers were about and none had attended the service. Yet curtains twitched and a few heads were looking over the churchyard wall . . . no doubt wondering if their secrets had gone to the grave with her.

'As we walked away leaving her in the ground, a formally dressed young man touched my arm and introduced himself as my aunt's lawyer. He gave me an ordinary manila envelope addressed in her writing. I undertook to contact him about the will in due course, and he got into his 14 h.p. Austin and drove off.

'I declined Sefton's invitation and returned to the cottage as I wanted to catch the afternoon train back to Craven Arms and college, if possible. Outside the pub, the landlord was shiftily watering his potted geraniums in the window boxes. He turned reluctantly as I spoke: "I found some notes of my aunt's concerning the business of folk in the village." He swallowed hard and eyed my tie-knot. "You may like to tell them that I have burned the lot and that their privacy is respected." He mumbled something, then – spontaneously – shook my hand and turned away as if in embarrassment. I guessed that at any rate, he and Maisie Bassett would sleep the easier now.

'My aunt's letter was brief and to the point, enclosing a copy of her will. "You have my gift of sight," she wrote. "Do what you will with it. Meantime you will find in my herb table" (here she gave directions for opening the drawer I had already discovered) "some books – use them as you see fit. If you should care to succeed me as a healer you will find that the villagers will support you because of the great knowledge in these books. My journal will explain that which mystified you as a child and I leave you to do what you think necessary." In essence, the will itself left the cottage and effects to me if I chose to occupy them, or – if sold – to divide the proceeds between Sefton and myself.

'Clearly, then, the journal that I had mistaken for an embryo novel was the one I wanted, so I settled down to read it there and then. As I did so, my hair began to rise.

'By this account, my uncle's ministry had not been confined to the spiritual plane where the females of his congregation were concerned. Certainly the decisive involvement with that farm lass – a distant relative – had deteriorated from spiritual to physical in remarkably short time, and the undue amount of spiritual guidance given to her alone in the chapel would have aroused suspicion in far less astute a person than Aunt Lucy, who had clearly put her peephole to good use. Her writing grew less and less legible as she vengefully recorded some of their inane utterances and the more sacrilegious aspects of their behaviour in the apparent security and privacy of the chapel. She bode her time and thus became aware of the girl's pregnancy as soon as her husband. Rage almost obliterated her meaning when she wrote of their plans to run away together, and I had a hard time deciphering the scrawl.

'Once they had arranged a rendezvous at the chapel gate for a certain evening, she acted with speed and decision. Suffice it to say that along with an appetite for the females of his flock, my uncle liked Welsh cakes, those unleavened sweet buns baked in the oven from flour and water. My

aunt simply substituted flour made from the roots of the hawthorn*
which contain a virulent poison that baking would reduce in toxicity to
a general paralytic agent.

'Inert as he was, paralysed, but horribly conscious, she had dragged
her offending spouse on a carpet out to the Wash House, humped him
upright, then – with the aid of the laundry basket hook and line –
upended him, head first, into the water butt. There she left him to
drown, upside down, while she returned the carpet to the cottage and
swept it clean.

'I was so horrified at this confession, that I could hardly continue
reading.

'However, the agitated, eccentric handwriting continued relentlessly
to relate how, later that night, the girl had arrived at the chapel gate to
rendezvous with my uncle. Aunt Lucy had put a thick sack over her head
and dragged her into the Wash House, where a hurricane lamp was lit.
The first thing the terrified girl saw when the sack was removed was the
flaccid body of her dead lover hanging upside down out of the big sink
– his inverted face toward her, eyes staring blankly and hair dripping on
to the floor. She had shrieked and fallen in a fit, which made it easy for
auntie to hoist her similarly into the butt – head first again, to prevent
any chance of her getting out even if she revived. And then went off to
make a cup of tea, gathering up the girl's bag of belongings en route. An
hour or so later she hoisted the sodden bundle of dead girl out with the
basket hook and reunited the lovers in the sink. It seemed incredible to
me, but she left them there all next day during which she instituted a
search for her missing husband and played the worried wife. Simultaneously the police were looking for the missing girl, and they soon
concluded – in the light of local opinion – that the two had run away
together. A report of a couple seen boarding an early train to Hereford
at Craven Arms seemed to confirm the theory. That night my aunt dug
up a portion of her herb garden and buried them both, bags and all,
beneath the thyme. When the local policeman came with tidings of the
Craven Arms couple she was placidly hoeing the topsoil around the
thyme plants – which (she said) were doing rather badly that year.'

Mr Cummings paused. We all sat in silence, surprised at the sudden
blunt turn of his narrative. With a heavy sigh, he continued.

* For obvious reasons this identity is incorrect. However, there are well-documented
  cases where multiple hawthorn scratches (hedging etc) have produced nausea and
  vertigo.

'I sat down for a long time, thinking over this chronicle of events which – if true – would scandalize Wenlock for years. On the other hand, the protagonists were all dead, with no direct links remaining. What possible benefit to anyone to stir up a mess of this nature, now? My prospect of catching the afternoon train vanished, for I needed a talk with Sefton: his commonsense would be a lifeline to my somewhat disordered wits.

'In the event, we left things as they were and burned the journal. Clearly, if the ground contained remains that could eventually be uncovered, then it was best kept in the family. Sefton turfed over the herb garden, and we let the cottage to his brother-in-law, and then to a cousin. Neither stayed, both moving out soon after arrival, claiming the place was haunted and that they could not stay. Since then we have not even been able to get a local jobber to tend the gardens – word has spread, you see – and they have run wild. The cottage is fast going to ruin, though of course the chapel has remained in use and they keep their path clear. There you have it, gentlemen: the story, of the skeletons that literally lurk in our family garden, if not cupboard.

As Mr Cummings concluded his narrative, Fr O'Connor became fidgety and flushed. Now he looked decidedly uncomfortable and exchanged glances with the Revd Timothy.

'It is embarrassing to say this, Mr Cummings, and please don't misunderstand me; I'm not quarrelling with your handling of this matter except in one respect. If they were indeed murdered, then I think you have wronged that couple by doing nothing.' (Revd Timothy made noises of assent.)

Mr Cummings looked surprised. 'You think we should exhume them, Father?'

'My dear chap, whatever we do, we must at least ensure their rest. See here now, this is no time for sectarian differences. Obviously I don't expect you to share my very real belief in purgatory, but if there is a haunting, and I suppose there must be – from your experiences and from those who won't stay there – then it's due to one of two things surely? Either a 'place memory': an emotional crisis recorded at that spot by the couple or your aunt; or else a genuine haunting and their spirits cannot rest. The usual reason I have found for the latter is lack of proper burial and absolution.'

The old priest leaned forward and patted Mr Cummings' hand. 'We will go to Longbury, you and I, and when it is dark, we will read the burial service over the ground, after praying for absolution of their sins, eh? If their poor bodies are not there; well, there's no harm done. If they are buried there, then it may be that we can help them to gain the rest they are seeking.'

Mr Cummings rose and held out his hand. 'Thank you, Father O'Connor. I believe you are right and I should value your company and your help in righting my neglect.'

They duly went, and I can only report what Cummings said subsequently. The cottage has been refurbished and occupied without incident. The Wash House has been demolished and his nephew and family are happily installed.

GAVON'S EVE

E. F. Benson

Edward Frederic Benson (1867–1940) is now
remembered not only for his many excellent
ghost stories, but also for the immortal 'Mapp
and Lucia' novels. The witchcraft motif is
featured in some of his more dramatic novels,
and he was undoubtedly fascinated by the
theme. In 1895 he published a scholarly essay
on the notorious 'Clonmel Witch Burning', now
widely regarded to be the last burning of a witch
in the history of Western Europe. This classic
tale of Scottish witchcraft first appeared in the
Illustrated London News, 13 January 1906.

I t is only the largest kind of ordnance map that records the existence
of the village of Gavon, in the shire of Sutherland, and it is perhaps
surprising that any map on whatever scale should mark so small and
huddled a group of huts, set on a bare, bleak headland between moor and
sea, and, so one would have thought, of no import at all to any who did
not happen to live there. But the river Gavon, on the right bank of which
stand this half-dozen of chimneyless and wind-swept habitations, is a
geographical fact of far greater interest to outsiders, for the salmon there
are heavy fish, the mouth of the river is clear of nets, and all the way up
to Gavon Loch, some six miles inland, the coffee-coloured water lies in
pool after deep pool, which verge, if the river is in order and the angler
moderately sanguine, on a fishing probability amounting almost to a
certainty. In any case during the first fortnight of September last I had no
blank day on those delectable waters, and up till the fifteenth of that

month there was no day on which some one at the lodge in which I was stopping did not land a fish out of the famous Picts' pool. But after the fifteenth that pool was not fished again. The reason why is here set forward.

The river at this point, after some hundred yards of rapid, makes a sudden turn round a rocky angle, and plunges madly into the pool itself. Very deep water lies at the head of it, but deeper still further down the east side, where a portion of the stream flicks back again in a swift dark backwater towards the top of the pool again. It is fishable only from the western bank, for to the east, above this backwater, a great wall of black and basaltic rock, heaved up no doubt by some fault in strata, rises sheer from the river to the height of some sixty feet. It is in fact nearly precipitous on both sides, heavily serrated at the top, and of so curious a thinness, that at about the middle of it where a fissure breaks its topmost edge, and some twenty feet from the top, there exists a long hole, a sort of lancet window, one would say, right through the rock, so that a slit of daylight can be seen through it. Since, therefore, no one would care to cast his line standing perched on that razor-edged eminence, the pool must needs be fished from the western bank. A decent fly, however, will cover it all.

It is on the western bank that there stand the remains of that which gave its title to the pool, namely the ruins of a Pict castle, built out of rough and scarcely hewn masonry, unmortared but on a certain large and impressive scale, and in a very well-preserved condition considering its extreme antiquity. It is circular in shape and measures some twenty yards of diameter in its internal span. A staircase of large blocks with a rise of at least a foot leads up to the main gate, and opposite this on the side towards the river is another smaller postern through which down a rather hazardously steep slope a scrambling path, where progress demands both caution and activity, conducts to the head of the pool which lies immediately beneath it. A gate-chamber still roofed over exists in the solid wall: inside there are foundation indications of three rooms, and in the centre of all a very deep hole, probably a well. Finally, just outside the postern leading to the river is a small artificially levelled platform, some twenty feet across, as if made to support some super-incumbent edifice. Certain stone slabs and blocks are dispersed over it.

Brora, the post-town of Gavon, lies some six miles to the south-west, and from it a track over the moor leads to the rapids immediately above the Picts' pool, across which by somewhat extravagant striding from boulder to boulder a man can pass dry-foot when the river is low, and make his way up a steep path to the north of the basaltic rock, and so to the village. But this transit demands a steady head, and at the best is a somewhat giddy passage. Otherwise the road between it and Brora lies in a long detour higher up the moor, passing by the gates of Gavon Lodge, where I was stopping. For some vague and ill-defined reason the pool itself and the Picts' Castle had an uneasy reputation on the country side, and several times trudging back from a day's fishing I have known my gillie take a longish circuit, though heavy with fish, rather than make this short cut in the dusk by the castle. On the first occasion when Sandy, a strapping yellow-bearded viking of twenty-five, did this he gave as a reason that the ground round about the castle was 'mossy', though as a God-fearing man, he must have known he lied. But on another occasion he was more frank, and said that the Picts' pool was 'no canny' after sunset. I am now inclined to agree with him, though, when he lied about it, I think it was because as a God-fearing man he feared the Devil also.

It was on the evening of September 14 that I was walking back with my host, Hugh Graham, from the forest beyond the lodge. It had been a day unseasonably hot for the time of year, and the hills were blanketed with soft, furry clouds. Sandy, the gillie of whom I have spoken, was behind with the ponies, and, idly enough, I told Hugh about his strange distaste for the Picts' pool after sunset. He listened, frowning a little.

'That's curious,' he said. 'I know there is some dim local superstition about the place, but last year certainly Sandy used to laugh at it. I remember asking him what ailed the place, and he said he thought nothing about the rubbish folk talked. But this year you say he avoids it.'

'On several occasions with me he has done so.'

Hugh smoked a while in silence, striding noiselessly over the dusky fragrant heather.

'Poor chap,' he said, 'I don't know what to do about him. He's becoming useless.'

'Drink?' I asked.

'Yes, drink in a secondary manner. But trouble led to drink, and trouble, I am afraid, is leading him to worse than drink.'

'The only thing worse than drink is the Devil,' I remarked.

'Precisely. That's where he is going. He goes there often.'

'What on earth do you mean?' I asked.

'Well, it's rather curious,' said Hugh. 'You know I dabble a bit in folklore and local superstition, and I believe I am on the track of something odder than odd. Just wait a moment.'

We stood there in the gathering dusk till the ponies laboured up the

[221]

hillside to us, Sandy with his six feet of lithe strength strolling easily beside them up the steep rise, as if his long day's trudging had but served to half awaken his dormant powers of limb.

'Going to see Mistress Macpherson again tonight?' asked Hugh.

'Aye, puir body,' said Sandy. 'She's auld, and she's lone.'

'Very kind of you, Sandy,' said Hugh, and we walked on.

'What then?' I asked when the ponies had fallen behind again.

'Why, superstition lingers here,' said Hugh, 'and it's supposed she's a witch. To be quite candid with you, the thing interests me a good deal. Supposing you asked me, on oath, whether I believed in witches, I should say "No." But if you asked me again, on oath, whether I suspected I believed in them, I should, I think, say "Yes." And the fifteenth of this month – tomorrow – is Gavon's Eve.'

'And what in Heaven's name is that?' I asked. 'And who is Gavon? And what's the trouble?'

'Well, Gavon is the person, I suppose, not saint, who is what we should call the eponymous hero of this district. And the trouble is Sandy's trouble. Rather a long story. But there's a long mile in front of us, if you care to be told.'

During that mile I heard. Sandy had been engaged a year ago to a girl of Gavon who was in service at Inverness. In March last he had gone, without giving notice to see her, and as he walked up the street in which her mistress' house stood, had met her suddenly face to face, in company with a man whose clipped speech betrayed him English, whose manner a kind of gentleman. He had a flourish of his hat for Sandy, pleasure to see him, and scarcely any need of explanation as to how he came to be walking with Catrine. It was the most natural thing possible, for a city like Inverness boasted its innocent urbanities, and a girl could stroll with a man. And for the time, since also Catrine was so frankly pleased to see him, Sandy was satisfied. But after his return to Gavon, suspicion, fungus-like, grew rank in his mind, with the result that a month ago he had, with infinite pains and blottings, written a letter to Catrine, urging her return and immediate marriage. Thereafter it was known that she had left Inverness; it was known that she had arrived by train at Brora. From Brora she had started to walk across the moor by the path leading just above the Picts' Castle, crossing the rapids to Gavon, leaving her box to be sent by the carrier. But at Gavon she had never arrived. Also it was said that, though it was a hot afternoon, she wore a big cloak.

By this time we had come to the lodge, the lights of which showed dim and blurred through the thick hill-mists that had streamed sullenly down from the higher ground.

'And the rest,' said Hugh, 'which is as fantastic as this is sober fact, I will tell you later.'

Now, a fruit-bearing determination to go to bed is, to my mind, as difficult to ripen as a fruit-bearing determination to get up, and in spite of our long day, I was glad when Hugh (the rest of the men having yawned themselves out of the smoking-room) came back from the hospitable dispensing of bedroom candlesticks with a briskness that denoted that, as far as he was concerned, the distressing determination was not imminent.

'As regards Sandy,' I suggested.

'Ah, I also was thinking of that,' he said. 'Well, Catrine Gordon left Brora, and never arrived here. That is fact. Now for what remains. Have you any remembrance of a woman always alone walking about the moor by the loch? I think I once called your attention to her.'

'Yes, I remember,' I said. 'Not Catrine, surely; a very old woman, awful to look at. Moustache, whiskers, and muttering to herself. Always looking at the ground, too.'

'Yes, that is she – not Catrine. Catrine! My word, a May morning! But the other – it is Mrs Macpherson, reputed witch. Well, Sandy trudges there, a mile and more away, every night to see her. You know Sandy: Adonis of the north. Now, can you account by any natural explanation for that fact? That he goes off after a long day to see an old hag in the hills?'

'It would seem unlikely,' said I.

'Unlikely! Well, yes, unlikely.'

Hugh got up from his chair and crossed the room to where a bookcase of rather fusty-looking volumes stood between windows. He took a small morocco-backed book from a top shelf.

'Superstitions of Sutherlandshire,' he said, as he handed it to me. 'Turn to page 128, and read.'

I obeyed, and read.

'September 15 appears to have been the date of what we may call this devil festival. On the night of that day the powers of darkness held pre-eminent dominion, and over-rode for any who were abroad that night and invoked their aid, the protective Providence of Almighty God. Witches, therefore, above all, were peculiarly potent. On this night any witch could entice to herself the heart and the love of any young man who consulted her on matters of philtre or love charm, with the result that on any night in succeeding years of the same date, he, though he was lawfully affianced and wedded, would for that night be hers. If, however, he should call on the name of God through any sudden grace of the Spirit, her charm would be of no avail. On this night, too, all witches had the power by certain dreadful incantations and indescribable profanities, to raise from the dead those who had committed suicide.'

'Top of the next page,' said Hugh. 'Leave out this next paragraph; it does not bear on this last.'

'Near a small village in this country,' I read, 'called Gavon, the moon at midnight is said to shine through a certain gap or fissure in a wall of rock close beside the river on to the ruins of a Pict castle, so that the light of its beams falls on to a large flat stone erected there near the gate, and supposed by some to be an ancient and pagan altar. At that moment, so the superstition still lingers in the countryside, the evil and malignant spirits which hold sway on Gavon's Even, are at the zenith of their powers, and those who invoke their aid at this moment and in this place, will, though with infinite peril to their immortal souls, get all that they desire of them.'

The paragraph on the subject ended here, and I shut the book.

'Well?' I asked.

'Under favourable circumstances two and two make four,' said Hugh. 'And four means—'

'This. Sandy is certainly in consultation with a woman who is supposed to be a witch, whose path no crofter will cross after nightfall. He wants to learn, at whatever cost, poor devil, what happened to Catrine. Thus I think it more than possible that tomorrow, at midnight, there will be folk by the Picts' pool. There is another curious thing. I was fishing there yesterday, and just opposite the river gate of the castle, someone had set up a great flat stone, which has been dragged (for I noticed the crushed grass) from the débris at the bottom of the slope.'

'You mean that the old hag is going to try to raise the body of Catrine, if she is dead?'

'Yes, and I mean to see myself what happens. Come too.'

The next day Hugh and I fished down the river from the lodge, taking with us not Sandy, but another gillie, and ate our lunch on the slope of the Picts' Castle after landing a couple of fish there. Even as Hugh had said, a great flat slab of stone had been dragged on to the platform outside the river gate of the castle, where it rested on certain rude supports, which, now that it was in place, seemed certainly designed to receive it. It was also exactly opposite that lancet window in the basaltic rock across the pool, so that if the moon at midnight did shine through it, the light would fall on the stone. This then was the almost certain scene of the incantations.

Below the platform, as I have said, the ground fell rapidly away to the level of the pool, which owing to rain on the hills was running very high, and, streaked with lines of greyish bubbles, poured down in amazing and ear-filling volume. But directly underneath the steep escarpment of rock on the far side of the pool it lay foamless and black, a still backwater of great depth. Above the altar-like erection again the ground rose up seven rough-hewn steps to the gate itself, on each side of which, to the height of about four feet, ran the circular wall of the castle. Inside again were the remains of partition walls between the three chambers, and it was in the one nearest to the river gate that we determined to conceal ourselves that night. From there, should the witch and Sandy keep tryst at the altar, any sound of movement would reach us, and through the aperture of the gate itself we could see, concealed in the shadow of the wall, whatever took place at the altar or down below at the pool. The lodge, finally, was but a short ten minutes away, if one went in the direct line, so that by starting at a quarter to twelve that night, we could enter the Picts' Castle by the gate away from the river, thus not betraying our presence to those who might be waiting for the moment when the moon should shine through the lancet window in the wall of rock on to the altar in front of the river gate.

Night fell very still and windless, and when not long before midnight we let ourselves silently out of the lodge, though to the east the sky was clear, a black continent of cloud was creeping up from the west, and had now nearly reached the zenith. Out of the remote fringes of it occasional lightning winked, and the growl of very distant thunder sounded drowsily at long intervals after. But it seemed to me as if another storm hung over our heads, ready every moment to burst, for the oppression in the air was of a far heavier quality than so distant a disturbance could have accounted for. To the east, however, the sky was still luminously clear; the curiously hard edges of the western cloud were star-embroidered, and by the dove-coloured light in the east it was evident that the moonrise over the moor was imminent. And though I did not in my heart believe that our expedition would end in anything but yawns, I was conscious of an extreme tension and rawness of nerves, which I set down to the thunder-charged air.

For noiselessness of footstep we had both put on india-rubber soled shoes, and all the way down to the pool we heard nothing but the distant thunder and our own padded tread. Very silently and cautiously we ascended the steps of the gate away from the river, and keeping close to the wall inside, sidled round to the river gate and peered out. For the first moment I could see nothing, so black lay the shadow of the rock-wall opposite across the pool, but by degrees I made out the lumps and line of the glimmering foam which streaked the water. High as the river was running this morning it was infinitely more voluminous and turbulent now, and the sound of it filled and bewildered the ear with its sonorous roaring. Only under the very base of the rock opposite it ran quite black and unflecked by foam: there lay the deep still surface of the backwater. Then suddenly I saw something black move in the dimness in front of me, and against the grey foam rose up first the head, then the shoulders, and finally the whole figure of a woman coming towards us up the bank. Behind her walked another, a man, and the two came to where the altar of stone had been newly erected and stood there side by side silhouetted against the churned white of the stream. Hugh had seen too, and touched me on the arm to call my attention. So far then he was right: there was no mistaking the stalwart proportions of Sandy.

Suddenly across the gloom shot a tiny spear of light, and momentarily as we watched, it grew larger and longer, till a tall beam, as from some window cut in the rock opposite, was shed on the bank below us. It moved slowly, imperceptibly to the left till it struck full between the two black figures standing there, and shone with a curious bluish gleam on the flat stone in front of them. Then the roar of the river was suddenly overscored by a dreadful screaming voice, the voice of a woman, and from her side her arms shot up and out as if in invocation of some power. At first I could catch none of the words, but soon from repetition they began to convey an intelligible message to my brain, and I was listening as in the paralytic horror of nightmare to a bellowing of the most hideous and un-nameable profanity. What I heard I cannot bring myself to record; suffice it to say that Satan was invoked by every adoring and reverent name, that cursing and unspeakable malediction was poured forth on Him whom we hold most holy. Then the yelling voice ceased as suddenly as it had begun, and for a moment there was silence again, but for the reverberating river.

Then once more that horror of sound was uplifted.

'So, Catrine Gordon,' it cried, 'I bid ye in the name of my master and your's to rise from where ye lie. Up with ye – up!'

Once more there was silence; then I heard Hugh at my elbow draw a quick sobbing breath, and his finger pointed unsteadily to the dead black water below the rock. And I too looked and saw.

Right under the rock there appeared a pale sub-aqueous light, which waved and quivered in the stream. At first it was very small and dim, but as we looked it seemed to swim upwards from remote depths and grew larger till I suppose the space of some square yard was illuminated by it. Then the surface of the water was broken, and a head, the head of a girl, dead-white and with long, flowing hair, appeared above the stream. Her eyes were shut, the corners of her mouth drooped as in sleep, and the moving water stood in a frill round her neck. Higher and higher rose the figure out of the tide, till at last it stood, luminous in itself, so it appeared, up to the middle. The head was bent down over the breast, and the hands clasped together. As it emerged from the water it seemed to get nearer, and was by now half-way across the pool, moving quietly and steadily against the great flood of the hurrying river.

Then I heard a man's voice crying out in a sort of strangled agony.

'Catrine!' it cried; 'Catrine! In God's name; in God's name!'

In two strides Sandy had rushed down the steep bank, and hurled himself out into that mad swirl of waters. For one moment I saw his arms flung up into the sky, the next he had altogether gone. And on the utterance of that name the unholy vision had vanished too, while simultaneously there burst in front of us a light so blinding, followed by a crack of thunder so appalling to the senses, that I know I just hid my face in my hands. At once, as if the flood-gates of the sky had been opened, the deluge was on us, not like rain, but like one sheet of solid water, so that we cowered under it. Any hope or attempt to rescue Sandy was out of the question; to dive into that whirlpool of mad water meant instant death, and even had it been possible for any swimmer to live there, in the blackness of the night there was absolutely no chance of finding him. Besides, even if it had been possible to save him, I doubt whether I was sufficiently master of my flesh and blood as to endure the plunge where that apparition had risen.

Then, as we lay there, another horror filled and possessed my mind. Somewhere close to us in the darkness was that woman whose yelling voice just now had made my blood run ice-cold, while it brought the streaming sweat to my forehead. At that moment I turned to Hugh.

'I cannot stop here,' I said. 'I must run, run right away. Where is She?'

'Did you not see?' he asked.

'No. What happened?'

'The lightning struck the stone within a few inches of where she was standing. We – we must go and look for her.'

I followed him down the slope, shaking as if I had the palsy, and groping with my hands on the ground in front of me, in deadly terror of encountering something human. The thunder-clouds had in the last few minutes spread over the moon, so that no ray from the window in the rock guided our search. But up and down the bank from the stone that lay shattered there to the edge of the pool we groped and stumbled, but found nothing. At length we gave it up: it seemed morally certain that she, too, had rolled down the bank after the lightning stroke, and lay somewhere deep in the pool from which she had called the dead.

None fished the pool next day, but men with drag-nets came from Brora. Right under the rock in the backwater lay two bodies, close together, Sandy and the dead girl. Of the other they found nothing.

It would seem, then, that Catrine Gordon, in answer to Sandy's letter, left Inverness in heavy trouble. What happened afterwards can only be conjectured, but it seems likely she took the short cut to Gavon, meaning to cross the river on the boulders above the Picts' pool. But whether she slipped accidentally in her passage, and so was drawn down by the hungry water, or whether, unable to face the future, she had thrown herself into the pool, we can only guess. In any case they sleep together now in the bleak, wind-swept graveyard at Brora, in obedience to the inscrutable designs of God.

THE WITCH'S CAT

Manly Wade Wellman

Manly Wade Wellman (1903–86) was one of
the most popular and prolific American fantasy
authors of this century. He was nominated for a
Pulitzer prize for one of his Southern histories,
and towards the end of his career he received
the World Fantasy Convention's prestigious
Gandalf Award for Lifetime Achievement. He
wrote several entertaining tales dealing with
aspects of witchcraft, including 'Rouse Him
Not', 'A Witch for All Seasons', and 'The
Witch's Cat'. This last story appeared in the
magazine *Weird Tales* (October 1939) under the
pseudonym Gans T. Field, and was reprinted in
Wellman's omnibus collection *Worse Things
Waiting* (Carcosa, 1973).

Old Jael Bettiss, who lived in the hollow among the cypresses,
was not a real witch.

It makes no difference that folk thought she was, and walked
fearfully wide of her shadow. Nothing can be proved by the fact that she
was as disgustingly ugly without as she was wicked within. It is quite
irrelevant that evil was her study and profession and pleasure. She was no
witch; she only pretended to be.

Jael Bettis knew that all laws providing for the punishment of witches
had been repealed, or at the least forgotten. As to being feared and hated,
that was meat and drink to Jael Bettiss, living secretly alone in the hollow.

The house and the hollow belonged to a kindly old villager, who had
been elected marshal and was too busy to look after his property.
Because he was easy-going and perhaps a little daunted, he let Jael Bettiss

live there rent-free. The house was no longer snug; the back of its roof was broken in, the eaves drooped slackly. At some time or other the place had been painted brown, before that with ivory black. Now both coats of colour peeled away in huge flakes, making the clapboards seem scrofulous. The windows had been broken in every small, grubby pane, and mended with coarse brown paper, so that they were like cast and blurred eyes. Behind was the muddy, bramble-choked back yard, and behind that yawned the old quarry, now abandoned and full of black water. As for the inside – but few ever saw it.

Jael Bettiss did not like people to come into her house. She always met callers on the old cracked doorstep, draped in a cloak of shadowy black, with grey hair straggling, her nose as hooked and sharp as the beak of a buzzard, her eyes filmy and sore-looking, her wrinkle-bordered mouth always grinning and showing her yellow, chisel-shaped teeth.

The nearby village was an old-fashioned place, with stone flags instead of concrete for pavements, and the villagers were the simplest of men and women. From them Jael Bettiss made a fair living, by selling love philtres, or herbs to cure sickness, or charms to ward off bad luck. When she wanted extra money, she would wrap her old black cloak about her and, tramping along a country road, would stop at a cowpen and ask the farmer what he would do if his cows went dry. The farmer, worried, usually came at dawn next day to her hollow and bought a good-luck charm. Occasionally the cows would go dry anyway, by accident of nature, and their owner would pay more and more, until their milk returned to them.

Now and then, when Jael Bettiss came to the door, there came with her the gaunt black cat, Gib.

Gib was not truly black, any more than Jael Bettiss was truly a witch. He had been born with white markings at muzzle, chest and forepaws, so that he looked to be in full evening dress. Left alone, he would have grown fat and fluffy. But Jael Bettiss, who wanted a fearsome pet, kept all his white spots smeared with thick soot, and underfed him to make him look rakish and lean.

On the night of the full moon, she would drive poor Gib from her door. He would wander to the village in search of food, and would wail mournfully in the yards. Awakened householders would angrily throw boots or pans or sticks of kindling. Often Gib was hit, and his cries were sharpened by pain. When that happened, Jael Bettiss took care to be seen next morning with a bandage on head or wrist. Some of the simplest villagers thought that Gib was really the old woman, magically transformed. Her reputation grew, as did Gib's unpopularity. But Gib did not deserve mistrust – like all cats, he was a practical philosopher, who wanted to be comfortable and quiet and dignified. At bottom, he was amiable. Like all cats, too, he loved his home above all else; and the house in the hollow, be it ever so humble and often cruel, was home. It was unthinkable to him that he might live elsewhere.

In the village he had two friends – black-eyed John Frey, the storekeeper's son, who brought the mail to and from the county seat, and Ivy Hill, pretty blonde daughter of the town marshal, the same town marshal who owned the hollow and let Jael Bettiss live in the old house. John Frey and Ivy Hill were so much in love with each other that they loved everything else, even black-stained, hungry Gib. He was grateful; if he had been able, he would have loved them in return. But his little heart had room for one devotion only, and that was given to the house in the hollow.

One day, Jael Bettiss slouched darkly into old Mr Frey's store, and up to the counter that served for post office. Leering, she gave John Frey a letter. It was directed to a certain little-known publisher, asking for a certain little-known book. Several days later, she appeared again, received a parcel, and bore it to her home.

In her gloomy, secret parlour, she unwrapped her purchase. It was a small, drab volume, with no title on cover or back. Sitting at the rickety table, she began to read. All evening and most of the night she read, forgetting to give Gib his supper, though he sat hungrily at her feet.

At length, an hour before dawn, she finished. Laughing loudly and briefly, she turned her beak-nose toward the kerosene lamp on the table. From the book she read aloud two words. The lamp went out, though she had not blown at it. Jael Bettiss spoke one commanding word more, and the lamp flamed alight again.

'At last!' she cried out in shrill exultation, and grinned down at Gib. Her lips drew back from her yellow chisels of teeth. 'At last!' she crowed again. 'Why don't you speak to me, you little brute? . . . Why don't you, indeed?'

She asked that final question as though she had been suddenly inspired. Quickly she glanced through the back part of the book, howled with laughter over something she found there, then sprang up and scuttled like a big, filthy crab into the dark, windowless cell that was her kitchen. There she mingled salt and malt in the palm of her skinny right hand. After that, she rummaged out a bundle of dried herbs, chewed

[231]

them fine and spat them into the mixture. Stirring again with her forefinger, she returned to the parlour. Scanning the book to refresh her memory, she muttered a nasty little rhyme. Finally she dashed the mess suddenly upon Gib.

He retreated, shaking himself, outraged and startled. In a corner he sat down, and bent his head to lick the smeared fragments of the mixture away. But they revolted his tongue and palate, and he paused in the midst of this chore, so important to cats; and meanwhile Jael Bettiss yelled, 'Speak!'

Gib crouched and blinked, feeling sick. His tongue came out and steadied his lips. Finally he said: 'I want something to eat.'

His voice was small and high, like a little child's, but entirely understandable. Jael Bettiss was so delighted that she laughed and clapped her bony knees with her hands, in self-applause.

'It worked!' she cried. 'No more humbug about me, you understand? I'm a real witch at last, and not a fraud!'

Gib found himself able to understand all this, more clearly than he had ever understood human affairs before. 'I want something to eat,' he said again, more definitely than before. 'I didn't have any supper, and it's nearly—'

'Oh, stow your gab!' snapped his mistress. 'This book, crammed with knowledge and strength, that made me able to do it. I'll never be without it again, and it'll teach me all the things I've only guessed at and mumbled about. I'm a real witch now, I say. And if you don't think I'll make those ignorant sheep of villagers realize it—'

Once more she went off into gales of wild, cracked mirth, and threw a dish at Gib. He darted away into a corner just in time, and the missile crashed into blue-and-white china fragments against the wall. But Jael Bettiss read aloud from her book an impressive gibberish, and the dish reformed itself on the floor; the bits crept together and joined and the cracks disappeared, as trickling drops of water formed into a pool. And finally, when the witch's twig-like forefinger beckoned, the dish floated upward like a leaf in a breeze and set itself gently back on the table. Gib watched warily.

'That's small to what I shall do hereafter,' swore Jael Bettis.

When next the mail was distributed at the general store, a dazzling stranger appeared.

She wore a cloak, an old-fashioned black coat, but its drapery did not conceal the tall perfection of her form. As for her face, it would have stirred interest and admiration in larger and more sophisticated gatherings than the knot of letter-seeking villagers. Its beauty was scornful but inviting, classic but warm with something in it of Grecian sculpture and Oriental allure. If the nose was cruel, it was straight; if the lips were sullen, they were full; if the forehead was a suspicion low, it was white and smooth. Thick, thunder-black hair swept up from that forehead, and backward to a knot at the neck. The eyes glowed with strange, hot lights, and wherever they turned they pierced and captivated.

People moved away to let her have a clear sweeping pathway forward to the counter. Until this stranger had entered, Ivy Hill was the loveliest person present; now she looked only modest and fresh and blonde in her starched gingham, and worried to boot. As a matter of fact, Ivy Hill's insides felt cold and topsy-turvy, because she saw how fascinated was the sudden attention of John Frey.

'Is there,' asked the newcomer in a deep, creamy voice, 'any mail for me?'

'Wh–what name, ma'am?' asked John Frey, his brown young cheeks turning full crimson.

'Bettiss. Jael Bettiss.'

He began to fumble through the sheaf of envelopes, with hands that shook. 'Are you,' he asked, 'any relation to the old lady of that name, the one who lives in the hollow?'

'Yes, of a sort.' She smiled a slow, conquering smile. 'She's my – aunt. Yes. Perhaps you see the family resemblance?' Wider and wider grew the smile with which she assaulted John Frey. 'If there isn't any mail,' she went on, 'I would like a stamp. A one-cent stamp.'

Turning to his little metal box on the shelf behind, John Frey tore a single green stamp from the sheet. His hand shook still more as he gave it to the customer and received in exchange a copper cent.

There was really nothing exceptional about the appearance of that copper cent. It looked brown and a little worn, with Lincoln's head on it, and with a date – 1917. But John Frey felt a sudden glow in the hand that took it, a glow that shot along his arm and into his heart. He gazed at the coin as if he had never seen its like before. And he put it slowly into his pocket, a different pocket from the one in which he usually kept change, and placed another coin in the till to pay for the stamp. Poor Ivy Hill's blue eyes grew round and downright miserable. Plainly he meant to keep that copper piece as a souvenir. But John Frey gazed only at the stranger, raptly, as though he were suddenly stunned or hypnotized.

[233]

The dark, sullen beauty drew her cloak more tightly around her, and moved regally out of the store and away toward the edge of town.

As she turned up the brush-hidden trail to the hollow, a change came. Not that her step was less young and free, her figure less queenly, her eyes dimmer or her beauty short of perfect. All these were as they had been; but her expression became set and grim, her body tense and her head high and truculent. It was as though, beneath that young loveliness, lurked an old and evil heart – which was precisely what did lurk there, it does not boot to conceal. But none saw except Gib, the black cat with soot-covered white spots, who sat on the doorstep of the ugly cottage. Jael Bettiss thrust him aside with her foot and entered.

In the kitchen she filled a tin basin from a wooden bucket, and threw into the water a pinch of coarse green powder with an unpleasant smell. As she stirred it in with her hands, they seemed to grow skinny and harsh. Then she threw great palmfuls of the liquid into her face and over her head, and other changes came . . .

The woman who returned to the front door, where Gib watched with a cat's apprehensive interest, was hideous old Jael Bettiss, whom all the village knew and avoided.

'He's trapped,' she shrilled triumphantly. 'That penny, the one I soaked for three hours in a love-philtre, trapped him the moment he touched it!' She stumped to the table, and patted the book as though it were a living, lovable thing.

'You taught me,' she crooned to it. 'You're winning me the love of John Frey!' She paused, and her voice grew harsh again. 'Why not? I'm old and ugly and queer, but I can love, and John Frey is the handsomest man in the village!'

The next day she went to the store again, in her new and dazzling person as a dark, beautiful girl. Gib, left alone in the hollow, turned over in his mind the things that he had heard. The new gift of human speech had brought with it, of necessity, a human quality of reasoning; but his viewpoint and his logic were as strongly feline as ever.

Jael Bettiss' dark love that lured John Frey promised no good to Gib. There would be plenty of trouble, he was inclined to think, and trouble was something that all sensible cats avoided. He was wise now, but he was weak. What could he do against danger? And his desires, as they had been since kittenhood, were food and warmth and a cosy sleeping-place, and a little respectful affection. Just now he was getting none of the four.

He thought also of Ivy Hill. She liked Gib, and often had shown it. If she won John Frey despite the witch's plan, the two would build a house all full of creature comforts – cushions, open fires, probably fish and chopped liver. Gib's tongue caressed his soot-stained lips at the savoury thought. It would be good to have a home with Ivy Hill and John Frey, if once he was quit of Jael Bettiss . . .

But he put the thought from him. The witch had never held his love and loyalty. That went to the house in the hollow, his home since the month that he was born. Even magic had not taught him how to be rid of that cat-instinctive obsession for his own proper dwelling-place. The sinister, strife-sodden hovel would always call and claim him, would draw him back from the warmest fire, the softest bed, the most savoury food in the world. Only John Howard Payne could have appreciated Gib's yearnings to the full, and he died long ago, in exile from the home he loved.

When Jael Bettiss returned, she was in a fine trembling rage. Her real self shone through the glamour of her disguise, like murky fire through a thin porcelain screen.

Gib was on the doorstep again, and tried to dodge away as she came up, but her enchantment, or something else, had made Jael Bettiss too quick even for a cat. She darted out a hand and caught him by the scruff of the neck.

'Listen to me,' she said, in a voice as deadly as the trickle of poisoned water. 'You understand human words. You can talk, and you can hear what I say. You can do what I say, too.' She shook him, by way of emphasis. 'Can't you do what I say?'

'Yes,' said Gib weakly, convulsed with fear.

'All right, I have a job for you. And mind you do it well, or else—' She broke off and shook him again, letting him imagine what would happen if he disobeyed.

'Yes,' said Gib again, panting for breath in her tight grip. 'What's it about?'

'It's about that little fool, Ivy Hill. She's not quite out of his heart . . . Go to the village tonight,' ordered Jael Bettiss, 'and to the house of the marshal. Steal something that belongs to Ivy Hill.'

'Steal something?'

'Don't echo me, as if you were a silly parrot.' She let go of him, and hurried back to the book that was her constant study. 'Bring me something that Ivy Hill owns and touches – and be back here with it before dawn.'

Gib carried out her orders. Shortly after sundown he crept through the deepened dusk to the home of Marshall Hill. Doubly black with the soot habitually smeared upon him by Jael Bettiss, he would have been almost invisible, even had anyone been on guard against his coming. But nobody watched; the genial old man sat on the front steps, talking to his daughter.

'Say,' the father teased, 'isn't young Johnny Frey coming over here tonight, as usual?'

'I don't know, daddy,' said Ivy Hill wretchedly.

'What's that daughter?' The marshal sounded surprised. 'Is there anything gone wrong between you two young 'uns?'

'Perhaps not, but – oh, daddy, there's a new girl come to town—'

And Ivy Hill burst into tears, groping dolefully on the step beside her for her little wadded handkerchief. But she could not find it.

For Gib, stealing near, had caught it up in his mouth and was scampering away toward the edge of town, and beyond to the house in the hollow.

Meanwhile, Jael Bettiss worked hard at a certain project of wax-modelling. Any witch, or student of witchcraft, would have known at once why she did this.

After several tries, she achieved something quite interesting and even clever – a little female figure, that actually resembled Ivy Hill.

Jael Bettiss used the wax of three candles to give it enough substance and proportion. To make it more realistic, she got some fresh, pale-gold hemp, and of this made hair, like the wig of a blonde doll, for the wax head. Drops of blue ink served for eyes, and a blob of berry-juice for the red mouth. All the while she worked, Jael Bettiss was muttering and mumbling words and phrases she had gleaned from the rearward pages of her book.

When Gib brought in the handkerchief, Jael Bettiss snatched it from his mouth, with a grunt by way of thanks. With rusty scissors and coarse white thread, she fashioned for the wax figure a little dress. It happened that the handkerchief was of gingham, and so the garment made all the more striking the puppet's resemblance to Ivy Hill.

'You're a fine one!' tittered the witch, propping her finished figure against the lamp. 'You'd better be scared!'

For it happened that she had worked into the waxen face an expression of terror. The blue ink of the eyes made wide round blotches, a stare of agonized fear; and the berry-juice mouth seemed to tremble, to plead shakily for mercy.

Again Jael Bettiss refreshed her memory of goetic spells by poring over the back of the book, and after that she dug from the bottom of an old pasteboard box a handful of rusty pins. She chuckled over them, so that one would think triumph already hers. Laying the puppet on its back, so that the lamplight fell full upon it, she began to recite a spell.

'I have made my wish before,' she said in measured tones. 'I will make it now. And there was never a day that I did not see my wish fulfilled.' Simple, vague – but how many have died because those words were spoken in a certain way over images of them?

The witch thrust a pin into the breast of the little wax figure, and drove it all the way in, with a murderous pressure of her thumb. Another pin she pushed into the head, another into an arm, another into a leg; and so on, until the gingham-clad puppet was fairly studded with transfixing pins.

'Now,' she said, 'we shall see what we shall see.'

Morning dawned, as clear and golden as though wickedness had never been born into the world. The mysterious new paragon of beauty – not a young man of the village but mooned over her, even though she was the reputed niece and namesake of that unsavoury old vagabond, Jael Bettiss – walked into the general store to make purchases. One delicate pink ear turned to the gossip of the housewives.

Wasn't it awful, they were agreeing, how poor little Ivy Hill was suddenly sick almost to death – she didn't seem to know her father or her friends. Not even Doctor Melcher could find out what was the matter with her. Strange that John Frey was not interested in her troubles; but John Frey sat behind the counter, slumped on his stool like a mud idol, and his eyes lighted up only when they spied lovely young Jael Bettiss with her market basket.

When she had heard enough, the witch left the store and went straight to the town marshal's house. There she spoke gravely and sorrowfully about how she feared for the sick girl, and was allowed to visit Ivy Hill in her bedroom. To the father and the doctor, it seemed that the patient grew stronger and felt less pain while Jael Bettiss remained to wish her a quick recovery; but, not long after this new acquaintance departed, Ivy Hill grew worse. She fainted, and recovered only to vomit.

And she vomited – pins, rusty pins. Something like that happened in old Salem Village, and earlier still in Scotland, before the grisly cult of North Berwick was literally burned out. But Doctor Melcher, a more modern scholar, had never seen or heard of anything remotely resembling Ivy Hill's disorder.

[237]

So it went, for three full days. Gib, too, heard the doleful gossip as he slunk around the village to hunt for food and to avoid Jael Bettiss, who did not like him near when she did magic. Ivy Hill was dying, and he mourned her, as for the boons of fish and fire and cushions and petting that might have been his. He knew, too, that he was responsible for her doom and his loss – that handkerchief that he had stolen had helped Jael Bettiss to direct her spells.

But philosophy came again to his aid. If Ivy Hill died, she died. Anyway, he had never been given the chance to live as her pensioner and pet. He was not even sure that he would have taken the chance – thinking of it, he felt strong, accustomed clamps upon his heart. The house in the hollow was his home for ever. Elsewhere he'd be an exile.

Nothing would ever root it out of his feline soul.

On the evening of the third day, witch and cat faced each other across the table-top in the old house in the hollow.

'They've talked loud enough to make his dull ears hear,' grumbled the fearful old woman – with none but Gib to see her, she had washed away the disguising enchantment that, though so full of lure, seemed to be a burden upon her. 'John Frey has agreed to take Ivy Hill out in his automobile. The doctor thinks that the fresh air, and John Frey's company, will make her feel better – but it won't. It's too late. She'll never return from that drive.'

She took up the pin-pierced wax image of her rival, rose and started toward the kitchen.

'What are you going to do?' Gib forced himself to ask.

'Do?' repeated Jael Bettiss, smiling murderously. 'I'm going to put an end to that baby-faced chit – but why are you so curious? Get out, with your prying!'

And, snarling curses and striking with her claw-like hands, she made him spring down from his chair and run out of the house. The door slammed, and he crouched in some brambles and watched. No sound, and at the half-blinded windows no movement; but, after a time, smoke began to coil upward from the chimney. Its first puffs were dark and greasy-looking. Then it turned dull grey, then white, then blue as indigo. Finally it vanished altogether.

When Jael Bettiss opened the door and came out, she was once more in the semblance of a beautiful dark girl. Yet Gib recognized a greater terror about her than ever before.

'You be gone from here when I get back,' she said to him.

'Gone?' stammered Gib, his little heart turning cold. 'What do you mean?'

She stooped above him, like a threatening bird of prey.

'You be gone,' she repeated. 'If I ever see you again, I'll kill you – or I'll make my new husband kill you.'

He still could not believe her. He shrank back, and his eyes turned mournfully to the old house that was the only thing he loved.

'You're the only witness to the things I've done,' Jael Bettiss continued. 'Nobody would believe their ears if a cat started telling tales, but anyway, I don't want any trace of you around. If you leave, they'll forget that I used to be a witch. So run!'

She turned away. Her mutterings were now only her thoughts aloud:

'If my magic works – and it always works – that car will find itself idling around through the hill road to the other side of the quarry. John Frey will stop there. And so will Ivy Hill – for ever.'

Drawing her cloak around her, she stalked purposefully toward the old quarry behind the house.

Left by himself, Gib lowered his lids and let his yellow eyes grow dim and deep with thought. His shrewd beast's mind pawed and probed at this final wonder and danger that faced him and John Frey and Ivy Hill.

He must run away if he would live. The witch's house in the hollow, that had never welcomed him, now threatened him. No more basking on the doorstep, no more ambushing wood-mice among the brambles, no more dozing by the kitchen fire. Nothing for Gib henceforth but strange, forbidding wilderness, and scavenger's food, and no shelter, not on the coldest night. The village? But his only two friends, John Frey and Ivy Hill, were being taken from him by the magic of Jael Bettiss and her book . . .

That book had done this. That book must undo it. There was no time to lose.

The door was not quite latched, and he nosed it open, despite the groans of its hinges. Hurrying in, he sprang up on the table.

It was gloomy in that tree-invested house, even for Gib's sharp eyes. Therefore, in a trembling fear almost too big for his little body, he spoke a word that Jael Bettiss had spoken, on her first night of power. As had happened then, so it happened now; the dark lamp glowed alight.

Gib pawed at the closed book, and contrived to lift its cover. Pressing it open with one front foot, with the other he painstakingly turned leaves, more leaves, and more yet. Finally he came to the page he wanted.

Not that he could read; and, in any case, the characters were strange in their shapes and combinations. Yet, if one looked long enough and levelly enough – even though one were a cat, and afraid – they made sense, conveyed intelligence.

And so into the mind of Gib, beating down his fears, there stole a phrase:

Beware of mirrors . . .

So that was why Jael Bettiss never kept a mirror – not even now, when she could assume such dazzling beauty.

Beware of mirrors, the book said to Gib, *for they declare the truth, and truth is fatal to sorcery. Beware, also, of crosses, which defeat all spells . . .*

That was definite inspiration. He moved back from the book, and let it snap shut. Then, pushing with head and paws, he coaxed it to the edge of the table and let it fall. Jumping down after it, he caught a corner of the book in his teeth and dragged it to the door, more like a retriever than a cat. When he got it into the yard, into a place where the earth was soft, he dug furiously until he had made a hole big enough to contain the volume. Then, thrusting it in, he covered it up.

Nor was that all his effort, so far as the book was concerned. He trotted a little way off to where lay some dry, tough twigs under the cypress trees. To the little grave he bore first one, then another of these, and laid them across each other, in the form of an X. He pressed them well into the earth, so that they would be hard to disturb. Perhaps he would keep an eye on that spot henceforth, after he had done the rest of the things in his mind, to see that the cross remained. And, though he acted thus only by chance reasoning, all the demonologists, even the Reverend Montague Summers, would have nodded approval. Is this not the way to foil the black wisdom of the *Grand Albert*? Did not Prospero thus inter his grimoires, in the fifth act of *The Tempest*?

Now back to the house once more, and into the kitchen. It was even darker than the parlour, but Gib could make out a basin on a stool by the muddy wall, and smelled an ugly pungency – Jael Bettiss had left her mixture of powdered water after last washing away her burden of false beauty.

Gib's feline nature rebelled at a wetting; his experience of witchcraft bade him to be wary, but he rose on his hind legs and with his forepaws dragged at the basin's edge. It tipped and toppled. The noisome fluid drenched him. Wheeling, he ran back into the parlour, but paused on the doorstep. He spoke two more words that he remembered from Jael Bettiss. The lamp went out again.

And now he dashed around the house and through the brambles and to the quarry beyond.

It lay amid uninhabited wooded hills, a wide excavation from which had once been quarried all the stones for the village houses and pavements. Now it was full of water, from many thaws and torrents. Almost at its lip was parked John Frey's touring-car, with the top down, and beside it he lolled, slack-faced and dreamy. At his side, cloak-draped and enigmatically queenly, was Jael Bettiss, her back to the quarry, never more terrible or handsome. John Frey's eyes were fixed drearily upon her, and her eyes were fixed commandingly on the figure in the front seat of the car – a slumped, defeated figure, hard to recognize as poor sick Ivy Hill.

'Can you think of no way to end all this pain, Miss Ivy?' the witch was asking. Though she did not stir, nor glance behind her, it was as though she had gestured toward the great quarry-pit, full to unknown depths with black, still water. The sun, at the very point of setting, made angry red lights on the surface of that stagnant pond.

'Go away,' sobbed Ivy Hill, afraid without knowing why. 'Please, please!'

'I'm only trying to help,' said Jael Bettiss. 'Isn't that so, John?'

'That's so, Ivy,' agreed John, like a little boy who is prompted to an unfamiliar recitation. 'She's only trying to help.'

Gib, moving silently as fate, crept to the back of the car. None of the three human beings, so intent upon each other, saw him.

'Get out of the car,' persisted Jael Bettiss. 'Get out, and look into the water. You will forget your pain.'

'Yes, yes,' chimed in John Frey, mechanically. 'You will forget your pain.'

Gib scrambled stealthily to the running board, then over the side of the car and into the rear seat. He found what he had hoped to find. Ivy Hill's purse – and open.

He pushed his nose into it. Tucked into a little side-pocket was a hard, flat rectangle, about the size and shape of a visiting card. All normal girls carry mirrors in their purses – all mirrors show the truth. Gib clamped the edge with his mouth, and struggled to drag the thing free.

'Miss Ivy!' Jael Bettiss was commanding, 'get out of this car, and come and look into the water of the quarry.'

No doubt what would happen if once Ivy Hill should gaze into the shiny black abyss; but she bowed her head, in agreement or defeat, and began slowly to push aside the catch of the door.

[241]

Now or never, thought Gib. He made a little noise in his throat, and sprang up on the side of the car next to Jael Bettiss. His black-stained face and yellow eyes were not a foot from her.

She alone saw him; Ivy Hill was too sick, John Frey too dull. 'What are you doing here?' she snarled, like a bigger and fiercer cat than he; but he moved closer still, holding up the oblong in his teeth. Its back was uppermost, covered with imitation leather, and hid the real nature of it. Jael Bettiss was mystified, for once in her relationship with Gib. She took the thing from him, turned it over, and saw a reflection.

She screamed.

The other two looked up, horrified through their stupour. The scream that Jael Bettiss uttered was not deep and rich and young; it was the wild, cracked cry of a terrified old woman.

'I don't look like that,' she choked out, and drew back from the car. 'Not old – ugly—'

Gib sprang at her face. With all four claw-bristling feet he seized and clung to her. Again Jael Bettiss screamed, flung up her hands, and tore him away from his hold, but his soggy fur had smeared the powdered water upon her face and head.

Though he fell to earth, Gib twisted in mid air and landed upright. He had one glimpse of his enemy. Jael Bettiss, no mistake – but a Jael Bettiss with hooked beak, rheumy eyes, hideous wry mouth and yellow chisel teeth – Jael Bettiss exposed for what she was, stripped of her lying mask of beauty!

And she drew back a whole staggering step. Rocks were just behind her. Gib saw, and flung himself. Like a flash he clawed his way up her cloak, and with both forepaws ripped at the ugliness he had betrayed. He struck for his home that was forbidden him – Marco Bozzaris never strove harder for Greece, nor Stonewall Jackson for Virginia.

Jael Bettiss screamed yet again, a scream loud and full of horror. Her feet had slipped on the edge of the abyss. She flung out her arms, the cloak flapped from them like frantic wings. She fell, and Gib fell with her, still tearing and fighting.

The waters of the quarry closed over them both.

Gib thought that it was a long way back to the surface, and a longer way to shore. But he got there, and scrambled out with the help of projecting rocks. He shook his drenched body, climbed back into the car and sat upon the rear seat. At least Jael Bettiss would no longer drive him from the home he loved. He'd find food some way, and take it back there each day to eat . . .

With tongue and paws he began to rearrange his sodden fur.

John Frey, clear-eyed and wide awake, was leaning in and talking to Ivy Hill. As for her, she sat up straight, as though she had never known a moment of sickness.

'But just what did happen?' she was asking.

John Frey shook his head, though all the stupidity was gone from his face and manner. 'I don't quite remember. I seem to have wakened from a dream. But are you all right, darling?'

'Yes, I'm all right.' She gazed toward the quarry, and the black water that had already subsided above what it had swallowed. Her eyes were puzzled, but not frightened. 'I was dreaming, too,' she said. 'Let's not bother about it.'

She lifted her gaze, and cried out with joy. 'There's that old house that Daddy owns. Isn't it interesting?'

John Frey looked too. 'Yes. The old witch has gone away – I seem to have heard she did.'

Ivy Hill was smiling with excitement. 'Then I have an inspiration. Let's get Daddy to give it to us. And we'll paint it over and fix it up, and then—' She broke off, with a cry of delight. 'I declare, there's a cat in the car with me!'

It was the first she had known of Gib's presence.

John Frey stared at Gib. He seemed to have wakened only the moment before. 'Yes, and isn't he a thin one? But he'll be pretty when he gets through cleaning himself. I think I see a white shirt-front.'

Ivy Hill put out a hand and scratched Gib behind the ear. 'He's bringing us good luck, I think. John, let's take him to live with us when we have the house fixed up and move in.'

'Why not?' asked her lover. He was gazing at Gib. 'He looks as if he was getting ready to speak.'

But Gib was not getting ready to speak. The power of speech was gone from him, along with Jael Bettiss and her enchantments. But he understood, in a measure, what was being said about him and the house in the hollow. There would be new life there, joyful and friendly this time. And he would be a part of it, for ever, and of his loved home.

He could only purr to show his relief and gratitude.

ACKNOWLEDGMENTS

The Publisher has made every effort to contact the copyright holders of material reproduced in this book, and wishes to apologize to those he has been unable to trace. Grateful acknowledgment is made for permission to reprint the following:

'The Fenstanton Witch' by M. R. James, reproduced by permission of N. J. R. James.

'Furze Hollow' by A. M. Burrage, reproduced by permission of J. S. F. Burrage.

'One Remained Behind' by Marjorie Bowen, reproduced by permission of Hilary Long.

'Catnip' by Robert Bloch, reprinted by permission of the author and the author's agents, Scott Meredith Literary Agency, Inc., 845 Third Avenue, New York, NY 10022.

'The Yew Tree' by Shamus Frazer, reproduced by permission of Mrs Joan N. Frazer.

'Gramma' by Stephen King, reproduced by permission of the author.

'The Day of the Underdog' by Ronald Chetwynd-Hayes, reproduced by permission of the author.

'The Executor' by David G. Rowlands, reproduced by permission of the author.

'The Witch's Cat' copyright © 1939 by Weird Tales for *Weird Tales*, October 1939. Reprinted by permission of Karl Edward Wagner, Literary Executor for the Estate of Manly Wade Wellman.

The following stories are reproduced by permission of the authors: 'The Toad Witch' © 1991 by Jessica Amanda Salmonson; 'Carven of Onyx' © 1991 by Ron Weighell; 'The Taking' © 1987, 1991 by Roger Johnson.